Permanent Seminar Studies

No. 3

OFFICIAL MINISTRY IN A NEW AGE

edited by

James H. Provost

Canon Law Society of America
The Catholic University of America
Washington, D.C. 20064

Contents

SIGLA

The following abbreviations are used in this set of studies.

AA	"Apostolicam actuositatem," Decree on the Apostolate of the Laity, Second Vatican Council.
AAS	*Acta Apostolicae Sedis.*
Abbott	Walter M. Abbott, ed., *The Documents of Vatican II.*
AG	"Ad gentes divinitus," Decree on the Missionary Activity of the Church, Second Vatican Council.
ASS	*Acta Sanctae Sedis.*
CD	"Christus Dominus," Decree on the Pastoral Office of Bishops in the Church, Second Vatican Council.
DH	"Dignitatis humanae," Declaration on Religious Liberty, Second Vatican Council.
DV	"Dei Verbum," Dogmatic Constitution on Divine Revelation, Second Vatican Council.
Flannery	Austin Flannery, ed., *Vatican Council II: The Conciliar and Post Conciliar Documents.*
GS	"Gaudium et spes," Pastoral Consitution on the Church in the Modern World, Second Vatican Council.
LG	"Lumen gentium," Dogmatic Constitution on the Church, Second Vatican Council.
PO	"Presbyterorum ordinis," Decree on the Ministry and Life of Priests, Second Vatican Council.
SC	"Sacrosanctum Concilium," Constitution on the Sacred Liturgy, Second Vatican Council.
UR	"Unitatis redintegratio," Decree on Ecumenism, Second Vatican Council.

PREFATORY NOTE

The Permanent Seminar of the Canon Law Society of America is an effort at research into foundational issues in canon law and theology. The present studies are the result of the third Permanent Seminar project and first appeared as a special issue of *The Jurist*, volume 41, number 2 (1981).

The C.L.S.A. expresses its appreciation to the participants in the Seminar for their scholarly contributions, and to the editors of *The Jurist* for their cooperation in making the papers of the Permanent Seminar available initially.

OFFICIAL MINISTRY IN A NEW AGE
AN INTRODUCTION

Seven years have passed since the Canon Law Society of America determined as one of its ten-year goals to research basic issues in Church life where law and theology meet. The C.L.S.A. Permanent Seminar was established to help pursue this goal. It was designed to develop conceptual tools which might be of assistance to canon lawyers, theologians, church administrators, and others. The Seminar was assigned several major areas of research. Two of these related to ways of thinking about the Church, the working concepts of Church as a communion and as mission. A third related to ministry, which after centuries of stable canonical ordering was showing signs of developing new forms and structures.

The Permanent Seminar has already published studies on its first two assignments. "The Church as Communion" appeared in THE JURIST 36 (1976): 1-245; "The Church as Mission" appeared in THE JURIST 39 (1979): 1-288. Within the tradition of this ecclesiological framework a third set of studies is now presented, "Official Ministry in a New Age." These papers move from considerations about the nature of the Church to the nature and function of official ministry within that renewed sense of Church.

The methodology of the Permanent Seminar process may explain some of the limitations as well as some of the strengths in these studies. Each project has involved a different set of scholars drawn from various disciplines, including scripture, theology, canon law, and related fields. The general topic of the project was mandated by the Canon Law Society of America, but the individual elements within the project and suggestions for participants were refined in consultation with a cross section of canon lawyers, theologians, and persons with known expertise in the topic area. A tentative outline of the work accompanied the invitation to participate; eventually a project team formed, and

1

with their help a more formal outline and assignment of topics was achieved.

Participants drafted initial studies as a condition for attending the first Seminar session. Most papers were circulated in advance. The initial three-day meeting concentrated on a review of each paper beginning with an explanation by the author and followed by detailed analysis in which the entire group engaged. Several common insights developed from this effort and were incorporated in the various papers. A second round of writing and distribution of most papers preceded the second three-day session, where further analysis and critique enabled the authors to refine their positions and to relate them to each other's efforts. A final polishing of the papers preceded this publication. It should be noted that the studies remain the work of their respective authors, although enriched and refined through the seminar process.

Unlike the previous Permanent Seminar projects, this one had no preconceived focus. Instead, it aimed to explore the situation of official ministry at a time when major changes are taking place in the practice of ministry. Non-ordained persons are assuming functions previously limited to the ordained. The traditional distribution of functions among ordained ministers is being questioned. The concept of "official ministry" in the name of the Church and specially mandated by church authorities, has been called into question and demands at least a re-examination in light of renewed understandings of the Church itself. Many of the papers focus on ordained ministry, and to some extent on the episcopacy, in an effort to begin with existing structures and understandings of official ministry and to explore what may be developing for a new age of the Church.

The Papers

"The Public Language of Ministry" is analyzed with particular reference to liturgical texts of ordination in the opening study by Mary Collins, associate professor of religion and religious education at The Catholic University of America. Ordination takes place in rites which use status-elevation terminology. The limits of this kind of language are explored, for the well-being of the community can be threatened when official ministry is isolated in ways this terminology may imply.

Ordination is not the only way in which persons engage in activity to serve the community. Vatican II speaks of the rights and duties which flow from being graced with a charism. Scripture scholar Carolyn Osiek, assistant professor at the Catholic Theological Union in Chicago, studies the "Relation of Charism to Rights and Duties in the New Testament Church" and relates this to the Vatican II teaching. There were important links between charisms and ministry in the early church, as there are today; but the concepts of rights and duties in New Testament times appear from her analysis to be different from twentieth-century concepts.

"The Basis for Official Ministry in the Church" is examined by David N. Power, associate professor of systematic theology at The Catholic University of America. Focusing on the episcopacy and drawing on historical evidence to develop his theological reflections, he explores a flexible notion of ministry which may integrate various forms of office and leadership.

The more recent forms of active participation of the laity in the pastoral ministry of the Catholic Church have raised the question concerning the extent to which the non-ordained can be incorporated into the hierarchical ministry. In "Lay Participation in the Apostolate of the Hierarchy" Edward J. Kilmartin, professor and director of the graduate program in Liturgical Studies at the University of Notre Dame, analyzes the responses to this problem which are based on Vatican II's theology of ordination and on ecclesiological perspectives which emerge from the conciliar documents.

Harry McSorley, professor of theology at St. Michael's College, University of Toronto, examines a key element of official ministry from an ecumenical perspective in "Determining the 'Validity' of Orders." The term "validity" itself is part of the difficulty, although ecclesiological and charismatic approaches to the concept can put the juridical questions in a better setting.

"Fullness of orders" is another key concept for official ministry. Bernard Cooke, professor of theology at Holy Cross College, Worcester, begins his "'Fullness of Orders': Theological Reflections" with an analysis of the ambiguities found in Vatican II's use of this term. Theological reflections on what fullness of orders means as it applies to the episcopate lead him to pose questions for further exploration concerning authority and power.

Joseph A. Komonchak, associate professor of religion and religious education at The Catholic University of America, argues the key to understanding ministry lies in the approach taken to the relationship of the Church and the world. He questions the assigning of "typical" roles to clergy, religious and laity as if they could be isolated, some into purely church-type roles and others into strictly worldly concerns.

The underlying attitude toward official ministry in the United States is examined by James H. Provost, assistant professor of canon law at The Catholic University of America. In "Toward a Renewed Canonical Understanding of Official Ministry" he explores the tension between professionalism and bureaucracy in the American church as a way of understanding what meaning of official ministry others are likely to encounter as they join the ranks of official ministers now dominated by priests.

How to organize such ministry is the concern of James A. Coriden, academic dean at the Washington Theological Union. In light of the complexity which marked the organization of ministry in the early Church he explores "Options for the Organization of Ministry" as these are found today in the third Church, in charismatic groups, through collaborative ministry, or in proposals for a uniting Church.

Some Implications

These studies have clarified at least this, that concern for ministry today has mainly been voiced in terms of attention to ministers. The content of ministry—what it means in practice—deserves greater study. When this is done the concept of the local church will be crucial, for ministry in the Church is fundamentally a localized experience, whether addressed in terms of the *cura animarum*, preaching the Word, celebrating the sacraments, or acting on behalf of justice.

Some abiding concerns have been addressed in these papers not with a view to providing definitive solutions, but in hopes of suggesting perspectives that may lead to greater insight. Such are the questions of orders and jurisdiction, the relationship of clergy and laity in ministry, and the priest-bishop relationship. The Second Vatican Council did not resolve these, and in many instances merely placed side-by-side various approaches to them. Despite their seemingly abstract character, these issues touch intimately the experience of ministry and the future of official ministers in the Church.

Some new concerns have also been identified. The very language we use concerning ministry and ministers asserts a worldview and carries meanings beyond the immediate intent. This calls for careful attention to language and its connotations.

Substantively, the relationship of Church and world appeared through these studies as perhaps more fundamental to understanding ministry than the distinctions of clergy-laity, charism-office, or institution-event. Vatican II suggested some important openings on this issue; subsequent theological and practical Church experience has broadened this understanding. The implications for ministry have yet to be fully appreciated.

The impact of cultural realities on the meaning and structure of ministry have once again been highlighted. Despite the world-wide character of the Church, or perhaps because of it, adaptations to local cultures constitutes a major project for effective official ministry.

Ecclesiology, therefore, continues to be at the core of discussions on ministry. Issues of celibacy, the ordination of women, lay involvement in official ministries—all these are rooted in the approach taken to the question, what is the Church? Diverse ecclesiologies are found in conciliar teaching; they continue to contend as underlying factors in discussions on ministry questions. Until a greater working consensus is achieved in the Church on ecclesiological questions, ministry questions will remain unresolved.

One approach to developing such a consensus may be to go beyond our immediate context and, within a wider ecumenical setting, seek a broader consensus. These studies have suggested that issues of validity, the organization of ministry, and the significance of key experiences such as eucharistic celebrations may be placed in a more productive context when discussed with those beyond the immediate communion of the Roman Church.

Finally, there are some issues we did not address, partly because of the limitations in the Permanent Seminar design, partly because some issues go beyond the scope envisioned in this project. Further theological probing is needed on the Christological basis for ministry. Second, the implications of civil political processes for ministry in the Church deserve further study; democracy, in addition to other political systems now used in the Church, may have beneficial implications for several ministerial questions, such as the selection of ministers. Third, greater attention deserves to be given to what one does in doing ministry (praxis)—how one does ministry, what functions are rightly termed "ministry." Finally, greater nuancing ought to be provided for the term "lay ministry."

These papers have been developed in an academic fashion, but their purpose is certainly more than academic. The Church prepares to enter a new millennium. It may already have entered a new age for official ministry. The actual experience of ministry in local communities throughout the world is changing, leading to tensions, frustration, and no little confusion. It is the hope of the Permanent Seminar project that added clarification of the underlying concepts and theoretical framework for ministering may assist church administrators and all who are interested in promoting official ministry in this new age.

This effort of the Seminar also expresses the continuing commitment of the Canon Law Society of America to serve the Church, its people and its structures, in such a new age. Members of the Seminar project express their appreciation for the support of the Society which has made the following studies possible, and the continued interest of the editors of THE JURIST in this work.

James H. Provost, Director
C.L.S.A. Permanent Seminar

THE PUBLIC LANGUAGE OF MINISTRY

MARY COLLINS, O.S.B.
The Catholic University of America

The phenomenon of status orientation in the language of ministry is apparent in the liturgical texts for the ordination of bishops, priests and deacons set out in the 1968 *Pontificale Romanum*. Those texts themselves reflect a long tradition within the Church of making status distinctions within the community of believers and among those who serve it. This essay will investigate what is at issue in the phenomenon reflected in those texts. The investigation will have three parts. First, the liturgical texts themselves will raise the human question of ordering and community, and the function of language in the process of ordering. Next, selected historical data will be used to consider sacralization of ministry as an event in the institutional history of the Church. This will lead finally to some theological reflection on the present situation of the language of ministry in the Roman Catholic ecclesial community.

I. LITURGICAL TEXTS

The language of ministry used in rites of ordination can be presumed to express the official self-understanding of the group which uses the language. Public ritual language sets out for all who participate in the rites the relationships which are known and affirmed within the group. Roman Catholic ordination rites are rites of passage according to their structure and function. In typical passage rites, some members of a community enter into a new set of relationship with the group, and in the process, all the relationships within the group are modified and then reaffirmed.[1] The texts of the ordination rites use language which identifies as one of the outcomes of the liturgical action the status-elevation of the *ordinandi*.

---

[1]V. W. Turner, *Dramas, Fields, and Metaphors: Symbolic Action in Human Society* (Ithaca, N.Y.: Cornell University Press, 1974), pp. 273-275.

A. The Texts

Each ordination rite in the 1968 *Pontificale Romanum* contains a unit in which the presiding minister addresses the assembly and asks them to focus on the meaning of the event in which they are participants. Language about elevation is prominent. At the ordination of a bishop, the assembly is enjoined:

> Pay careful attention to the position in the Church to which our brother is about to be promoted. (. . . *sedulo attendite, ad qualem in Ecclesia gradum frater noster sit provehendus.*)[2]

At the ordination of a presbyter, the episcopal injunction to the assembly is:

> Give careful consideration to the position to which they are to be promoted. (. . . *attente perpendite ad qualem in Ecclesia gradum sint ascensuri.*)[3]

A similar injunction is spoken to those gathered for the ordination of deacons:

> Reflect thoughtfully on the ministerial rank to which they are to be promoted. (. . . *attente cogitate ad qualem ministerii gradum sint ascensuri.*)[4]

The new situation into which the ordinand is moving is in each case characterized as involving an ascent, a step upward, a promotion.

The candidates, too, are addressed with speech about elevation. The deacon-elect is told:

> ". . . you are being raised to the order of deacon." (. . . *vobis autem, filii dilectissimi, ad ordinem Diaconi provehendi. . . .*)[5]

The candidates for the presbyterate hear:

> You are now to be advanced to the order of the presbyterate.

[2]*Pontificale Romanum. De Ordinatione Diaconi, Presbyteri, et Episcopi.* Editio Typica (Typis Polyglottis Vaticanum, 1968; henceforth *PR*): Ordination of a Bishop, 18. English translations are the author's unless otherwise noted. Those of the International Commission for English in the Liturgy (ICEL) are given in footnotes. ICEL: "Consider carefully the position in the Church to which our brother is about to be raised."

[3]*PR*: Ordination of a Presbyter, 14. ICEL: "Consider carefully the position to which they are to be promoted."

[4]*PR*: Ordination of a Deacon, 14. ICEL: "Consider carefully the ministry to which they are to be promoted."

[5]Ibid. ICEL translation given.

(*Vos autem . . . ad ordinem Presbyterii provehendi. . . .*)[6]

The words spoken publicly to the bishop-elect break the pattern in an interesting way:

> Beloved brother, keep in mind that you are chosen by the Lord, raised up from among the people, and appointed to act on their behalf in matters related to God. The designation bishop refers to a job to be done, not an honor. Therefore, it is necessary that a bishop should serve rather than rule. . . . (*Tu autem, frater carissime, electus a Domino, cogita te ex hominibus esse assumptum et pro hominibus constitutum in iis quae sunt ad Deum. Episcopatus enim nomen est operis, non honoris, et Episcopum magis prodesse quam praeesse oportet . . .*)[7]

At the moment of reaching top rank, the one advancing is told, in phrases borrowed from the description of the levitical high priestly role fulfilled perfectly in Christ Jesus (Heb 5:1), that his is an extraordinary mediatorial role. Accordingly, he is cautioned about the paradoxical purpose of his elevated status: to be among the people as one who serves. This theme of service complements the theme of advancement, promotion, upward mobility in the rite. However, it is only the latter theme which is the focus of this study.

The ritual address to the assembly and the ritual address to the *ordinandi* are not the only uses of language of ascent. In the consecratory prayers spoken on behalf of the *ordinandi*, God is proclaimed as the one who authorizes and maintains the work of selecting and promoting men for special purposes. The prayer of consecration of the deacon declares:

> Almighty God . . . you are the giver of preferments, the assigner of roles, the one who arranges official appointments. (*Deus . . . honorum dator, ordinem distributor officiorumque dispositor . . .*)[8]

The consecratory prayer continues, celebrating the existence of a three-

---

[6]*PR*: Presbyter, 14. ICEL translation given.

[7]*PR*: Bishop, 18. ICEL: "You . . . have been chosen by the Lord. Remember that you are chosen from among men [sic; Latin: *hominibus*] and appointed to act for men and women [sic; Latin: *hominibus*] in relation to God. The title of bishop is not one of honor, but of function, and therefore a bishop should strive to serve rather than to rule. . . ."

[8]*PR*: Deacon, 21. ICEL: "Almighty God . . . You are the source of all honor, you assign to each his rank, you give each his ministry."

fold ministry as one of the *mirabilia dei* for which God will be glorified.

The prayer of consecration of the presbyter affirms the same reason for praise of God:

> [you are] . . . the source of preferments, the one who assigns all ranks, the one through whom the whole world advances and everything is made secure . . . (. . . *honorum auctor et distributor omnium dignitatum, per quem proficiunt universa, per quem cuncta firmantur* . . .)[9]

God's gift of a structured order is further elaborated on this occasion, too:

> . . . when you appointed high priests to rule your people, you chose other men next to them in rank and dignity, to be with them and help them in their task . . . (. . . *ut cum Pontifices summos regendis populis praefecisses, ad eorum societatis et operis adiumentum sequentis ordinis viros et secundae dignitatis eligeres.*)[10]

In this particular prayer, the order is explicitly acknowledged to be both sacral and hierarchical. Not all the uses of elevation language cited up to this point have distinguished ranks among those who have been promoted. But here, the presbyter is "next . . . in rank" to the "high priests," that is, the bishops.

All of this is credited to divine action. Thus the rite of ordination of a bishop culminates in the proclamation:

> May God, who has brought you to share the high priesthood of Christ, pour out on you the oils of mystical anointing. May he nourish you with spiritual blessings. (*Deus, qui summi Christi sacerdotii participem te effecit, ipse te mysticae delibutionis liquore perfundat, et spiritualis benedictionis ubertate fecundet.*)[11]

As the consecratory prayer unfolds, the act of consecration is said to bring the ordinand to a spiritual summit. Divine election which began with Abraham, which continued in the choice of the rulers and priests of Israel, which culminated in the election of Jesus, and which was

---

[9]*PR*: Presbyter, 22. ICEL: ". . . you are the source of every honor and dignity, of all progress and stability. . . ."

[10]Ibid. ICEL translation given.

[11]*PR*: Bishop, 28. ICEL: "God has brought you to share the high priesthood of Christ. May he pour out on you the oil of mystical anointing and enrich you with spiritual blessings."

extended to apostles chosen personally by Jesus, has now been revealed again in this choice.[12]

The texts of the ordination rites deserve thorough examination for the total vision of Christian ministry they set out, and also for what they omit speaking of, namely the prior election of all the baptized. They are being investigated here only insofar as they exhibit a sustained understanding that ordination involves status elevation. That understanding is reflected in the verb choices that describe the nature of the transaction in which the ordinand is engaged; e.g., *sit provehendus* and *sint ascensuri*. The outcomes of the ritual actions are identified in terms of status—*honor, dignitas, officium, ordo,* and *gradus*—rather than in functional language, despite the admonition to the bishop. Furthermore, the texts express an understanding that those who participate in these rites are also distinguishable among themselves according to a scheme of ranking; e.g., *ad qualem in Ecclesia gradum; ad qualem ministeriis gradum; secundae dignitatis.* Finally, they convey a conviction that both the status elevation and the distinctions are the work of God; e.g., *Deus . . . auctor . . . et distributor; Deus . . . dator . . . distributor . . . dispositor.*

The history of this language deserves thorough examination. It is almost as old as the Church; but it is not the language of the New Testament. The task of this essay is not to undertake a fully historical study of language traditions concerning ministry within the Church. The focus will be rather on the human phenomenon of ranked or hierarchical ordering which is reflected in the language of the 1968 rites of ordination. While the language itself attributes the phenomenon it describes to divine wisdom and divine intervention, it is nevertheless human language and so invites reflection on the human community, which uses language in several ways: to name experience, to structure it, and to define it.

B. Human Community

Cultural anthropology characterizes human society as a process in which communities use ritual acts to express, among other things, the paradoxical twin truths of the *mythos* within which they live together: what unites them is prior to and is more fundamental than the distinctions among them, and yet the distinctions among them are essential to their continued existence as a people. The human community must live within the pull exerted by the truth of structure and the truth of pre-

[12]Ibid., 26.

structural realities which gives value to any ordered common life. Human communities are constituted and maintained through corporate symbolic acts which assert this vital tension as the basic condition of human social existence.[13]

Rites of ordination within the Church are examples of this larger social phenomenon. The Christian community which gathers to ordain ministers for the community intends to affirm and to sanction distinctions among the members which are perceived to be essential to the very existence of the Church. Ecclesial existence itself is valued because those who call themselves *ekklēsia* and ordain ministers for themselves believe themselves to be a holy people set apart from all other peoples for a mission. Accordingly, the factual phenomenon or ordering within the ecclesial community is not the matter under investigation here. What is under investigation is language which reflects the perceptions that some of those set apart for distinct ministries vital to the well-being of the community have been divinely elevated, and that rank exists within the elevated group so that the relationships among the ordained are between superiors and inferiors. In the language of ecclesiastical documents, the Church is not simply an ordered community, but one which is hierarchically ordered. Those not ordained into any of the ranks of the hierarchy are inferior to them all.

C. Language: Naming, Structuring and Defining Reality

The study of the many uses of language has dominated recent western philosophical inquiry. This essay cannot engage in a thorough exploration of such a major area of study. We must be content simply to point out and to summarize several considerations about the uses of language which are pertinent to our focus: status orientation in the public language of ministry in the Roman Catholic Church.

Original language is spoken language. In the kind of speaking which occurs within the situations of life, language provides the speaker the opportunity to take up a relationship with the experiences of corporate and personal life. Such speaking also allows the speaker the opportunity of structuring the experience in order to render it intelligible. Language used in the first way involves "naming." Language used for the second purpose involves "handling" experience.

Speakers use ordinary words, available language, for both the naming and the cognitive structuring of experience. In actual life situations, words inevitably function as metaphors. They are capable of partial

---

[13]Cf. Turner, pp. 292-298. His terms for the polarity are structure and anti-structure.

discernments of truth, but the reality of unprecedented experience inevitably exceeds the structuring capabilities of available words. Thus, ordinary words have a wide range of approximate uses. In this lies their power and their weakness. Conceptual clarity can be achieved only if and when ordinary words are transformed into terms. Terminological language is a language of restricted meanings, of definition and precision.[14]

These considerations draw our attention to the fact that the original language of ministry in the formative stages of the Church is a language of naming and structuring the unprecedented experience of ministry within the community. As the next section of the paper will show there is no single tradition of the original language of ministry. Only slowly does a consensus build about a common set of words to name the experience of ministry. Only slowly does a common set of ministerial experiences undergird the emerging common language. Even more slowly does the language of ministry receive precise definition which restricts its applicability in the speech of the community.

The related matter of the public use of a single set of words to name, handle, and define ecclesial experience is a particularly complex matter. The liturgical event as a moment of religious celebration of the saving mystery of Christ quite rightly uses language which is rich with metaphoric ambiguity. Language which is expansive in its applicability allows ritual participants to recognize through the words of their common life their own participation in the ministry of the Church. At the same time the liturgical event of ordination, a rite of passage, is an occasion designed to introduce structural distinction and difference and limit into the community. It may thereby seem to demand language which defines, language which is technical and restricted in its applications. Words and ceremonial behavior joined together serve as language in this regard. Furthermore, the language proclaimed in the liturgical assembly inevitably carries with it a divine warrant. The community which speaks and listens and acts together in worship believes that what is said and done there reflects the intent of God for them and calls for faithful and obedient response.

How is the status-oriented language of ministry found in public rites to be understood? Is it allusive, descriptive, prescriptive, restrictive? A brief survey of the development of the original language of ministry is a

[14]F. J. van Beeck, *Christ Proclaimed: Christology as Rhetoric* (New York: Paulist, 1979), pp. 64-104. This chapter contains a useful summary of pertinent issues in the functioning of language.

necessary foundation for any reflection on the theological significance of the traditional language of ministry.

II. Sacralization of Ministry

Much New Testament research in the past decade has been directed to the matter of tracing the development of the gospel ministry. However, less scholarly attention has been focused on the process whereby some of the NT language came to define a sacral order. That process will be the subject of the middle section of this essay.

A. Flux in Forms and Language: The NT Evidence

Scholarly consensus exists that the communities of the New Testament period were indeed organized or ordered. There is also agreement that several patterns of institutional order coexisted and evolved independently in the churches reflected in the New Testament. It is not the purpose of this section of the essay to weigh the merits of each of several possible interpretations offered to explain the data on which this exegetical consensus is based.[15] One position, that of Andre Lemaire, will be followed for convenience in the presentation of pertinent material. Lemaire proposes on the basis of his own extensive studies that the distinctive institutional patterns of ministry reflect not only different epochs in the life of the churches but also different ethno-cultural settings of the earliest communities. Whatever the case, different clusters of words name and interpret distinctive experiences of ministry within local communities. The language for speaking of ministry in the New Testament is neither technical nor precise. Thus, the ranking of fixed ministries hierarchically necessarily postdates the witness of the New Testament.[16]

What are the data that invite Lemaire to these judgments? A schematization of three time periods (30-45; 45-65; and 65-100) and three settings (Jerusalem, Antioch, and Asia Minor) provides him some insight into the development of public language for the gospel ministry.

The Jerusalem community in the years 30-45 A.D. comprised two

---

[15]See, for example, R. E. Brown, "Episkopē and Episkopos—The New Testament Evidence," *Theological Studies* 41 (1980): 322-338; J. Delorme, *Le ministère et les ministères selon le Nouveau Testament* (Paris: Editions du Seuil, 1974); A. Lemaire, "The Ministries in the New Testament: Recent Research," *Biblical Theology Bulletin* 3 (1973): 138.

[16]A. Lemaire, "L'Eglise apostolique et les ministères," *Revue de Droit Canonique* 23 (1973): 28.

ethno-cultural groups, the "Hebrews" (Palestinian Jews who spoke Aramaic) and the "Hellenists" (Greek-speaking Jews of the Diaspora). The original Jerusalem ministry of "the Twelve" spawned the parallel Jerusalem ministry of "the Seven" as a response to the internal ethno-cultural conflict attested to in Acts. Each group brought the good news of God's action in Jesus to the synagogues of its own people. Each developed its own treasury for the poor (Acts 6:1-11). And each provoked violent persecution from within the synagogues. The "Hebrews" Peter, James and John were arrested; the "Hellenist" Stephen was stoned.

Under these pressures the early order at Jerusalem gave way. When the Hellenists scattered, the institution of "the Seven" vanished, leaving its traces only in language. Language also preserved the memory of "the Twelve," an institution evidently rooted in the Galilean ministry of Jesus himself. Paul, for example, referred to "the Twelve" in the primitive credal formula of 1 Cor 15:3-5.[17] But when Paul actually dealt with the Jerusalem church, the leadership he knew in the decade of the '50's consisted of a council of elders.

A second period of ministerial development occurred in the period 45-65 A.D. Two centers, responding to local circumstances, had begun to speak in distinctive ways about the exercise of the gospel ministry. The church in Antioch faced for the first time the task of incorporating non-Jews; its leading ministries were those of prophet and teacher. At Jerusalem, leadership among Jewish Christians developed through the innovative appropriation and adaptation of the existing Jewish institution of the presbyterate or council of elders to meet new needs.

At Antioch, the prophet's task was to exhort, to console, and to build up the "Christian" community. The setting for this ministry was the Christian assembly. The forms the ministry took included the opening up of the scripture as the living Word of God addressed to the gathered community and the proclamation of the great thanksgiving prayer, the *eucharistia*.[18] The teacher at Antioch was rather something of a technical specialist working in a non-liturgical setting. The teacher's exposition, *didachē*, provided formal knowledge of scripture according to Jewish methods of interpretation. Teaching was Paul's first ministry in the church at Antioch.

The prophets and teachers secured the community at Antioch. The community so secured inaugurated the mission to the Diaspora and to

[17]Ibid.: 20-21.
[18]Ibid.: 24.

the Greek-speaking world in general. The ministry of the apostle emerged to provide this missionary service. Barnabas and Paul were among those set apart for apostolic mission. Their first task was to announce the gospel, then to form a community of those who accepted the good news; but they were to remain only until an organized community was established, and then move on, maintaining contact through letters and visits by co-workers. Paul's account to the Corinthian church of the basic ministerial structure may reflect the Antiochene scheme of values during this great missionary era: first are apostles, then prophets, then teachers (I Cor 12:28).[19]

During the same era James and the elders ministered to the Jerusalem community as its presbyters. In Palestinian Judaism the presbyterate was a familiar institution, a college or assembly which exercised power within a political community. The elders of a village as well as the elders of the whole people exercised legislative power through interpretations of Torah in both civil and religious matters. They regularly exercised judicial power through excommunication.

In the *mythos* of late Judaism the "elders of the whole people," the Jewish Sanhedrin, were understood to have divine authority. The origins of the Sanhedrin, a literal "council of Seventy," were found in the express command of YHWH to Moses to share some of his Spirit (Num 11:16-30). These "elders of the whole people" were drawn from among both priestly and non-priestly families. Thus the presbyterate included laymen, regularly pharisees. The president of the Sanhedrin was the High Priest.[20] Elsewhere, the head of a local council was simply the chief *hēgoumenos*.

The emerging "presbyterate" of the Jerusalem church served the beleagured new community by guarding its teaching and practice so that these were faithful to and did not negate the scriptures, and also by taking care of the treasury and disbursements for the poor.[21] Ironically, to give dignity, meaning, and credibility to their efforts to build and to maintain a new community of faith in the holy city this marginal group of Jewish sectarians either boldly or naively had appropriated the identity of the Jerusalem council of elders. The name *presbyteroi* resonated with reference to the great Jewish religious-legal institution; the overtones were heard in later stages of development.

---

[19]Ibid.: 22-23; also "Recent Research," p. 144.

[20]A. Lemaire, *Les Ministères aux origines de l'Eglise: Naissance de la triple hiérarchie: évêques, presbytres, diacres,* Lectio Divina 68 (Paris, 1971), pp. 21-27.

Still these two centers at Jerusalem and Antioch did not provide comprehensive ministerial models in this expansionist era of early Christianity. Thus, a third pattern of ministry took shape among the churches of the apostolic mission in which Paul was a principal actor; it left its linguistic traces in the New Testament phrase *episkopoi kai diakonoi* (Phil 1:1). The words were taken from the language of daily life. In ordinary speech, the generic word *episkopos* was available for designating anyone who exercised a function of supervision or inspection.[22] It had no particular or peculiar religious usage. *Diakonos* was a word of wide-ranging usefulness in ordinary Greek speech. While it might designate persons with social inferiority, e.g., employees and domestics, it was also used for merchants and for pagan priests whose work was service to the whole people. It was used indiscriminately to name male and female. When it was used in a religious context, sometimes but not always the Greek *diakonos* names one who was involved in the sacred meals of the cult.[23] Accordingly, in this middle era of ecclesial development, two ordinary Greek words, *episkopos* and *diakonos* were expanded in their reference. Christians employed them to name the new social and religious reality of the first century: the gospel ministry being exercised within the churches outside Jerusalem and Antioch, but united with these centers through the itinerant apostles.

Language remained fluid throughout the era, directed always to naming and handling evolving ministerial experiences. Evidence indicates that Paul and Barnabas, for example, organized the local ministers of the gospel into a quasi-presbyterate (Acts 14:23; cf. I Thess 5:12). Yet it is unlikely that councils of elders in the churches born from the apostolic mission could have imitated in every aspect the presbyteral ministry as it was exercised at Jerusalem. On the contrary, differences in understanding about the requirements of the gospel ministry are what precipitated the crisis of missionary expansion. The conflict was resolved through agreement that the one ministry of guiding the church must have flexibility in its exercise (Gal 2:1-8; cf. Acts 15).

In a third stage of ecclesial organization and development, 65-100 A.D., the presbyteral institution and the word "presbyter" spread

---

[21]Lemaire, "L'Eglise apostolique," p. 24.

[22]Lemaire, "Recent Research," pp. 145-146; cf. "Les Ministères aux origines," pp. 27-30.

[23]Lemaire, "Les Ministères aux origines," pp. 31-34; cf. "Recent Research," pp. 145-146.

from the Jewish-Christian center through the whole Church.[24] It was a period of consolidation in matters of organization and ministry. What was at issue was assuring both the authenticity and the strength of the local churches after the deaths of the original Twelve and of the first apostles. Some in each local community were needed to direct the *ekklēsia* according to the norm of the gospel message, which was still unfolding in its implications through their teaching. Presbyteral organization provided a needed structure.

The word "presbyter" had had a long history of technical use within Judaism to designate the institution of authority, dating from the word choice of the translators of the Septuagint. But the word had also survived in the ordinary language of the Greek-speaking world. The word itself is a comparative. The *presbyteros* is elder in comparison with the *presbys*, an old one. So it designated the senior among peers or colleagues or adults in a family. *Presbyteros* was also commonly used for another comparative purpose, namely to distinguish the failing and defects of *neōteros*—the younger—from the experience, wisdom, and ability to guide which is characteristic of the *presbyteros*.

The word scarcely had a technical use in the Hellenistic world of the first century. When it was employed in the political sphere, in Asia Minor and Greece, it meant to designate maturity and wisdom. However, the word had gained some capacity for definition of social structures in Egypt. Evidence exists that members of a representative or administrative group within a community or an association were called *presbyteroi*.[25] So a social and linguistic context existed outside Judaism and the church of the "Hebrews" for using the word *presbyteros* to designate those responsible for gospel ministry.

The need for an identifiable head or chief of the local presbyterate also intensified when the apostle to a church was no longer living. The function of local headship had, of course, begun to emerge earlier. Language is again a chief witness to the development. Verbal substantives like *proistamenos*, *prōtokathedritēs*, and *prokathēmenos* point to the emergence of someone from within the assembly. Consensus about the naming of that one apparently came more slowly. The use of *hēgoumenos* and *prohēgoumenos* in Hebrews (13:7, 17, 24), in the first letter of Clement (XXI, 6) and in the *Shepherd* of Hermas (II/2,6 and III/9,7) support the hypothesis that *hēgemōn* was an early word choice

---

[24]Lemaire, "L'Eglise apostolique," p. 20; "Recent Research," p. 153.
[25]Lemaire, "Les Ministères aux origines," pp. 17-21.

of the church at Rome, where that literature originated.[26] In the church
at Antioch, Ignatius was clear and decisive about an alternative word
choice: the one who is first or head is the one called *episkopos*. Ignatius' preference eventually prevailed. However, that development
is reflected outside New Testament texts, and so discussion of it must
be deferred.

In summary, current research on New Testament texts related to the
original language of ministry yields the following data. Clusters of
words appear which designate various operative arrangements within
the local churches for maintaining the gospel ministry. The Twelve and
the Seven ministered at Jerusalem in an early period, perhaps 30-
45 A.D. The apostles, prophets, and teachers emerge as the ministers
of the gospel in Antioch in the missionary era of 45-65 A.D. The
episkopoi kai diakonoi, dependent on the apostles, were the contem-
poraries and counterparts of the prophets and teachers in the local
churches established through the apostolic mission. In Jerusalem *presbyteroi* administered the community. The extension of a local presbyteral order throughout the entire Church occurred in the period 65-
100 A.D. In the meeting of the two patterns of ministry, both were
transmuted. Slowly, with the deaths of the apostles, local leadership
established itself within the presbyteral structure. No early consensus
developed over the naming of this ministry of local leadership. Thus,
New Testament literature uses a range of words like *episkopos*, *presbyteros*, *hēgoumenos*, *proistamenos*, to designate local leadership
without any technical precision or any clear definition.

The phenomenon of community organization is everywhere evident.
Some within the *ekklēsia* clearly have special responsibility for the
gospel ministry, precisely because the good news revealed in Jesus is
what undergirds the community's existence. Along those in the *ekklēsia* with ministerial responsibility, there are further specifications of
different ministries. But all forms of ministry, including the ministry of
leadership, rise and recede according to what is needed for the different
communities to be maintained in the gospel hope.

The language of ministry does accord different relative values to the
ministries—e.g., "first are apostles, then prophets, then teachers"—and
it acknowledges the inevitability of a focus of leadership within a
group. But the value placed on different ministries reflects the community's perception of how the gospel is to be served. Among conceiv-

[26]Lemaire, "Recent Research," pp. 145-146; cf. "Les Ministères aux origines," pp. 27-
30, 169, 193.

able alternatives some form of ordering ministry had to shape the life of the local church at each given moment. But the language does not warrant conclusions about a single order, divinely mandated, or of any absolute ranking among those who serve the community.

B. Good Order: The Second and Third Centuries

If neither a stable language, a normative church order, nor a formal hierarchy among ministers is evident in the New Testament literature all of these realities find expression in the literary witness of the next several Christian generations. These three developments will be considered in turn.

The seeds of stability in the language of ministry, normative church order, and hierarchy are all clearly planted in the letters of Ignatius of Antioch written at the turn of the second century. In his correspondence, Ignatius advocated a well-delineated ministerial structure for the local church. At the head is the one named *episkopos*; he is surrounded by the council of presbyters; he is assisted by deacons. The people for their part are to submit themselves (*hypotassomenon*) to this arrangement.[27]

Although Ignatius' choice of *episkopos* and *diakonos* might be explained in terms of the *koinē* usage evident in the New Testament, he clearly intended to expand the field of meaning for these words beyond secular to specific religious usage, indeed even to venture sacralization. In his letter to the Trallians, for example, the *episkopos* is called "image of God," the *presbyteroi* are the "senate of God" and the "assembly of the apostles," and the deacons are to be "revered as Jesus Christ." His interpretative referents are not consistent, however. The Philadelphians are told that the bishop represents both God and Jesus Christ, the presyteral senate is a tribunal of reconciliation for sinners, and the deacons are envoys.[28] Clearly his vocabulary choices were well-established. How words were to be understood with reference to the divine work in and through the ministry of the local church was not yet so clear.

Ignatius of Antioch, himself an *episkopos*, held an unquestionably

[27]Lemaire, "Les Ministères aux origines," pp. 169-174, 199; cf. Ignatius of Antioch to Polycarp, VI, 1; to the Trallians, II, 1; Ephesians, II, 1.

[28]Lemaire, "Les Ministères aux origines," pp. 167-171; cf. Ignatius of Antioch to the Trallians, III, 1; to the Philadelphians, IV; VII, 1; VIII, 1; X, 20.

high regard for the role. Contemporary correspondence reveals that not all the local churches of his day shared either his administrative style or his estimate of its significance. When he wrote to the church at Smyrna, setting out his doctrine that the *episkopos* was the one through whom God attaches himself to the local church, he addresses it to Polycarp as *episkopos*. However, Polycarp's self-designation differed. When he wrote to the church of the Philippians, he wrote in his own name and in the name of those who were "presbyters with him," with no advertance to an *episkopos* functioning apart from or over them. In a fourth locale, Rome, the word *episkopos* was apparently not yet in use at the turn of the second century. In the extant writings from that church, leadership or headship was designated through the word *hēgoumenos*. Thus, only a retrospective reading of the early second-century witness can find an authoritative position in the teaching of Ignatius concerning a three-fold hierarchically ordered ministry. In his own era, he was one witness to the continuing evolution of language, structure, and function. Nevertheless, the position he advocated established the trajectory which extends to the church of Vatican II and the language of its rites of ordination. What circumstances fostered the developments?

Pierre Nautin proposes that it was the social realities pressing on the second and third century Christian communities which supported the consolidation of local church order under the headship of a monarchial *episkopos*. Alexandre Faivre maintains that it was growth in numbers and so in new ministerial needs that fostered development of "lesser ministries" in the same era, and created a correlative need for a scheme of distinction of status and definition of roles. A summary account of developments both "at the top" and "at the bottom" is in order.

Ignatius of Antioch had insisted that nothing was to be done by the presbyters and deacons of the churches without the approval of the bishop. Practically, this meant that the overseer or chief became the final arbiter in community disputes, approved choices of "marriage in the Lord" and made judgments about the distribution of alms to the poor and about wages for the presbyters and deacons from the treasury of the church. Because he had both patrons and clients, money and authority to make decisions, he acquired the social status of any powerful person. Civil authorities as well as church members dealt with him accordingly. The dynamic of episcopal ascendancy, says Nautin, was sociological in its origins. Yet a culturally grounded sacralizing tendency quickly gave episcopal ascendancy a foundation in divine wisdom.[29]

The Hellenistic cultural sense of divine order (*kosmos* or *taxis*) which is reflected in the hierarchical cosmologies of contemporary philosophical systems—Stoic, Neo-Platonic, and Hermetic—found its way into discussions of church order, too. Interest in such order is evident in the pastoral letters of the New Testament. However, this cultural assumption that the arrangement (*taxis*) of society was the work of God was a dominant motif in much Christian literature of the second and third centuries.[30] Early writers like Clement of Rome readily exploited the cultural horizon of divine cosmic arrangement to speak of the Christian realities of creation and redemption. Initially this use of *taxis* in Christian writing was non-technical, even exploratory, as authors sought to determine its usefulness for understanding the theological significance of the already operative three-fold ministry of bishop, presbyters, and deacons within the Church.

Latin writers of this era like Tertullian translated *taxis* through the common Latin *ordo*. In doing so they refocused the meaning field of *taxis* but also reinterpreted the word *ordo*. Previously, the Latin *ordo*, unlike the Greek *taxis*, had little cosmological valence. It specified a social group or an organized class, or some part of that group or class which had responsibility for its direction, or a social hierarchy.[31]

Thus, the common Latin *ordo* fitted the sociological phenomenon of ecclesial ministry on several scores. The bishops, presbyters and deacons together exercised a ministerial function in the local church. As a part within the whole they were immediately distinguishable from those who had no such public responsibility. They were equivalently an *ordo*. Furthermore, they were differentiated themselves, "arranged" according to roles and functions. Such arrangements were open to interpretation as a divinely constituted hierarchy when *taxis* and *ordo*

---

[29]P. Nautin, "L'evolution des ministères au IIe et au IIIe siècle," *Revue de Droit Canonique* 23 (1973): 48-50, 54-56; cf. Ignatius to Polycarp, V, 2.

[30]The role of the household codes in the development of church order is discussed in C. Osiek, "Relation of Charism to Rights and Duties in the New Testament Church," in this volume; See also Nautin, "L'evolution"; also R. Roques, *L'Univers Dionysien: Structure hiérarique du monde selon le Pseudo-Denys* (Paris: Aubier, 1954), p. 36; P. van Beneden, *Aux Origines d'une terminologie sacrementelle ordo, ordinare, ordinatio dans la littérature chrétienne avant 313* (Louvain: Spicilegium Sacrum, 1974), pp. 14-15. Cf. Clement to the Corinthians 20.2; 40.1; 48, 1.

[31]van Beneden, pp. 2-4, 13-14.

were played against each other in discussions of the significance of the *klēroi*.[32]

The first systematic presentation of Christian ministry as a manifestation of the hierarchical divine economy would come from the pen of the fifth century Pseudo-Dionysius, and would be taken up by successive generations of medieval thinkers. Between the second and the fifth centuries, socially induced developments in church order occurred which later seemed to warrant such a comprehensive interpetation. The *Apostolic Tradition* of Hippolytus, product of Roman church life in the late second and early third centuries, contains traces of what was happening. Faivre's interpretation of the document in the context of its derivatives offers a plausible account of the significance of those developments for the birth and eventual maturation of the institution of an ecclesiastical hierarchy.

What data from the *Apostolic Tradition* shed light on the matter? First, Hippolytus wrote of a church some of whose members were already clergy. He knew where the distinguishing line was to be drawn. *Klēroi* are those who take part in the offering. They were publicly recognized as a distinct group because the *episkopos* had laid hands on them in the assembly. Others whose service in the community was public but unrelated to the offering are not *klēroi*: widows, readers, virgins, sub-deacons, and healers.[33] According to Hippolytus, virgins had claimed their place in the community by their own choice; healers, by the evident truth of their service. Widows, readers, and sub-deacons were to be installed by the *episkopos* to render service. But he deliberately declined to lay his hands upon them.

Several developments are notable in Hippolytus' presentation of what he considers the proper arrangement of things. First, differences and limits were an acknowledged part of ecclesial life. Second, value judgments continued to be made about the services performed by community members, although the values were different from those established at Antioch in the first century, where "first were apostles, then prophets, then teachers." Now the focus of service is not the gospel but "the offering."[34]

---

[32]Ibid., pp. 14-15; cf. p. 44, n. 99.

[33]I. de la Potterie, "L'origine et le sense primitif du mot 'laïc'", *Nouvelle Revue Théologique* 80 (1958): 847-53. He notes the original identity of *laikos* as that part of the *laos* not consecrated for the service of cult.

[34]A. Faivre, *Naissance d'Une Hiérarchie: les Premières Etapes du Cursus Clérical* (Paris: Beauchesne, 1977), pp. 58-61.

In a third development, public demarcation of ecclesial status was being established through the use of a gesture or its absence. By it, the community had been differentiated into a top and a bottom. Even at the top, rank among the *klēroi* was further refined through this same gesture. While all had hands laid on them, only one rank had authority to extend the gesture. This assertion of episcopal prerogative implies a fourth development. The prerogative rests on a claim to divine power, which the bishop may confer and delegate as he sees fit for the good order of the community.[35]

If the claim to power calls for some explanation, Hippolytus provided it in his prayer for the ordination of the bishop. That explanation has more than antiquarian significance, since the ordination rite of 1968 draws deeply from the third century text as an expression of the faith of the Church even in the twentieth century. Hippolytus' prayer celebrated God's compassion preceding and establishing the order to all things, including the order of his Church.[36] In his compassion and for his glory God selected a people and then chose rulers of the people and priests for the sanctuary. These were to receive a share of his Spirit. The original world Hippolytus called upon for the language of his prayer is clearly that of the High Priest presiding over the Sanhedrin of late Judaism and officiating at the temple cult. His prayer also incorporated the self-understanding of the Sanhedrin, namely that they were descendant from the patriarchs and prophets. What Hippolytus might have, but did not evoke, is equally significant. He does not celebrate the divine disorder of Pentecost. For whatever reasons, his prayer celebrates an *ekklēsia* more orderly than the *ekklēsia* of the new age in which all the *laos* of God unexpectedly have received some share of the Spirit of God.[37]

Hippolytus' interpretative frame for the preferred order of the church at Rome at the turn of the new century is neither self-explanatory nor original. It represents one emphasis among available alternatives, evidently a culturally favored one. He is witness to the contemporary reinterpretation of the early "institutions" for the gospel ministry. The original patterns of apostles, prophets, and teachers, *episkopoi kai diakonoi*, and local presbyterates leading an odd sort of priestly people have been overlaid by the sacerdotal and sacralized

[35]Ibid., pp. 54-56.

[36]B. Botte, ed. *La Tradition Apostolique de Saint Hippolyte*, LQF 39 (Munster Westfalen: Aschendorffsche Verlagsbuchhandlung, 1963), p. 3. Cf. *PR*: Bishop, 26.

[37]de la Potterie, pp. 841-842.

images of late Judaism. Ranks of levites, priests, and a high priest presenting the offering had caught the imaginations of Hellenistic churches in the second century; it would capture them by the end of the fifth. This occurred even as Judaism was abandoning the horizon of a sacralized sacerdotal locus of spiritual power—albeit against its will—and risking the very possibility it had rejected in the original preaching of the gospel.

Whatever the irony, the Hellenistic church had to take shape and find language to express its self-understanding, and it did so. The image world of a sacralized social order, that found in the ancient scriptures and in defunct institutions, provided a conceptual buffer against cultural disorientation. But it also blocked memory of the radical newness of the original experience of resurrection faith with its unexpected breakthroughs of the Spirit of God. Hippolytus' church was still familiar with the possible disruptive choice of God's Spirit manifesting itself in the confessor of the faith. He himself did not try to suppress the phenomenon by presuming to lay hands on one whom God had chosen independently of the *episkopos*. However, he did insert the confessor within the local presbyterate, finding him a place within the established order. Genuine spiritual power had to be subordinated to the bishop, locus of all legitimate spiritual authority in the world of orthodox Hellenistic Christianity.

C. A World to Live In: Fourth to Sixth Centuries

In 313 A.D. the free exercise of religion was authorized in the empire; in 381 the emperor imposed the religion of the apostle Peter on all the peoples of the empire. These political developments challenged the Church structurally, pressing it to organize itself for its new public role. In addition to adjustments related to sheer numerical growth, key organizational developments contributed further to status orientation within church order and in the public language of ministry. First was the establishment of an expanded clerical *ordo* as a public institution. Accompanying it was the process of juridical, liturgical, and theological legitimization of a hierarchy within that new *ordo*. A summary of these developments is appropriate.

The exploratory and clearly metaphorical use of the word *ordo* among Christian writers of earlier generations—Tertullian tried *ordo episcoporum*, *ordo ecclesiae*, *ordo sacerdotalis*, *ordo ecclesiasticus*, *ordo viduarum*, and *ordo Melchisedec*—became precise technical language to identify a public institution in the late fourth and early fifth centuries.[38] An order of clerics gradually took its place alongside the old Roman *ordines* of senators and knights in the decaying empire. Clerics eventually formed a distinct social group, ranked internally, for the performance of distinct public service. The process of constituting the new *ordo* as a public institution was effected by both civil and ecclesiastical legislation. Law did not merely reflect life, but performed a creative function in this matter. Thus, the Theodosian Code (438), reflecting civil developments through the fourth century, specified: ". . . qui divino cultu ministeria impendunt, id est hi qui clerici appelantur" (16.2).[39]

Extant church orders document the development of the public *ordo* through their listings of who was to be named in the litanies, in what sequence members of the assembly were to receive communion, and how and by whom persons were to be ordained or installed in the various positions; church councils and synods legislated who were suitable candidates. In Gaudemet's judgment, the first ecclesiastical legislation in this formative era of "Christendom" may have served primarily for the emulation of imperial style itself, organizing, distinguishing and defining, and legislating. In any case, the practical impact of early rounds of legislation about clerics was not strong. Exceptions were common; regional differences flourished; new rounds followed on earlier decisions, repeating them and modifying them.[40]

But some ground was gained. An earlier understanding of *klēroi* as those who serve the offering was extended and then redefined through a series of distinctions. Early on, the group called *klēroi* had been coextensive with the ordained, those on whom hands had been laid by the bishop. But the *Apostolic Constitution* (Book VIII 2.12), dating from the end of the fourth century, witnesses to an expanded clerical group whose special standing in the community was publicly recognized in the arrangement for the distribution of the *eulogia* remaining after the celebration of the mysteries: the bishop received four portions, presbyters three, deacons two, and others one: sub-deacon, lector, psalmist, and deaconess. The distribution scheme, it was claimed, showed honor expressive of the dignity of each in a church which is not a school of disorder (*ataxias*) but of *eutaxias*, felicitous arrangement. Notably, even as the group of *klēroi* had expanded, it too had been

---

[38]J. Gaudemet, "De la liberté constantinienne à une Eglise d'Etat," *Revue de Droit Canonique* 23 (1973): 60-61; cf. van Beneden, p. 15.

[39]Faivre, pp. 279-292.

[40]Ibid., p. 64.

sorted into a top and bottom. Nevertheless, despite the protestations of the text, the bottom was not yet as clearly ordered as the top. That matter would occupy several more generations.

One of the points of uncertainty in the fourth and fifth centuries was the matter of women's place in a well-ordered imperial church. If the Syrian *Apostolic Constitutions* (VIII 19.2) had room for laying hands on women, situating them among the *klēroi*, albeit at the bottom, the Canons of Hippolytus (ca. 340), while ostensibly maintaining an old distinction, had actually introduced a new one. In that Egyptian schema for a well-ordered church, while the chosen (*klēroi*) included many groups, only bishops, priests, and deacons are ordained through the laying on of hands. However, the Canons also pronounce unequivocally that ordination is only for men.[42]

Gaudemet and others have noted that the process of excluding women altogther in the emerging scheme of things was not without its difficulties. Local monophysite and nestorian churches of Syria and priscillianist and montanist churches in the west certainly continued including women among their deacons and presbyters during this era. Moreover, repeated civil and ecclesiastical legislation through the fourth and fifth centuries, including explicit condemnations of clerics who allowed women ministerial functions reserved to men, suggests that the exclusion of women from the clerical *ordo* was disruptive of actual ministerial practice in many places in the empire.[43]

Uncertainty about good order was also evident in efforts to determine the relative significance of the various services among the lesser ministries "at the bottom" of the emerging clerical *ordo*. These were forming a pool from which the higher orders might draw as needed to maintain their numbers. Sub-deacon and reader vied for status, each gaining ascendancy or losing it in different local churches during the fourth century. The matter was apparently settled in favor of the sub-deacon according to a cultic scale of values in which the handling of

[41]Faivre, p. 81. Cf. F. X. Funk, ed., *Didascalia et Constitutiones Apostolorum* (Paderborn, 1895; reprint, Torino: Bottega d'Erasmo, 1959) Book VIII, 31,2.

[42]Faivre, pp. 71-73; cf. J. M. Hanssens, *La Liturgie D'Hippolyte,* Orientalia Christiana Anelecta 155 (Roma: Pont. Institutum Orientalium Studiorum, 1959), pp. 73-75.

[43]Gaudemet, p. 63; cf. R. Gryson, *The Ministry of Women in the Early Church* (Collegeville: Liturgical Press, 1976); also E. Schüssler-Fiorenza, "Word, Spirit, and Power: Women in Early Christian Communities," in R. Ruether and E. McLaughlin, ed., *Women of Spirit* (New York: Simon and Schuster, 1979), pp. 30-70.

sacred vessels for the offering had greater significance than the presentation of the sacred text.[44]

Consolidating the *cursus* for clerics occupied bishops of the fifth and early sixth centuries. At Rome, with no women under consideration to disturb the metaphor, Sosimus, Celestine, and Leo cast the matter in military terms in which good performance and good conduct at entry ranks were rewarded with promotion and perhaps eventually admission to the highest.[45] At the close of the period, the bureaucratic notion of an orderly *cursus* through which men could advance by grades was firmly in possession. The notion was supported by a range of decretals and other legal texts (many falsified for the sake of advocacy, according to the custom of the day) and effected through liturgical rites marking each step of advancement.[46]

What has not yet been addressed directly is the specific role of concepts of hierarchy in the process of sacralization of the gospel ministries. This sacralization process was concurrent with but not identical to the development of the clerical *ordo* as a public institution. Since the idea of sacred hierarchy is captured linguistically throughout the texts of the 1968 Roman Catholic ordination rites cited earlier, it needs to be accounted for. It is no more self-explanatory, from a twentieth century perspective, than Hippolytus' presentation of gospel ministry in the superimposed sacerdotal images borrowed from an obsolescent Jewish institution or the fifth century presentation of Christian ministry as a graded public *ordo*, a form of civil service system in which males who meet specific qualifications ascend by degrees.

In reflecting on the phenomenon of ranked ministries, Faivre asserts that it is a fact of the ancient world that groups were composed of unequal members who were inevitably ordered hierarchically. L. Dumont, citing the sociologist Talcott Parsons for support, argues that social stratification necessarily occurs in all epochs.[47] What distinguishes the "ancients" from Parsons is the interpretation given to the phenomenon of internal ranking in a group. Contemporary sociological theory explains stratification within a group in functional terms. Every group distinguished from others by some self-understanding and some goals makes practical judgments about what has relative signifi-

---

[44]Faivre, p. 96.

[45]Ibid., p. 330.

[46]Ibid., pp. 327-352.

[47]Ibid., p. 57; cf. L. Dumont, *Homo Hierarchicus* (University of Chicago Press, 1970), pp. 19-20.

cance for promoting its good and its goals. Groups necessarily organize to survive. Contemporary anthropological theory explains that social groups are always in process, maintaining themselves precisely to the degree that they attend not only to group structure but also to the prior reality which gives them identity as a group for which the internal order exists and because of which it may change.

Hellenistic cosmological theories provided a different account of the significance of ranked ministries. They were earthly manifestations of heavenly hierarchies. Although Dionysius, pseudonymous author of the extant fifth century treaties on this topic, has been credited with having introduced the *mythos* of neoplatonic hierarchy as a useful construct for interpreting the ecclesiastical developments of his day,[48] he did not create a new field of experience. Rather, he provided culturally congenial language to name and to handle theologically the organizational and aspirational realities of the late Hellenistic *ekklēsia*. Through the appropriation of the language of hierarchies, subtle but significant shifts occurred in the understanding of the purpose of ranked ministries.

Consensus exists among scholars that the mystical neo-platonic ideas which had gained authority in the east in this period reflected broad cultural concerns about nearness to God.[49] Accordingly, in the grand design of Ps-Dionysius' text, the purpose of the earthly ecclesiastical hierarchies was to assure progressive divinization: assimilation to, participation in, and union with God.[50]

The triadic form of neo-platonic schemata had to be trimmed to the empirical phenomenon of the Church. So Ps-Dionysius posited a double, not a triple, triadic form for the ecclesiastical hierarchy. An active triad, the bishop, priests, and deacons, worked on the passive triad of monks, laity, and the catechumens along with their penitential counterparts, in proportion to the powers each had received. In the active triad, the episcopal hierarch was said to possess a triple spiritual power to purify, to illuminate, and to unify. He conferred two shares of that power on the next in rank but only one share on the deacon. They in turn used these powers on those in the inferior receptive hierarchy.[51]

[48]Ibid., p. 172.

[49]G. Tellenbach, *Church, State and Christian Society in the Time of the Investiture Contest* (Oxford: B. Blackwell, 1948), p. 8; cf. Y. Congar, "The Sacralization of Western Society in the Middle Ages," *Concilium* 47 (New York: Paulist, 1969), p. 67; also Congar, "Les Ministères d'Eglise dans le monde féodal jusqu'à la reforme gregorienne," *Revue de Droit Canonique* 23 (1973): 82.

[50]Roques, *L'Univers Dionysien*, pp. 92-100.

[51]Faivre, p. 174; cf. Roques, pp. 99-100.

Orthodox theologian John Meyendorff has called Ps-Dionysius' hierarch a Gnostic because his spiritual power was not a function of the inner structure of his ecclesial community but his personal possession. Meyendorff goes further, attributing the "magical clericalism" of the west to the later influence of Ps-Dionysius on medieval speculations about the progressive powers of the ecclesiastical hierarchy. He suggests that further research is needed in order to establish the measure of considered and of unreflective Ps-Dionysian influence on the development of western ecclesiology in both the scholastic and post-scholastic periods.[52] Certainly, his scheme of progressive hierarchical power is not unfamiliar in western theology. Nor is his localized interpretation of ministerial mediation as residing squarely in the person of the hierarch. The episcopal ordinand who is told through the text of the 1968 Roman Pontifical that it is his responsibility to act for people in matters pertaining to God is a linear descendant of Dionysius' hierarch.

As noted earlier, the range of concerns involved in Christian appropriation of neo-platonic schemes of hierarchy was broader than long-standing interest in orderly ministry in the *ekklēsia*. Nearness to God was an emerging preoccupation. Within the horizon of hierarchical interpretations of ministries, Ps-Dionysius was able to address this distinctive cultural interest. Nothing in the hierarchical world was accidental or optional; every arrangement was *taxis hiera*, holy disposition coming from God and so *thesmos*, norm or command. People and things had their place by divine choice. But the manifest ecclesiastical arrangement and the situation of each individual soul reflected the harmony of the heavenly realm. Rebellion against the given order was both futile and sinful. Ps-Dionysius even specified that burial sites were to be located according to this arrangement, so that at the moment of regeneration the deceased would be "in the right place." Hierarchical organization was, for him, both constitutive and expressive of intrinsic moral perfection.[53]

With this new interpretative overlay of divine-human intimacy and ultimacy superimposed onto the matter of ecclesiastical status, a cultural dynamism was confirmed. Paradoxically, that dynamic was *stāsis:*

---

[52]J. Meyendorff, *Christ in Eastern Christian Thought* (Washington: Corpus, 1969), pp. 79-82; cf. G. Thery, "L'entrée du Ps.-Denys en Occident," *Melanges Madonnet*, II. Bibl. Thomiste XIV (Paris, 1930), pp. 23-30.

[53]Faivre, p. 174. To this day, it is customary at the funeral of clergy to place the head of the deceased closest to the altar; a deceased layperson's head is away from the altar.

a divinely willed arrangement cannot change. If it seemed that the earlier generations of God's holy people had lived by other arrangements, more careful reflection would disclose the hidden presence of earthly hierarchies foreshadowing and anticipating the fullness of ecclesiastical hierarchy. Not only was church order holy gift; it is eternal, sacred, and inviolable harmony.

The sacralizing impulse was already noted in the episcopal ordination prayers and directives of Hippolytus, as it was in the second century letters of Ignatius of Antioch and in the fourth century *Apostolic Constitutions* (Book III). If neo-platonic churchmen like Ps-Dionysius gave it its first systematic form and comprehensive elaboration, the highly ceremonialized rites of ordination had been communicating the *mythos* of divine hierarchy for some time.

The *Apostolic Tradition* of Hippolytus had already presented an overt ceremonial distinction between those who had episcopal hands laid on them for the purpose of establishing a share in the Holy Spirit and those who did not.[54] The texts explained the ceremonial protocol in terms of distinctions between the bishop's authority to act in this matter and the presbyter's more limited authority either to receive the Holy Spirit through the bishop's act, or to confirm the bishop's act on behalf of other presbyters. Hippolytus' schema for establishing ecclesial order also provided for a ceremonial handing over of the paraphernalia of lesser ministries. Thus, the bishop was to give the reader the book.

The ceremonial impulse flourished as a way of effectively communicating differences, distinctions, and ranks in the ecclesial *ordo*. In the fifth century western document *Statuta Antiqua Ecclesiae* the ceremonial aspects of rites of ordering have been systematized and refined.[55] Many episcopal hands and the book of the gospels superimposed appropriately signify the empowerment of the new episcopal ordinand. The hands of one bishop and many presbyters are fitting for the empowerment of a new presbyter; for a deacon, the hands of one bishop only. The subdeacon received no such spiritual empowerment from episcopal hands. Instead, the bishop and the archdeacon hand over to his care cup and plate and oil and water cruets for the offering. The bishop instructs an acolyte but hands nothing over; the archdeacon hands him lamp and oil. The bishop only hands the exorcist the

---

[54]Botte, *Tradition Apostolique*, 2, 7-9; cf. 9-14.

[55]C. Munier, ed., *Statuta Ecclesiae Antiqua* (Paris: Presses Universitaires de France, 1960), nos. 90-98.

manual of exorcism; but he gives him authority to lay his own hands upon the possessed. The bishop hands the lector the book; he hands the doorkeeper the keys to the church building. A presbyter empowers the psalmist with a word of command to bring song and life into harmony.

Whether or not the third century *Apostolic Tradition*, the fifth century *Statuta Antiqua Ecclesiae* or Ps-Dionysius' *Ecclesiastical Hierarchies* were actually reflective of contemporary practices or were advocacy documents, they had vast influence on subsequent generations.[56] The tenth century Romano-Germanic pontifical incorporated ceremonies handed down from the *Statuta Antiqua Ecclesiae*. Provisions for distinguishing and ranking lesser ministers and superior ones either through direct episcopal agency or through the indirect agency of the archdeacon or presbyter are firmly embedded within even more elaborate ceremonies.[57] Each of these ritual exchanges publicly confirmed ecclesial relations; and all of them together established a well-ordered *ecclēsia* in which the bishop's authority in the empowerment of ministers was indisputable.

Congar maintains that the Roman church, even the whole western church, officially resisted the overlay of mystical hierarchical interpretations of ministries as personal spiritual powers until the twelfth century.[58] That calls for some distinctions. Power became an acute political issue in the eleventh and twelfth centuries in the wake of investiture controversies involving lords spiritual and lords temporal. In the fray, Pope Gregory VII asserted his claim to supreme power. His claim could be and was supported by appeal to the mystical cosmological scheme of earlier writers like Ps-Dionysius, whose works had been circulating for some time in scholastic circles. However, the medieval liturgical ceremonies long-established in the west effectively dramatized the *mythos* of degrees of power, controlled access to it, and personal appropriation of it. The churches east and west had long known, unsystematically even prethematically, but none the less cognitively, about the locus of spiritual power in the bishop, its conferral on others by degrees, and inexorable divine choice in the hierarchical scheme of

---

[56]Ibid.

[57]C. Vogel et R. Elze, ed., *Le Pontifical Romano-Germanique du Dixième Siècle I.* Studi e Testi 226 (Città del Vaticano: Bibl. Apostolica Vaticana, 1963), XV; cf. XVI. Also, Munier, *Statuta Ecclesiae Antiqua*, nos. 90-98.

[58]Y. Congar, "My Pathfindings in the Theology of Laity and Ministries," THE JURIST 32 (1972): 180.

things. The churches knew these things from the ceremonial language of the liturgy. The early medieval canonists and schoolmen did not create a new ecclesiastical order; they explicated the *mythos* of the hierarchical order in which they were already dwelling in a effort to control untimely harbingers of its collapse. Through an ironic final twist in the differentiation process, those members of the *ekklēsia* who had been excluded from the handlayings and the handings-over characteristic of the clerical holy *ordo* were judged spiritually impotent by the medieval churchmen.[59] At the high point of the medieval conflict over power, spiritual and temporal, Ps-Dionysius' imaginary hierarch took flesh in the west in the person of the Roman Pontiff.[60]

III. Language of Ministry Today

In order to evaluate the course of developments in the matter of language for speaking about ministry, it is necessary to recall premises stated earlier in the paper about the several uses of language and about the intentionality of all structuring within groups. Language serves to name, to handle, and to define experience. The handling of experience linguistically will mean interpreting that experience through available heuristic frames. One of the goals of the interpretative process will be establishing significance; another will be the shaping and controlling of world. The process of development of public language always has a touchstone. The reference point for authenticity will be the intentionality of the group which uses the language.

The preceding survey indicated that only a limited number of the words which accumulated in the original naming of the experience of Christian ministry have persisted as actual names of ministries: bishop, presbyter, and deacon. It also indicated that at least three interpretative overlays used in the first six centuries are firmly deposited in the texts of the 1968 rites for the ordination of bishop, presbyter, and deacon. The first draws upon the sacerdotal theocratic world of late Judaism; the second, the sacral and hierarchical schemes of platonism and neo-platonism; the third, the organizational wisdom of the public institutions of the Roman empire.

The Church's ordination prayers and rites have been the depository

---

[59]C. Lefebvre, "Les Ministères de direction dans l'Eglise à l'âge classique," *Revue de Droit Canonique* 23 (1973): 99-112; cf. Congar, "Les Ministères," pp. 80-88; Tellenbach, *Church, State and Society,* p. 38; cf. 6-8.

[60]H Mühlen, *Entsakralisierung* (Paderborn: Schöningh, 1970), pp. 393-394.

for the most cogent interpretive insights from this formative era about the larger significance of the ones who are called bishop, presbyter, and deacon. First, these ministers maintain the theocratic order intended for those chosen to be God's own people; among them can be found high priest, councillors, and cultic functionaries who together both rule the people and attend to the offering. Second, the triad are visible manifestations of invisible realities; together they act as earthly representatives of the Father, of Christ risen and glorified, of the apostles. In their very triadic form they attested to the ascending order of divine triads which serve as intermediaries between the heavenly summit and the earthly realm. In the person of the bishop these realms meet; divine power enters into the world and is disseminated through his activity. Third, this hierarchical triad which had essential public services to perform took on the organizational shape of known public service institutions, the Roman *ordines*. Positions were graded; personnel were classified. Candidates aspiring to the triad entered at lower levels according to qualifications, and were promoted on the basis of length of service, suitable performance and divine choice disclosed in the bishop's act.

Those who crafted the prayers of consecration for bishops, presbyters, and deacons, throughout this era gave selective emphasis to one or more of these themes of significance.[61] In Hippolytus' prayer texts the first image world, that of sacerdotal theocracy, dominates. However, his comprehensive church order reveals an operational mode for the bishop which also draws upon the platonic and neo-platonic preserve. His bishop tends to be a hierarch through whom power flows. So his ceremonial protocol for episcopal hand-layings and handings-over suggests. But the tendency is still checked by his consciousness of the charisms of confessor and healer in relation to which he had no *auctoritas*. He is at ease with the fact that such gifts, evident in the lives of some of the community, are the result of the direct action of God. As bishop, he is to acknowledge them and welcome them.

Hippolytus is an early witness to the interpretative process. However, the 1968 use of his prayer for the ordination of bishops is situated in another context which interprets the bishop's hierarchical role in a way which sets aside that early Roman's restraint. The official "homily" to be addressed to the assembly and the subsequent address to the ordinand assert publicly that the bishop is the one through whom

---

[61]See, for example, Apostolic Constitutions, Book VIII, 3; also, 46; cf. Book II, 25, 26, 30.

spiritual power will pass and who will mediate between heaven and earth.[62] Furthermore, apparently minor modifications of the original text of Hippolytus also serve to bring his prayer into line with the later, more fully elaborated, heuristic developments. For example, the extant Latin version of Hippolytus' prayer designates the episcopal ordinand *primatum sacerdotium*; the 1968 text substitutes a neo-platonic *summum sacerdotium*.[63] Similarly, Hippolytus' prayer designates among the bishop's tasks *dare sortes secundum praeceptum tuum,* the assigning of lots in the church, that is, the neo-platonic responsibility for constituting church order as a manifestation of divine law. The 1968 text has introduced canonical language acquired from the world of the imperial *ordo* to designate the neo-platonic task. The bishop *distribuat munera secundum praeceptum tuum.*

If such is the trajectory of western church interpretation of the significance of those called bishop, presbyter, and deacon, what of the authenticity of that process? Is truth served by maintaining it? The answers to those questions are basically ecclesiological. Any interpretative frame both discloses and conceals. This one is no different. Three issues must be addressed briefly to determine the implications for the Church of maintaining it. These are the Church as a group in process; sacralization and pseudo-sacralization; and the liturgical assembly as locus of power.

A. The Church as Group in Process

The Church necessarily functions as any human group. Its self-definition incorporates what distinguishes it from other groups; its structures protect and promote values which are judged essential for the life of the group. The received tradition of interpreting ministries in the Church has been directed to the latter function. However, that process is necessarily based on a prior perception of the distinctive characteristic of the group. Yet most of what has been written about the Church between the early apologists and *Gaudium et Spes* misplaces the initial distinction. The original church leaders knew that the important dividing line was between those who were chosen as the *ekklēsia tou theou* and those outside to whom they were to act as ambassadors of reconciliation and bearers of good news. Hippolytus is witness to the early emergence of a second dividing line between those chosen for "the service of the offering" and the rest of the Church. It

[62]*PR*: Bishop, 18.
[63]Botte, p. 3; *PR*: Bishop, 26.

matters which of those two frontiers is identified as decisive, for that judgment shapes the whole rest of the organizational and interpretative process. Ecclesiastical literature tends erroneously to treat the second distinction as primordial. As Heribert Mühlen notes, the difference between clerics and laity has been treated as though it were as significant as the distinction between the baptized and the unbaptized.[64]

Overcoming the error demands beginning at the right starting point. When the Church/not-church frontier was clear, as it was for the first Christian generations, there was room for organizational flexibility and imaginative response to new development. Ministerial forms shifted often in response to the dual needs of fulfilling the group vocation and serving group needs: so the Twelve and the Seven; so also, apostles, then prophets, then teachers; so also the presbyterium and *hēgoumenoi*; so even deacons and sub-deacons. The clarity of that Church/not-church frontier exists again at the end of the twentieth century at least for the so-called new churches in Asia and Africa. It seems to have produced the same need for local development of new ministerial structures, some to serve the well-being of the Church itself and others to serve the proclamation of the gospel directly.[65]

The right starting point theologically for establishing the Church/not-church frontier is pneumatology informing eschatology. The underdevelopment of these themes in the theology of Vatican II testifies to the malformation of the self-understanding of the Church and so its structuring and interpretation of ministries over many centuries.

B. Sacralization and Pseudo-Sacralization

Preoccupation with divine choice of an hierarchical *ordo* overshadows the significance of the divine choice of a Spirit-filled Church. The result has been what Mühlen calls pseudo-sacralization.[66] That disorder has had many witnesses through the centuries. Little official evidence yet exists that it is being eschewed.

In 1906 Pius X asserted, "In the hierarchy alone reside the power and authority necessary to move and direct all the members of the society to its end. As for the many, they have no other right than to let

---

[64]Mühlen, *Entsakralizierung*, p. 377.

[65]Federation of Asian Bishops Conferences, "Ministries: Heralding A New Era," Asian Colloquium on Ministries, Feb. 27-Mar. 6, 1977, *Origins* 8/9 (August 3, 1978): 129, 131-143.

[66]H. Mühlen, "Sakralität und Amt zu Beginn einer Neuen Epoche," *Catholica* (1973): 77-78; cf. *Entsakralizierung*, pp. 385-396.

themselves be guided and so follow their pastors in docility."[67] The 1918 Code of Canon Law made the point with less rhetorical flourish: *Ordo ex Christi institutione clericos a laicis in Ecclesia distinguet ad fidelium regimen et cultus divini ministerium* (Can 948). The revised Code has abandoned that directness but not the point:

> *Sacramento Ordinis ex Christi institutione inter christifideles quidam, charactere indelebili quo signantur, constituuntur sacri ministri, qui nempe eodem consecrantur et deputantur ut, pro suo quisque gradu, in persona Christi Capitis munera adimplentes Evangelium annuntiandi, christifideles regendi et divinum cultum celebrandi, Dei populum pascant.*[68]

The assertion that the ordained function *"in persona Christi"* resonates with the early sacralizing tendencies of an Ignatius of Antioch. Why is it pseudosacralization? Is there any authentic sacralization?

Mühlen's study of the sacralization phenomenon has led him to the judgment that humans inevitably tend toward sacralizing.[69] The tendency is good, for it is rooted in the relationship of creation and the Creator. Insofar as the Creator is called holy, whatever is created is alongside but outside, that is, profane. That very profanity is a manifestation of God's holiness, for in Mühlen's reading of the New Testament revelation, God's holiness means that God is not turned inward but outward. The genuine sacredness of the world lies in its corresponding ordination to the holiness of God.

Within this horizon the Church is necessarily profane, but the Church's vocation to holiness contains the imperative to announce to the whole world the self-giving holiness of God. Only when the Church is diaphanous, says Mühlen, is it sacred. By contrast, all theocratic claims of church authorities to possess the authority of God and to act in God's place, as vicar, as representative, *"in persona Christi,"* negate the difference between the holiness of God and the divinely willed profanity of every created thing.[70] The result is pseudosacralization. Mühlen proposes Mark 12:28-34 as a key gospel pericope for the pursuit of this aspect of the good news. In the dialogue between Jesus and

[67]Pius X, *"Vehementer Nos,"* Feb. 11, 1906: *ASS* 39 (1906): 8-9; cited in Congar, "Pathfindings," p. 171.

[68]Pont. Commissio Codici Iuris Canonici Recognoscendo, *Schema Codicis Iuris Canonici* (Vatican City: Libreria Editrice Vaticana, 1980), can. 961.

[69]Mühlen, "Sakralität" pp. 72-75; cf. *Entsakralizierung*, pp. 106-140.

[70]Mühlen, *Entsakralizierung*, pp. 393-395; cf. "Sakralität," pp. 74-80.

the lawyer, Jesus confirms the anti-sacralizing lawyer's insight: "You are right in saying God is one and beside him there is no other." Because of this truth, Jesus necessarily confronted the temple and sabbath ideologies of his own day. He redirected the aspirations of the pious to a radical truth: to revere God above all else is to love your neighbor.

This is a hard saying, because pseudo-sacralization serves some basic human needs.[71] First, what is chaotic is menacing. Whatever gives order and structure, whatever provides a world to live in is fascinating, worthy of admiration, even worship. It is saving; it seems divine. Secondly, as historians of religion note, ritual functions to master the chaotic and to disclose good order. Accordingly, cultic priesthood in every religion serves a stabilizing function for the community. Certain persons and places are inevitably set apart for priestly service. In their work, priests tend to look backward to "the beginning of the world" and inward to their own agency and responsibility for the maintenance of the divinely given order.

It is in this context that the "priesthood" of the new covenant is genuinely new. Those who gather to give thanks with bread and wine for *anamnēsis* of Jesus find themselves confronted with the unexpected disclosure that life poured out for others is only apparently menacing and chaotic. It is the source of the world's salvation, a manifestation of the holiness of God. The genuinely sacred character of the Church will be discernible if this disclosure is believed and responded to. Therefore the distinction between the holiness of God and the profanity of everything else, including the Church, must be preserved. So must be the distinction between the genuinely sacred revealed in Jesus and the pseudosacralizing self-protective schemes evident in human religiosity.

But the fact is that a pseudosacral horizon constrains the Church and finds expression in the public language, public worship, and public behavior in the matter of ministry. The distortion has consequences. The ecclesial community's well-being, perhaps even its being, is at stake. Social psychologist and communication theorist Gregory Bateson observes that potential for internal rupture exists whenever a community which starts with a shared ideology undergoes progressive and cumulative complementary differentiation. The process, which he calls complementary schismogenesis, is played out as the two sub-groups take up opposing or contrasting behaviors and goals and these

---

[71]Mühlen, "Sakralität," pp. 70-71.

effectively isolate the two groups. He notes: "Unless it is restrained, [it] leads to progressive unilateral distortion of the personalities of both groups, which results in mutual hostility between them and must end in the breakdown of the system."[72] The Roman Catholic Church has such a cumulative program for rupture in language about ministry which continues to draw the sacred/secular line between *klēroi* and *laikoi* and which continues to assert "*Sacram ordinationem valide recepit solus vir baptizatus*," thereby isolating men from women in the service of the gospel.[73]

Restraints and redressive action can reestablish equilibrium, Bateson notes. The isolated groups may actively introduce more symmetrical behavior to balance themselves and stabilize the situation. Or they may merely wait to respond to the "negative feedback" that moves through the group. Both these courses of action can be undertaken to repair and maintain the old system. But groups can also pursue them in ways that will eventually design a whole new organizational system. It is evident that the post-conciliar church has explored a growing range of pastoral responses in order to span the lay/clerical chasm, and more recently even to close the male/female breach. It is equally clear that both rationales—repairing the old or forming the new—are motivating factors in all groups.

C. The Liturgical Assembly as Locus of Power

Finally, however, the judgment about what is appropriate motivation for any action at all must be theological, just as the judgment about which are the radical frontiers for the Church's self-understanding and mission is theological. Nevertheless, because of the central role of liturgical rites in disclosing within a community the important delineations and for presenting the mysterious holiness of God, the liturgical assembly will continue to be, as it has been for centuries, decisive for the Church's self-understanding. It is in assembly that what the Church knows to be true can and must be celebrated, and the very physical shape this public praise of the holy God takes will contribute to the slower work of theological reflection.

The regular eucharistic assembly of the local Church is already the place where those named bishop, presbyters, deacons, and the many other named and unnamed ministers of the gospel may meet each other

---

[72]G. Bateson, *Steps Toward an Ecology of Mind* (New York: Ballentine Books, 1972), p. 68.

[73]*Schema Codicis Iuris Canonici*, can. 977.

and call each other to be a people filled with the Spirit of Jesus. Wherever that meeting takes place with openness and trust in God's holiness and their own vocation to be a holy people, the language of the current ordination rites will become progressively less intelligible. But the Church as a holy people will also know better by then how it must pray together—in an age preoccupied with national security, the nuclear arms race, and economic imperialism—for those it will designate specially for leadership in service of the gospel.

RELATION OF CHARISM TO RIGHTS AND DUTIES IN THE NEW TESTAMENT CHURCH

CAROLYN OSIEK, RSCJ
Catholic Theological Union
Chicago, Illinois

The Holy Spirit who sanctifies the People of God through the ministry and the sacraments gives to the faithful special gifts as well (cf. 1 Cor 12:7), "allotting to everyone according as he wills" (1 Cor 12:11). Thus may the individual, "according to the gift that each has received, administer it to one another" and become "good stewards of the manifold grace of God" (1 Pet 4:10), and build up thereby the whole body in charity (cf. Eph 4:16). From the reception of these charisms or gifts, including those which are less dramatic, there arise for each believer the right and duty to use them in the Church and in the world for the good of mankind and for the upbuilding of the Church. In so doing, believers need to enjoy the freedom of the Holy Spirit who "breathes where he will" (Jn 3:8). At the same time, they must act in union with their brothers in Christ, especially with their pastors. The latter must make a judgment about the true nature and proper use of these gifts, not in order to extinguish the Spirit, but to test all things and hold fast to what is good (cf. 1 Th 5:12,19,21).[1]

This overlooked text from Vatican II serves well to illustrate the Council's theology of charisms. These charisms are special gifts given according to the needs of the Church (LG 12) which complement the sacraments and ministries. The lay apostolate is none other than the exercise of charismatic gifts given by the Holy Spirit for the good of all (AA 30). Even the missionary vocation is a charismatic gift (AG 23). Just as no part of a living body is passive, so no member of the Church is without an essential function (AA 2), which brings to Christians rights and duties flowing from union with Christ their head (AA 3).

[1]*AA* 3; Abbott, pp. 492-493.

41

The text quoted above illuminates for us both the challenge and the problem. It contains a clear call to the laity to claim their rights and assume their responsibility as apostles on the basis of the charisms given to the community by the Holy Spirit. That is the challenge. The problem is that this mission of the laity is held separate from ministry, *sacrum ministerium*, which throughout the documents of Vatican II is normally associated only with ordination. Thus the laity are defined as those not in holy orders or a properly approved religious congregation. While at times those in holy orders may engage in secular work, their principal responsibility is the *sacrum ministerium* (LG 31), and a distinction is to be made between sacred ministers and the rest of the People of God (*inter sacros ministros et reliquum Populum Dei*— LG 32).[2] Gray areas do occur in special circumstances: the laity do their best to provide *officia sacra* when sacred ministers are lacking due to persecution, etc. (LG 35); certain priests, religious, and laity have a special call to missionary labor, and when sent by legitimate authority, are *ministri Evangelii* (AG 23—but this is under the influence of Rom 15:16); some members of the laity can also be delegated after the example of Paul's co-workers to more direct cooperation in the work of the hierarchy through the exercise of certain ecclesiastical functions, for a spiritual purpose (*munera ecclesiastica, ad finem spiritualem exercenda*—LG 33).[3] But generally the assumption is operative that the spiritual gifts or charisms given to the People of God do not include that of ministry, which belongs only to those in sacred orders. One of the purposes of this paper is to demonstrate that the New Testament [NT] evidence cannot support such a distinction between ministry and charisms.

A second purpose is to trace briefly the early Church's understanding of "charismatic" leadership and to cast a glance at its traditional tension with "hierarchical" leadership in the first Christian centuries. As

[2]This may reflect simply the ambiguity of use of the word *munus* in the Council documents. Elsewhere it seems to mean what is conferred in the sacrament of holy orders. See E. Sigurbjörnsson, *Ministry within the People of God: The Development of the Doctrines on the Church and on the Ministry in the Second Vatican Council's* DE ECCLESIA, Studia Theologica Lundensia 34 (Lund: C.W.K. Gleerup, 1974), pp. 120-122.

[3]All members of the Church share in the priestly, prophetic, and royal office of Christ (LG 31; AA 2) and in the royal priesthood of the whole People of God (1 Pet 2:4,9; AA 3; LG 34). This is an entirely different theological theme with different biblical roots, and should not be brought into discussion about distinctive types of service within the Church. See J. H. Elliott, *The Elect and the Holy: An Exegetical Examination of 1 Peter 2:4-10 and the Phrase* BASILEON HIERATEUMA (Leiden: Brill, 1966).

will be seen, this is a tension that post-dates the NT and may be more of a modern invention than a meaningful category of experience in the early Church. As we shall also see, however, the basis for rights and duties shifts in the early Church and even within the NT itself.

Restrictions of space and time necessitate that two related contemporary questions not be dealt with in this paper: the modern charismatic movement and the charism of a religious community. While it is my opinion on the basis of the NT text that at least some of the Pauline communities bore close resemblances to today's charismatic groups, the reality of spiritual gifts inherent in the Christian community is a far broader question, and my remarks are addressed to the good of the whole Church. So too the attempt to identify the distinctive charism(s) of a religious founder, habitually present in his or her order, is a valid effort, but one which is not relevant here. My use of the terms "charism" and "charismatic" should therefore not be associated with these two issues, but should be understood in a more general and more original sense.

CHARISM IN THE NEW TESTAMENT

The word *charisma* with its NT meaning is practically a Pauline innovation; at least his is the earliest and heaviest surviving literary evidence of its use in Christianity. The only NT use of the word outside the Pauline corpus is in 1 Pet 4:10. Though it occurs a few times in Hellenistic Greek writers contemporary to and later than Paul meaning "ingratiation" or "something freely bestowed," it seems to have been he who expanded and developed its meaning into a more specific concept related to the tangible manifestation of the Spirit in the Christian community. Its etymological relationship to *charis* (grace), *chara* (joy), and *eucharistia* (thanksgiving), all important Pauline ideas related to the work of the Spirit, should be kept in mind. Even for Paul there is a range of meaning, however. God's free and gracious gift of salvation is *charisma* (Rom 5:15-16; 6:23), as was the original divine gift of election to Israel (Rom 11:29). But it is also more concretely deliverance in time of danger (2 Cor 1:11). In all these usages, *charism* can aptly mean simply the gift and realization of divine grace. Even Paul does not always speak of charisms in the technical sense upon which we are about to focus.[4]

---

[4]For a more detailed discussion of the varied uses of the word, see H. Conzelmann, "Charisma," G. Kittel and G. Friederich, eds., *Theological Dictionary of the New Testament* [*TDNT*] 9 (1974): 402-406; U. Brockhaus, *Charisma und Amt: Die paulinische*

The more specialized meaning of charism occurs principally in the following passages: 1 Cor 12:9-10,28-31; Rom 12:6-8; Eph 4:11; 1 Pet 4:10-11; 1 Tim 4:14; 2 Tim 1:6. It is generally agreed that here a charism is understood to be *a gift of the Holy Spirit bestowed upon an individual Christian for the sake of the building up of the community.* This is the technical meaning usually given to the word both by Paul and in modern religious language. The basis for the presence of such gifts is quite clear: it is the continually abiding presence of the Holy Spirit in the Christian community. Indeed the charisms can be seen as the manifestation or proof of that presence. But they have no validity or claim to existence apart from the Spirit.

When one thinks of gifts of the Spirit in the NT, Luke's description of the Pentecost event in Acts 2:1-36 comes readily to mind. Surely the spectacular manifestations of prophecy, tongues, interpretations, and preaching demonstrated in that narrative, as well as the continued boldness of the apostles and their ability to work signs and wonders (2:43; 3:1-10, etc.) are all spiritual gifts that Paul recognized. Yet the Lukan narrative is difficult to work with for our purposes: it describes a spectacular and unrepeatable foundational event of the Church in language indicative of a great deal of retrospective theological reflection. It is questionable, therefore, how helpful such passages are for understanding how charisms are present and active in everyday life in the first century or in any other.

When we turn to the pages of Paul's first letter to the Corinthians, however, we find advice that is directed to a concrete Gentile Christian community attempting to live in fidelity to its risen Lord in the day-to-day world of a busy commercial center. True, the Corinthian Christians were strongly apocalyptic in their expectation of an imminent end to all of this, but in the meantime, Paul's obvious exasperation with them in some parts of the letter shows that there are real-life problems that do not get swept away in a blaze of apocalyptic fervor.

The Spiritual Gifts

In 1 Cor 12 Paul gives his most detailed teaching on spiritual gifts. In verses 4-6 he refers to them rhetorically under three different aspects, as *charismata, diakoniai* (forms of service), and *energēmata* (divine workings), linked with the Spirit, the Lord, and God respectively. Rather

---

Charismenlehre auf dem Hintergrund der frühchristlichen Gemeindefunktionen (Wuppertal: R. Brockhaus, 1972), pp. 128-142.

than mutually exclusive categories or a trinitarian division of labor, these verses should be understood as a literary method of making the same point in three different ways: though the gifts show great diversity, the source is One. Verse 7 underscores the other two important characteristics of the gifts: the Spirit gives them to individual persons for the sake of the common good. Indeed 1 Cor 12:7 might be considered a synthesis of Paul's whole teaching on charisms.

Verses 8-10 give a suggestive but by no means exhaustive list: utterance of wisdom and of knowledge; faith (under its community-building aspect); healing (probably both by what we would call "natural" and "extraordinary" methods); the working of other kinds of wonders (which may include exorcism); prophecy; discernment of spirits; tongues; interpretation of tongues. Of the nine gifts enumerated here, only five reappear in another listing of equal length at the end of the chapter. Verses 28-30, a more administratively oriented list, add apostleship, teaching, assistance, and governance (the word originally meant the ability to pilot a ship—a most apt comparison). Significantly, what has occupied the whole center of the chapter between the two lists is a discussion of the mutual relationship of community members to one another, under the image of the body. The context says eloquently what the gifts are all about.

Later in his apostolic career Paul again gave a partial list of *charismata* in Rom 12:6-8: prophecy; service (*diakonia*); teaching; encouragement or exhortation; generosity in giving aid; zeal in giving subsidy; cheerful mercy. Again the context is the body of Christ and mutual responsibilities of the members (verses 3-5).

Many attempts have been made to classify the Pauline *charismata* in order to see their interaction with one another. All are gifts of service, but in different ways. Some gifts manifest the quiet and abiding power of the Spirit, e.g., knowledge, wisdom, faith; governance, generosity, mercy. They are not merely "natural" virtues, but real gifts of grace which enable the recipient to contribute to the upbuilding of the community in his or her unique way. Others, however, manifest the power of the Spirit in a spectacular way, e.g., prophecy, tongues, discernment of spirits; miraculous healing, exorcism, working of wonders.[5]

---

[5]For other attempts at classification, see for instance H. Küng, *The Church* (N.Y.: Sheed and Ward, 1967), p. 184: preaching, service, leadership; or A. Bittlinger, *Gifts and Ministries* (Grand Rapids: Eerdmans, 1973), p. 16: proclamation, service, special power, prayer.

These more striking gifts are what Paul seems to call *pneumatika*, gifts of *pneuma*, "of inspired utterance or discernment."[6] They are those phenomena which exhibit *enthousiasmos*, ecstatic or parapsychological characteristics indicative of divine possession: visions, ecstatic speech, etc. If a careful reading of 1 Cor 12 and 14 indicates that for Paul the *pneumatika* are these kinds of gifts (see 1 Cor 12:1 and 14:1 in context), still the *pneumatika* are one kind of *charismata*. In Rom 1:11 Paul expresses his longing to see the Roman Christians in order to share with them some kind of *charisma pneumatikon* which will strengthen them. While we would wish that Paul had been more specific here, what is at least clear is that the pneumatic gift to which he refers is one kind of *charisma*. All gifts, whether of inspired speech or daily upbuilding, are of the Spirit. All are *charismata*.[7]

In spite of the foregoing, it must also be said that Paul had a special preference for the pneumatic gifts, that is, those of inspired speech, with priority on prophecy. It is probably no accident that in the three listings of gifts given by Paul himself (1 Cor 12:8-10,28-30; Rom 12:6-8) the single constant is prophecy. This gift is not only that of inspired speech given to individual persons. It is seen by NT writers as an essential characteristic of the Church itself (Eph 2:20; Acts 2 where prophecy is exercised by the whole community; etc.). Hence those who possess the gift manifest in their lives the presence of the Holy Spirit which guarantees the Church's legitimacy.[8]

After the sublime and poetic exhortation to love in 1 Corinthians 13 Paul returns to the subject of the "better" *charismata*, which had been left off at 12:31. Chapter 13 reveals Paul's own admiration for and possession of pneumatic gifts. Though he is proficient in speaking in tongues (14:18), prophecy and interpretation are to be preferred precisely because of the criterion he had already carefully laid down in chapter 12: the upbuilding of the community.

Paul also recognizes the tendency to chaos in the exercise of the pneumatic gifts; hence his concern in the second half of 1 Corinthians

---

[6]E. E. Ellis, *Prophecy and Hermeneutic in Early Christianity* (Grand Rapids: Eerdmans, 1978), p. 23.

[7]On the other hand, it does seem as if *pneumatika* are more than just a synonym for *charismata*, but represent one kind of *charismata*. This is with Ellis, *Prophecy and Hermeneutic*, pp. 23-24; against H. Conzelmann, *1 Corinthians*, Hermeneia (Philadelphia: Fortress, 1975), p. 208.

[8]E. Cothenet in "Prophétisme dans le NT," *DBSup* 8 (1972): 1222-1337 suggests (1223 and passim) that a distinction should be made between prophecy as a foundational element of the Church and the exercise of the gift of prophecy.

14 for order and harmony. God is the giver of all authentic spiritual gifts, but the same God is one of peace, not chaos (1 Cor 14:33).

Effects of Charisms

The spiritual gifts bring about a unique effect on the persons who receive them and on the community as a whole, according to Paul. To understand this we must again return to the description given at the beginning of this discussion: they are gifts of the Holy Spirit given to individuals for the building up of the whole community. The effect on the recipients is one of individuation: the manifestation of the unique gifts of each brings out the distinctiveness of a person's contribution to the life of the whole. At this level the possession of a *charisma* influences the shape of a person's life as a Christian. Those with gifts of teaching or prophecy, for instance, will order their lives differently from those with gifts of administration or healing.[9]

At this point another of Paul's uses of *charisma* can be appropriately considered: 1 Cor 7:7. After expressing his opinion on the importance of conjugal rights in marriage and his own preference for celibacy, he remarks that "each has a proper charism from God, some one, some another." It is disputed whether Paul intends that marriage also be called a charism here. He may be saying that both marriage and celibacy are charisms given to different people, or he may more likely intend that some have the charism of celibacy and others have some other kind, for instance of those named in 1 Corinthians 12. There is no doubt, however, that he is calling celibacy a charism. Leaving aside later disputes about the relative status of various states in life, we still gain a new insight into the effect of charisms on the person through Paul's remark in this passage. A charism orders one's life in profound ways.

The effect of the *charismata* on the community is one both of ordering and inspiring. As Paul stresses in 1 Cor 14:33, they ought not to cause confusion, but rather peace. The frequently raised question of tension between "charismatic" and "hierarchical" leadership, while relevant for later periods, is not appropriate in the Pauline churches or even in the deutero-Pauline literature. It follows therefore that there is no tension in the NT between charism and ministry or charism and

---

[9]For further discussion of this individuating effect, see J. Koening, *Charismata: God's Gifts for God's People* (Philadelphia: Westminster, 1978), pp. 108-110; J. H. Schütz, "Charismata and Social Reality in Primitive Christianity," *Journal of Religion* 54 (1974): 51-70 (59).

office (though as we shall see, there is a tendency in the later Pauline literature to absorb charism into office). Rather, for Paul *some* charisms are expressed in leadership and governance while others are expressed in other ways, all equally constructive for the community. A charism by its very nature brings with it a certain authority, but of many different kinds. Each charism in its ordering aspect may indeed be considered a form of "the interpretation of power,"[10] and on the other hand, every form of leadership is "charismatic." Rather than there being a question of struggle between charismatic and authority figure, the manifestation of a charism is "an interchange between the unpredictable . . . and the institutional," "the social or institutional form which is assumed by the gratuitousness of grace."[11]

OFFICE IN THE NEW TESTAMENT

Since a working definition of charism has been previously established, some attempt must be made at this point to describe what is indeed an extremely difficult concept, that of office. B. Holmberg offers the following description of office as it may have been understood in Pauline communities: "permanent acknowledged function in local churches filled by stable groups of persons who lead and serve and take responsibility for their congregations in different ways, in some cases even having a designation or title and some form of material support." If two more characteristics suggested by Brockhaus are added, namely, that of "setting apart" in authority or dignity, and commissioning by imposition of hands, we have enumerated the characteristics of any NT office.[12] The important thing to remember, however, is that these functions are seen as kinds of charisms.

The one passage from the authentic Pauline letters which is sometimes raised in support of a Pauline notion of office distinct from charism is 1 Cor 12:28: "For God has established in the church first apostles, second prophets, third teachers, then miracle workers, healers, . . ." etc. The ordinal ranking of three functions before the others

---

[10]Schütz, "Charisma and Social Reality," p. 67.

[11]C. Duquoc, "Charism as the Social Expression of the Unpredictable Nature of Grace," *Charisms in the Church*, Concilium 109 (New York: Seabury, 1978), p. 92.

[12]See the listing of characteristics of office and charism as understood by various modern authors in Brockhaus, pp. 24-25, n. 106; discussion in B. Holmberg, *Paul and Power: The Structure of Authority in the Primitive Church as Reflected in the Pauline Epistles* (Philadelphia: Fortress, 1980), pp. 109-112.

could be seen as setting these off as separate and distinct. Such is not the case, however, for in the next verse the triad is again inserted into a list of charisms with no distinction of literary structure. Verse 28 names three charisms among many as having a priority of importance in the work of building the body of Christ. Paul himself possesses that of apostleship; he demonstrates his own predilection for prophecy in 1 Corinthians 14; and teachers were the most reliably systematic workers in a local church. There can be no question of more "official" or "institutional" functions than the others. A careful reading of 1 Corinthians 14 indicates that the Pauline prophets were anything but official or institutional. Moreover, prophecy and teaching appear as equals in the charismatic list of Rom 12:6-8.

The Letter to the Ephesians, probably a post-Pauline meditation on the mystery of the Church, is more conscious of leadership roles. Its recognized charisms are more in line with an ecclesiology of official witness and authority. Hence its list of gift-holders includes apostles, prophets, evangelists, pastors, and teachers (Eph 4:11). It must be stressed, however, that these are *not* office holders as distinct from those possessing charisms. Though the functions are not called *charismata*, they are nevertheless gifts (*dōrea*) and grace (*charis*) bestowed on each one through the exaltation of Christ (verses 7, 8, 11) for the purpose of building the Church (verses 12-16). The same factors are present in this description as were laid down by Paul in 1 Cor 12:7. Moreover, the ecclesiological motif of the body of Christ is also present here (verses 4, 12) as it is in 1 Corinthians 12 and Romans 12. The charisms singled out for mention are those already established in apostolic times (no longer the time of the author—see 2:20) which stress governance and for the most part stabilization.

The author of the First Letter of Peter shows his familiarity on a number of points with Pauline theology. One of them is his reference to charism and some brief elaboration in 1 Pet 4:10-11. In a context of warning and exhortation about mutual charity, the readers are reminded of the individual gift (*charisma*) that each has received. Only two gifts are specified: that of speaking (*lalia*), which may be a technical term for preaching, prophecy, and tongues;[13] and service (*diakonia*), which probably includes administration, assistance, healing, etc. What are being named here are essentially two kinds of charisms, those of word and of deed.

---

[13]Consider use of the related verb in 1 Cor 14:2-6,9-13, etc. See Liddell-Scott-Jones, *Greek-English Lexicon*, s. v. *laleō* II, "chatter, opp. articulate speech."

The Pastoral Epistles portray a developing notion of ecclesiastical office for bishop, deacons (probably male and female—cf. 1 Tim 3:11), perhaps presbyters as distinct from bishops, and widows. In the Pastorals the notion of *charisma* remains, but only in a restricted context. Prophecy, that gift so highly preferred by Paul in 1 Corinthians 14, also remains, but it too is at the service of a limited vision of church leadership. *Charisma* is the spiritual gift which Timothy has received that enables him to serve his congregation as its leader, to proclaim sound teaching and to lead the community in reading and prayer. Prophecy has indicated Timothy as possessor of this charism (1 Tim 1:18; 4:14), bestowed with the imposition of hands of the presbyterate (1 Tim 4:14) or of Paul himself (2 Tim 1:6), a gesture already indicated in Acts 6:6 and 13:3 as commissioning for a special church role.

The charism possessed by Timothy is dynamic: he is exhorted to stir it up, for the Spirit given him is one of power, love, and discretion, not fear (2 Tim 1:7). Yet there is something strangely different here from the world of 1 Corinthians, where prophecy is one gift among many given by the Spirit for the Church. In 2 Timothy the charism to perform his leadership functions is given to Timothy *by means of* prophecy with imposition of hands (1 Tim 4:4), or *by means of* imposition of hands (2 Tim 1:6) in a public ritual (1 Tim 6:12). The differences in language between 1 Tim 4:14 and 2 Tim 1:6 are probably not significant, but the difference between them and 1 Corinthians is. Whereas in 1 Corinthians prophecy legitimates the authority of the prophet and in a more general sense of the community as a whole, so too it legitimates the authority of the one receiving the imposition of hands in the Pastorals. Here, however, it legitimates him to perform a function much larger than that of prophecy. Timothy is to be above all *teacher* of reliable doctrine (1 Tim 4:6,11,13; 6:2; 2 Tim 4:2); administrator of community goods and policies; and leader of public prayer (1 Tim 4:13). This last function may be the one most closely associated with the role of prophets in the Pauline churches and elsewhere (1 Cor 11:4-5; 14:6,13-15,26-32; cf. *Did.*10.7),[14] though certainly the function of teaching is also connected with prophecy (1 Cor 14:26; Acts 13:1; *Did.* 11.10).

---

[14]See G. Friedrich, "Prophētēs, ktl," *TDNT* 6 (1968): 852-853 on the relationship of public prayer and prophecy; A. Lemaire, "Les ministères dans l'Eglise," in J. Delorme, ed., *Le ministère et les ministères selon le Nouveau Testament* (Paris: Editions du Seuil, 1974), pp. 104-105. Lemaire interprets the prophecy pronounced "upon" (*epi*) Timothy as a reference to an official liturgical prayer.

Prophecy in the Pauline churches is the manifestation of the Spirit through the ecstatic speech of one who speaks comfort or challenge for the spiritual growth of the community. The impression is given in the Pastorals as in Ephesians that "prophecy" and "prophets" are no longer the ecstatic utterances and speakers of 1 Corinthians, and that perhaps the authors do not even know such pneumatic manifestations first-hand—at least ones they would recognize as authentic.

In the Pastorals the primary locus for the manifestation of a charism is that of delegated and authoritative leadership, a view not totally alien to the earlier Pauline ecclesiology but certainly one which represents only a small portion of it. "Theologically this can be characterized as the 'charismatization' of the incipient institutionalization of authority,"[15] as religious language and experience adjust to changed social reality. The assimilation of roles and terms shows, however, that opposing office to charism would have been unthinkable in this context.

RIGHTS AND DUTIES

It is time now to begin to consider the question of rights and duties flowing from the possession of charisms. The language of rights and duties for the most part does not appear in the NT but this does not mean that the concepts are alien to the social experience of early Christians. Greco-Roman society was tightly structured along the lines of family relationships within the framework of the household model, with clear lines of authority possessed by the powerful, and of submission as response of those over whom power was exercised. At every level of society—domestic, neighborhood, civil, provincial, and imperial (even the emperor was *pater patrium*)—the *auctoritas* of paternal position required the exercise of benevolent responsibility over others and the possession of correlative rights to respect and obedience. Correspondingly, those in social positions of receptivity exercised their responsibility of *pietas*—reverence, submission, and support—and could expect as their legal right protection, material provision and legal advocacy, in a patronage system before which any modern political machine pales. If by the first century of the Christian era access to wealth in Roman society was less predictable than it had previously been, structures of access to social power and privilege remained

---

[15]Holmberg, *Paul and Power*, p. 191.

remarkably uniform for some time to come.[16] Though the society which produced the NT was by no means a democracy, and the notion of citizenship was limited to the privileged (at least in the early years of the Empire), rights and duties corresponding to one's social position were familiar to all.

It was characteristic of small non-institutional religious groupings to operate on something other than the patriarchal pattern of social organization, and Pauline Christianity was no exception. In spite of the "house church" basis of organization, the ecclesial images used by Paul, field, building, temple (1 Cor 3:6-17), and body (1 Cor 12) are indicative of his attempt to create a society in which the limitations of secular social structures do not apply (see Gal 3:27-28; 1 Cor 7:22-23). The basis for the exercise of rights and duties is for Paul the outpouring of the Spirit in baptism as it is manifested in each person through his or her own *charisma*. Yet the appeal to rights based on accepted functions is inescapable: Paul himself raises the issue in one of his many defenses of his actions as apostle (1 Cor 9:4-5).

The later household codes (*Haustafeln*), which never appear in the undoubtedly authentic Pauline writings, return to a greater emphasis on the reciprocal nature of rights and responsibilities based on the most recognizable social unit: the extended family. The household codes of the NT (Col 3:18-4:1; Eph 5:21-6:9; 1 Pet 2:13-3:8) are powerful propaganda pieces for both internal and external consumption which show that the boundaries of *auctoritas* and *pietas* are being respected by Christians. These codes lay the foundation for the extension of the structure to the whole community (1 Tim 2:1-15; 5:1-6:2; Titus 2:1-10) as one big happy family under the fatherly governance of the bishop and his deacons (1 Tim 3:1-13; cf. esp. verses 4-5; compare Ign. *Magn.* 3.1; 6.1; *Trall.* 3.1, etc.)

In the *Didache* rights and duties of charismatics are described. The itinerant leaders of *Did.* 10-13 seem to have been recognized as persons possessing special gifts or authority. They are generally called prophets, with the added title of apostles in 11.3, and the job description of teachers in 11.1-2. Thus they may have combined all three functions of the triad in 1 Cor 12:28. They have the right to lead eucharistic celebrations improvisationally (10.7); to teach (11.1-2); to be received with

---

[16]See for instance M. I. Finley, *The Ancient Economy* (Berkeley and Los Angeles: U. of California Press, 1973); G. Gagé, *Les classes sociales dans l'Empire romain* (Paris: Payot, 1964); P. Garnsey, *Social Status and Legal Privilege in the Roman Empire* (Oxford: Clarendon, 1970).

honor (11.4); to have their ecstatic prophecy received (11.7); to receive the first fruits of produce (13.3). Likewise they have the responsibility to teach the truth (11.1-2), and to live simply and according to certain fixed norms so that their authenticity can be known by their conduct (11.5-6, 8-12). The authority of these charismatic leaders is not seen to be in tension with resident authorities. Rather, in this unique document, it is the bishops and deacons who are introduced with the assurance that they too can be worthy ministers along with the apostles and prophets (15.1-2)!

MARTYRDOM

As we move toward consideration of the rights and duties that flow from possession of charisms, one more historical glimpse beyond the NT will provide a helpful example. While the exercise of charisms to build community as Paul had conceived of it dwindled in the first Christian centuries because the model of community changed, a new situation arose which enabled the recognition of a distinct charism in the Church: martyrdom. Whether one was fortunate enough to give one's life, or only to be able to witness by imprisonment and torture, the martyr or confessor was seen at least in the North African Church of the second and third centuries as one having the Holy Spirit in a special way. From this presence of the Spirit flowed the right to grant peace and reconciliation to those who sought forgiveness through the intercession of the imprisoned confessors. Their subsequent death brought about the assurance of forgiveness for those for whom they interceded.

This practice is first witnessed by Tertullian.[17] He protests that the martyrs themselves do not have the power to forgive sins, but only to intercede. But by this time Tertullian the Montanist reveals the tension inherent in such a policy between "charismatic" and "hierarchical" authority: it is the Church of the Spirit, not the Church of the bishops, which has the power to forgive sins.[18]

A similar belief in the charismatic authority of the potential martyr is reflected in the Roman Church at about the same time: Hippolytus' *Apostolic Tradition* rules that a true confessor who has suffered chains

---

[17] *Ad mart.* 1.3; 1.6; *De pen.* 19.

[18] *De pud.* 21,22. According to Tertullian's interpretation, the power to forgive sins granted by Christ to Peter in Matt 16:18-19 was meant for Peter personally, because he was a "spiritual" man.

and imprisonment and has survived needs no ordination to join the ranks of the diaconate or presbyterate (though he still does to the episcopate). He has already sufficient status (*timē*) through his confession of faith and life (*homologia*).[19] This practice reflects thinking closer to that of the Pastoral Epistles: charism, here specifically the charism of martyrdom missed, has its own validity but is placed at the service of office. The only evidence from Hippolytus of the continued existence of pneumatic charisms respected and left alone by hierarchical authority is the prescription that one who has a "charism of healing through revelation" has an obvious grace and therefore needs no laying on of hands, presumably for the healing ministry.[20] But these are isolated instances that survive in an otherwise well ordered community.

Half a century after Tertullian the situation in North Africa was getting out of hand in the judgment of Cyprian of Carthage, in the wake of the controversy about readmission of the *lapsi*—those who had apostasized under pressure and later sought reconciliation and readmission to the Church. The imprisoned confessors—some of whom turned out later to live less than edifying lives themselves[21] —were taking it upon themselves to grant pardon to whomever they pleased, in at least one instance even granting it in the name of a dead martyr. Some wrote letters of peace specifying certain names but including "all of his friends" as well, so that there was no limit to the number of *lapsi* included. Some presbyters then moved to admitting the recipients of these letters to the Eucharist without waiting for the consent of the bishop.[22]

While Cyprian concedes that any of the lapsed in danger of death may be admitted to communion immediately by a presbyter or even a deacon when necessary, and that those who are sick may be treated with special consideration, his general policy is that the lapsed may be

[19] *Ap. Trad.* 10.1-2. But one who has only been derided publically and not imprisoned must still be ordained. The same occurs in later dependent texts: *Testamentum Domini* 39; *Canons of Hippolytus* 43-45; and *Apostolic Constitutions* 8.23, which seems to distinguish between the honor (*timē*) and use (*chreia*) of office. Thus even the *Ap. Trad.* may be speaking of an "honorary" presbyterate in this case. It must be remembered, however, that at this point the presbyters are more the bishop's council than his representatives. The function of priesthood as it later came to be should not be read back into these documents with regard to presbyters.

[20] *Ap. Trad.* 15. In the parallel text of *Ap. Const.* 8.26.2, it is a *charisma iamatōn* (Paul's term in 1 Cor 12:9,28) *di' apokalypseōs*.

[21] *De unitat.* 20,21; *Ep.* 13.4-5; 14.3 (*The Ante-Nicene Fathers* [ANF] 6.4-5; 5.3).

[22] *Ep.* 15; 17.2; 27 (ANF 10;11.2; 22).

readmitted to full communion only through episcopal approval and satisfactory performance of appropriate penance.[23] Here charismatic and episcopal authority seem to clash head-on. Cyprian objects that the confessors are taking upon themselves a power of forgiveness that is against the law of God (e.g., Lk 12:8) as interpreted by episcopal authority. At the same time he is careful not to belittle the dignity and power of martyrdom. His position is that indiscriminate readmission of the lapsed without hierarchical authorization violates the very gospel in the name of which the martyrs die.[24] As is to be expected by the third century, Cyprian's hierarchical authority eventually predominates and the confessors agree that they will henceforth not give letters of peace declaring reconciliation, but will only recommend suppliants to the bishop.[25]

In spite of the way it may seem, however, this is not a clear-cut case of charism vs. office. What clouds the issue is the way the tradition stemming from 1 Tim 4:14 finds expression in Cyprian's ecclesiology, for Cyprian the bishop portrays himself as one who believes in the prophetic power of dreams and visions, and what is more, acts on their suggestions. The champion of episcopal authority and legitimacy is also a charismatic visionary.[26] This situation again reveals that a supposed opposition between charism and hierarchy is simplistic. The tension is rather between different ways in which charism is thought to be manifested and to operate.[27]

This phenomenon in the African Church is instructive. In a milieu in which pneumatic manifestations became increasingly suspect because of the Montanist problem, martyrdom functioned in popular faith as a charism in the Pauline sense: a gift bestowed by the Holy Spirit on an individual person for the building up of the community. The literature of martyrdom in these centuries clearly reveals its strongly communal

---

[23]*Ep.* 18.1; 19.2; 20.3 (ANF 12.1; 13.2; 14.2).

[24]*De lap.* 15-20.

[25]*Ep.* 23; 31.6; 36.2 (ANF 16; 25.6; 29.2).

[26]See *Ep.* 11 (7).3,4,5,6; 16(9).4; 39(33).1; 40(34).1; 73(72).13; 78.2; especially 66 (68).10, where he defends his trust in dreams by appeal to the example of Joseph in Genesis; A. Harnack, "Cyprian als Enthusiast," *Zeitschrift für die neutestamentliche Wissenschaft* 3 (1902) 177-91; M. Fahey, "Cyprian's Dreams and His Decision-Making," communication given at International Patristics Conference, Oxford, Sept. 3-8, 1979; and at AAR Annual Meeting, 1979. Compare Ig. *Phld.* 7.

[27]Helpful in this regard is J. H. Schütz, *Paul and the Anatomy of Apostolic Authority.* SNTSMS 26 (Cambridge: University Press, 1975), pp. 249-280; and another study upon which he partially relies (pp. 274-278): E Shils, "Charisma, Order and Status," *American Sociological Review* 30 (1965): 199-213.

dimension: its power to encourage and unite a community and be a tangible sign of the Spirit's presence. The Acts of Perpetua and Felicitas, a document contemporary with Tertullian, underscore the relationship between martyrdom and pneumatic manifestations. The problem is that at some point the charism of martyrdom became as destructive of community as it was constructive. The rights attributed to confessors on the basis of their charism eventually came into conflict with the rights attributed to episcopal authority on the basis of its charism. While it is certainly true at one level that there can be no conflict between two different manifestations of one and the same Spirit abiding in the Church, that seems to be ultimately where history led. The spontaneous response of course is that such conflict arises only when there are abuses: the charismatic danger of chaos, the hierarchical danger of stultification. From a distance of centuries and with only partial evidence, it is difficult to discern which abuse was the greater.

MINISTRY

We can now turn to a consideration of rights and duties associated with Pauline charisms in light of our overall concern for the question of ministry. It has been argued above that the Vatican II distinction between ministry and charism as reflected in AA is untenable for the NT in general and for Paul in particular. Certainly a theology of the gift and presence of the Spirit in the Church is pervasive in the Gospels and other major NT books, but the notion of charism as developed by Paul is distinctive to his writings. There is a rich theological variety in the NT, and Paul's ecclesiology is no more normative than, say, Matthew's or John's, or that of the deutero-Pauline letters. But if it is accepted as part of the basis of a contemporary ecclesiology, then it must be taken seriously for what it is, and not too easily assimilated to other theological systems.

For Paul the charisms are the means whereby the life of the community coheres and thereby the Body of Christ is built up. They are the visible sign of the Spirit's presence even in their most everyday aspects. J. Dunn has suggested seven characteristics. A charism is: (1) an *event* in which God's gracious action is shown; (2) a specific *act of God* that is given, not achieved; (3) an *experience* in which something is accomplished through human means; (4) not the same as human talent and natural ability, but rather an expression of the *transcendent*; (5) one of many given in unlimited diversity as need arises; (6) not limited to the liturgical sphere but embracing all of life's possibilities; (7) not confined to sacramental and hierarchical channels.[28]

The responsibility to give expression to charisms is that of responding to grace bestowed. There can be no escaping the relentless force of God's Spirit that arises from the depth of prayer and urges to action: "We cannot refrain from speaking of what we have seen and heard" (Acts 4:20).

The right that flows from the possession of a charism is to have that gift recognized and discerned by the community, which must heed the advice of Paul not to extinguish the Spirit, not to despise prophecy, but to "test everything and keep what is good" (1 Thess 5:18-21). The thorny problems arise when in a different historical situation, ways of discerning and testing need to be formulated. AA's procedure of leaving it to the pastors to "make a judgment about the true nature and proper use of these gifts" is an incomplete appropriation of the original Pauline vision of community. Yet the document and those who stand behind it have appropriated Paul's theology of charism and so must reckon with all of his ecclesiology.

In the Pauline community rights and duties are founded on two complementary insights which must also accompany any adoption of the Pauline notion of charisms: freedom in Christ as gift of the Spirit, and the Church as Body of Christ. Both elements are present in our passage from AA. One who has a charism is to exercise it in "the freedom of the Holy Spirit" . . . . "At the same time, they must act in communion with their brothers [and sisters] in Christ, especially with their pastors." The tension between freedom and communion was already keenly felt in Paul's day; it is evident in the pages of 1 Corinthians and Galatians especially. The Christian's newfound freedom in Christ, itself a gift of the Holy Spirit, is no invitation to selfishness, irresponsibility, and license. Those who abuse freedom in this way Paul would hold just as culpable as those who overly restrict it through law.

"Christ has freed us for freedom. See to it then lest you take on again a yoke of slavery." The ringing tones of Gal 5:1 refer at the first level to Paul's conflict with proponents of the Mosaic Law. But already within Paul's consciousness, there is more to it than that. The yoke of slavery is not only that of useless external observance; it is also submission to the dark forces within human nature which produce "the works of the

---

[28]J. D. G. Dunn, *Jesus and the Spirit* (Philadelphia: Westminster, 1975), pp. 253-58.

flesh" (Gal 5:19-21). Modern psychological discoveries would necessitate a very different theory of cause and effect in human weakness than Paul would have held, but the results remain the same. This way of behavior is the very opposite of freedom.

True freedom in Paul's view is that integrity of spirit which enables a person to move spontaneously under the influence of grace, and therefore to experience "the fruits of the Spirit" (Gal 5:22-23) and fulfill "the law of Christ" by mutual corresponsibility. The freedom of the Spirit is essential for the personal exercise of charisms. It brings with it both the right to be recognized as one who has received gifts from the Spirit, and the responsibility to live faithful to the impulse of the same Spirit.

The Christian freedom that Paul envisions is realized within a context: the communion of the Church, the Body of Christ. For Paul the *ecclēsia* was primarily the local community, in which bonds of friendship and mutual assistance were easily forged and the organic relationship of members to one another was more easily seen than in today's vision of a universal Church—or even a parish with 500 families. This is our problem, not Paul's. It surely is not coincidental, however, that all four lists of charisms in the Pauline corpus occur as elaboration of a reference to the Church as body of Christ: 1 Cor 12; Rom 12: 4-8; Eph 4:4-16. For Paul the charisms are *the* concrete way in which the community experiences itself as the Body of Christ through the Holy Spirit. Membership in the Body of Christ bears with it the rights and responsibilities necessary for its continued growth: the right of each member to full consideration and the responsibility of each to give the same full consideration to others; the right to be as fully accepted in the community as a part of the body is in the whole organism, and the responsibility to accept others as fully into the community as one would part of one's own body. The rights and responsibilities inherent in membership in the Body are the same ones inherent in the possession of charisms, for the charisms are simply the expression of the reality of the Body. To consider one without the other is a hopeless mistake, one that AA happily avoids.

Though the very notion of rights and duties is a juridical category in which the NT does not operate, nevertheless the functions are present implicitly, as they must be in any ordered community. For Paul, then, the basis for rights and duties is the gift of the Spirit given to each person in the Church. This vision of community represents an alternative to the prevailing social structure of his time. In the household codes of the deutero-Pauline writings, the rights and duties of Christians are of course ultimately grounded in the grace of baptism, but they are at the same time mediated through one's position in a carefully articulated social framework. Some of the discussion surrounding the new Code of Canon Law comes nearer to the Deutero-Pauline view in its suggestion that rights flow from responsiblities.[29]

This too is a viable approach, but it is not the position of the Vatican II texts under consideration, with their Pauline language. Two different ecclesiologies are in conflict here.

To return to our own situation, AA advises the faithful of their "right and duty to use (the charisms) in the Church and in the world for the good of mankind and for the upbuilding of the Church." Because of the restricted notion of ministry which is only gradually changing and which, as we have seen, is not part of the Pauline picture, more emphasis has been placed in recent years on the expending of lay apostolic energy for the good of the world than for the good of the Church. Certainly Vatican II encouraged more initiative in that direction. Perhaps this is because it has not been seen clearly enough that the exercise of charisms, that is, of ministry in the Pauline sense, brings with it not only duties but rights as well. Indeed the right to exercise charisms seems to be the only right mentioned in the council documents which is not included in the new Code of Canon Law.[30] If we are going to continue to rely on Paul's ecclesiology and to believe in the reality of charisms as he understood them, then we must take the whole of his ecclesial vision seriously. This will necessitate far deeper questioning of our expression of freedom and communion than we as Church have so far been willing to do.[31]

[29]*Communicationes* 12(1980): 78. I owe this reference to Prof. Joseph Komonchak.

[30]*Communicationes* 12 (1980): 43-44 reports a discussion in the coetus on the *Lex Ecclesiae Fundamentalis* about the proposal of a new canon to acknowledge the right to the exercise of personal charisms. The passage from AA 3, however, was recognized in the discussion as "good, but not juridical." It was further decided to make some mention of charisms in the "theological introduction" rather than in the Code itself.

[31]The author gratefully acknowledges a collection of articles on this subject published by the CLSA twelve years ago, which paved the way and still makes good reading: J. A. Coriden, ed., *The Case for Freedom: Human Rights in the Church* (Washington & Cleveland: Corpus, 1969). Also helpful for further reading are G. W. MacRae, "Shared Responsibility—Some NT Perspectives"; R. B. Eno, "Shared Responsibility in the Early Church," both in *Chicago Studies* 9 (1970): 115-127; 129-141.

THE BASIS FOR OFFICIAL MINISTRY IN THE CHURCH

DAVID N. POWER, O.M.I.
The Catholic University of America

In treating of official ministry, it has to be recognized from the outset that the notion of office is not theologically a very clear one. Usually it is employed in reference to the ordained, but in the wake of the Second Vatican Council it has become clear that lay persons may hold special office in the Church, in keeping with the order and rights of the baptized. The best known canonical and ritual provisions for this are those affecting the ministries of acolyte and reader and special (or extraordinary) ministers of communion. There are also, however, many cases of local practice and discipline which pertain to a wide variety of ministries and which blur the distinction between the office of the ordained and the office of the laity. The forms of appointment in these cases are quite diverse, including designation by official appointment, liturgical installations, special blessings of various kinds, and the practical recognition of leaders by a community without formal ceremony.[1]

The purpose of this essay is to explore a flexible notion of office which is consonant with tradition and at the same time pertinent to contemporary experience and developments. In exploring the question historically, much attention has to be given to the episcopacy as the most important form of church office known to us. A serious interpretation of historical data together with theological reflection is the best way to grasp the place of the episcopacy in the believing community and at the same time open new possibilities for the integration of other forms of office and leadership.

PASTORAL MINISTRY IN CONTEMPORARY THOUGHT

Even though the theology of the Church underwent considerable development in the course of the Second Vatican Council, the position

---

[1] I have recently endeavored to assess some of these developments. See D. N. Power, *Gifts That Differ: Lay Ministries Established and Unestablished* (New York: Pueblo, 1980).

taken on the episcopacy in the Constitution on the Church was on the conservative side. This can be seen, for example, from this statement:

> This sacred synod, following in the steps of the First Vatican Council, teaches and declares with it that Jesus Christ, the eternal pastor, set up the holy Church by entrusting the apostles with their mission as he himself had been sent by the Father. He willed that their successors, the bishops namely, should be the shepherds of the Church until the end of the world.[2]

This seems to suppose not only an apostolic origin to church office but a rather definite form as well, even though we know that the council did not wish to resolve the issue of the historical origins of the episcopacy. Its pronouncement, however, on the sacramentality of the episcopacy made it possible to determine the intimate unity which exists between the three ministries of liturgy, teaching and pastoral care. By way of clarifying the position which the episcopacy has in the practical life of the Church, the council made a distinction between office (*munus*) and power (*potestas*), as well as between office and power on the one hand and their exercise on the other. These distinctions serve to clarify the difference between the authority which comes with ordination and the practical canonical directives which govern the exercise of that authority. A shortcoming in the distinctions, however, is that they allow for a rather abstract conception of the office of bishop, as though the office could exist without relation to the particular church for which a person is ordained.

By way of contrast with these positions of the Vatican Council, a statement on the ministry by the Faith and Order Commission of the World Council of Churches in 1974 emphasises the intimate relation between the minister and the community for which one is ordained, as well as the plurality of forms of ministry which legitimately exist in christian churches:

> The plurality of ecclesial cultures and ministerial structures does not diminish the one ministerial reality found in Christ and constituted by the Holy Spirit in the commission of the Apostles. Among the various ministerial structures the three-fold ministry of bishop, presbyter-priest and deacon predomi-

---

[2]*Lumen Gentium*, 18; Flannery, pp. 369-370.

nates. But it would be wrong to exclude other patterns of ministry which are found among the churches . . . [3]

Theology cannot proceed only from doctrinal statements but has to reckon with experience and church practice as well. What is of particular importance in our present age is the phenomenon of grass-roots communities and the types of leadership which emerge from this experience. Many theologians are therefore ready to look for the points of continuity and of legitimate discontinuity in the form and exercise of official ministry in the Church.[4] Among Catholic theologians, the situation has been recently summarized by Karl Rahner in this way:

> According to a Catholic understanding of pastoral ministry in the Church, it is obvious that there must be a ministry of leadership in the Church as a historical and social reality. The characteristics, tasks and powers of this ministry have to be understood and explained on the basis of the Church's nature . . . (This) is all that can and must be said about the office of church ministry with absolute dogmatic binding force.[5]

This rapid survey of current trends at the outset of this essay makes it possible to list a number of important questions which describe the subject matter of our investigation. (1) In what way is the episcopacy, as the primary form of church office, related to the apostolic church, and what other forms of office are consonant with christian tradition and apostolic beginnings? (2) What is the link between community and ordination, and to what extent does ordination in and for, and with the recognition of, a community pertain to the legitimacy of church office? (3) What is the link between charism and office, or to what extent may charism be said to precede appointment to office, and what does this have to say to the question of the power exercised by an office-holder? (4) Can there be offices which are directly related to baptism, rather than to the structures of leadership associated with ordination, and what are the appropriate forms of recognition for such offices?

[3]Faith and Order Paper No. 73, *One Baptism, One Eucharist and a Mutually Recognized Ministry* (Geneva: World Council of Churches, 1975), p. 35.

[4]See Power, *Gifts That Differ*, and the important work by E. Schillebeeckx, *Ministry: Leadership in the Community of Jesus Christ* (New York: Crossroad, 1981).

[5]K. Rahner, "Open Questions in Dogma Considered by an Institutional Church to be Definitively Answered," *Catholic Mind* n. 1331, 77 (1979): 12.

HISTORICAL DATA: EARLY BEGINNINGS OF OFFICE

In Catholic doctrine and theology, the concepts of "twelve apostles" and "succession to the twelve apostles" are often used to express the legitimacy and power of episcopal authority, even to the point of granting it the title of "apostolic ministry." If done indiscriminately, this approach risks presenting a false picture of New Testament history and understanding.

Since the work of J. B. Lightfoot it is accepted among scholars that "apostle" and "the twelve" are names that ought not to be interchanged. They do not refer to the same reality, nor even necessarily to the same persons. It is in what is generally known as the Pauline corpus that the meaning developed which came to be customarily attached to the word "apostle" and which underlies the sense in which the term "twelve apostles" is often taken. It may even be this meaning which served Luke in writing of the twelve apostles instead of, as in Matthew, of the disciples, or simply of the twelve. The Pauline influence on this notion is summarized as follows by J. H. Schütz:

> A study of recent literature on the apostolic idea reveals clearly that no basic normative concept of the apostle was available in the time of Paul. We cannot make Luke the norm, nor can we take refuge in the *Shaliach* hypothesis. As it happens, we have only Paul himself as witness to one form of apostolic self-consciousness in his own time. Paul's sense of what it means to be an apostle is etched sharply enough in his letters to make it clear that apostles are something special. He belongs to a group of apostles, however ill-defined that group may be, and his claims are intimately connected to his temporal primacy as one who establishes the communities through his missionary preaching activity . . . For reasons and in ways not entirely clear, he is gradually incorporated into a somewhat fuzzy picture of an earlier apostolate.[6]

The power of the apostle is to preach the gospel and to form communities on the basis of this preaching. In the Pauline writings, this is presented as a formalized power, or authority, in as much as it rests on the vision of the Risen Lord and on the call to preach received from

---

[6]J. H. Schütz, *Paul and the Anatomy of Apostolic Authority* (London and New York: Cambridge University Press, 1975), p. 252.

him. While Paul recognizes the authority of the leaders in Jerusalem, he does not see them as the source of his own authority.

Whatever nuances have to be kept in mind in reading Luke's narrative, it would appear that Paul exercised the power of appointing persons as heads and office-holders in communities whose qualities could be relied upon to guarantee fidelity to the apostolic teaching and to keep order.[7] The vocabulary of office is indefinite but by and large it may be said that the *episkopé* has to do with maintaining a community practice that is faithful to the apostolic teaching. In that sense, it does not equate the task of the apostle but continues the task by another form of ministry. Indeed, the formal authority of apostle attached to the name in Pauline and Lucan writings cannot be used directly to legitimize power in the post-apostolic church, since it comes from the vision and command of the risen Lord. The concept of "apostle" has to be changed in its meaning in order to serve as one which expresses the formal authority of office in post-New Testament times.

It is because the apostle could no longer serve as a prototype for ecclesial authority in the post-apostolic age that questions arose about the legitimacy of office and were couched in terms of the office's relation to the apostle or apostles. These questions concerned the teaching that was transmitted, the church structures that developed, and the authority of office-holders. They also affected the position of charismatics in the community and their relation to office-holders.

A relatively early form in which such matters were resolved appears in the Pastoral Letters of the New Testament. The office-holders are the second generation apostles such as Timothy or Titus, bishop-presbyters and deacons. The authority which they hold is not one that comes from a vision of the Lord, but it has a twofold basis. The first is the life of faith of the person who holds office, summed up in the moral qualities which make him respected both within and without the household of the faith (1 Tim 3:1-7; Tit 1:5-9). The second is the fact that the authority he has is given to him by Paul, or by some other person established in authority by Paul. This authority, however, does not accrue to him automatically but is subject to the test of fidelity to the apostolic teaching, for in the final analysis it is this fidelity which is the source of the power exercised (1 Tim 3:2; Tit 1:9). As Schütz writes, "the ministry is a service to the apostolicity [of the Church], and for

---

[7]Acts 14: 23. For a survey of recent literature on the development of office in the New Testament times, see R. Brown, "Episkopē and Episkopos: The New Testament Evidence," *Theological Studies* 41 (1980): 322-338.

this reason can itself be called apostolic, especially as a service to the apostolic community with its apostolic gospel."[8]

Episcopacy and the Teaching Office[9]

By the time of Irenaeus of Lyons, the threefold office of bishop, presbyterium, and deacons was well established. Yet when he wrote against the gnostics on investigating the true faith, he remained in line with the thought that what makes a community apostolic is its apostolic teaching. The lists of bishops which he offers, especially that of the great church founded by the apostles Peter and Paul, are a guarantee of authentic teaching rather than of office. The apostolic teaching was given to apostolic churches, and Irenaeus guarantees to his readers that it has been kept faithfully by them rather than by the gnostic churches, which rely on esoteric knowledge and privileged initiation.

The meaning which he thus attaches to the episcopacy is complemented by what he writes of the presbyter or elder, when he uses this designation for persons outside the official church structure.[10] The elder has particular status in the community from the fact that he knew the early disciples of the apostles, and is consequently closer to the original apostolic teaching and able to give witness to it. It would seem in fact that the office of bishop has acquired something of the role of the elder, modified of course by the lapse of time. His role is to give witness to the apostolic faith and his charism is to lead the people in fidelity to this tradition. Thus it is that outside the unity of the bishop and of the Church, as in the gnostic sects, the true teaching does not prevail. It is on these grounds that we can understand the importance of the teaching office of the bishop and the meaning of its symbol, the *cathedra*.

At the same time, teaching in the early church was not confined to the bishop, but continued to be considered as a charism which might fit a person for the office of bishop but could also be exercised by other members of the church. Liturgical evidence alone suggests that the

---

[8]Schütz, *Paul and the Anatomy*, p. 31.

[9]See H. von Campenhausen, *Ecclesiastical Authority and Spiritual Power in the Church of the First Three Centuries* (Stanford: Stanford University Press, 1969), pp. 149-177.

[10]See Irenaues, *Adversus Haereses* III, 2,2, ed. F. Sagnard (Paris: Cerf, 1947), p. 100, where *presbyter* is used of bishops; and V, 5,1, ed. W. Harvey (Cambridge: Cambridge University Press, 1857), p. 331, where it refers to the disciples of the apostles.

reader was a teacher.[11] In other words, reading the scriptures in the assembly included explaining them. We are also aware of the importance of the kind of teacher of whom Origen is the outstanding example.

Eucharistic Presidency and Community Presidency

Safeguarding the unity of the Church in the one apostolic tradition, presiding over its essential unity, and presiding over its Eucharist all go together. Presidency of the Eucharist was not something for which a person was explicitly ordained, but it went with the office of bishop because of his relation to the community. H. M. Legrand summarizes a considerable amount of historical evidence in these terms:

> If we summarize the testimonies of the pre-Nicene church, a general perspective emerges. The bond between the apostles and presidents of the Eucharist is to be found only with Clement and secondarily with Hippolytus. The perception of the president of the Eucharist as an explicitly sacerdotal figure is not attested before the beginning of the third century (Hippolytus, Tertullian, Cyprian). On the other hand, with all the witnesses we note that it is a fact, and most often it is axiomatic (Clement, Ignatius, Justin, Tertullian, Hippolytus, Cyprian and the canonical tradition deriving from Hippolytus) that those who preside over the life of the church preside at the Eucharist.[12]

While this evidence, then, does indicate that the role of the bishop and the presidency of the Eucharist go together, it also shows that the bishop is ordained for a community and not to an abstract function. For this reason, the role of the community in his choice and in the legitimation of his authority is an important issue. Several studies have shown that the candidate's choice or at least approval by the people is necessary for appointment both to the episcopate and to the presbyterate. The principle of episcopal election was general and was formulated canonically in Canon 6 of the Council of Chalcedon.[13] The ordination

[11]See A. Faivre, *Naissance d'une Hiérarchie: les Premières Etapes du Cursus Clérical* (Paris: Beauchesne, 1977), pp. 58-62.

[12]H. M. Legrand, "The Presidency of the Eucharist According to the Ancient Tradition," *Worship* 53 (1979): 407.

[13]See Y. Congar, "Ordinations 'invitus, coactus' de l'Eglise Antique au Canon 214," *Revue des Sciences Philosophiques et Théologiques* 50 (1966): 169-197; E. Schillebeeckx, "The Christian Community and Its Office-Bearers," in E. Schillebeeckx and J. B. Metz, eds., *Right of the Community to a Priest, Concilium* 133 (New York: Seabury, 1980) pp. 95-133; Schillebeeckx, *Ministry*, pp. 38-48.

ceremony as it is known to us in several churches of early and medieval Christianity shows how the bishop's office was considered in relation to the community. The ceremony was a community action in which the Spirit was invoked so that the bishop might be guided in his ministry, the people affirmed their choice and approval, and the laying-on of hands by bishops of other churches signified the communion of all churches in the one apostolic faith. The exact relation between charism, appointment, people's choice and laying-on of hands cannot be demonstrated on the sole basis of the ordination rite, but its history shows that these were all necessary factors in the process of accession to the episcopal office.

The appointment of presbyters did not follow exactly the same lines as that of bishops, but in their case also the intervention of the faithful was an integral part of the process.[14] More initiative might be taken by the bishop in proposing a candidate for the ordination but the rite provided for the people's voice to be heard. The case of Paulinus of Nola is an interesting one. He was ordained a presbyter at Barcelona almost by force, but when he left there he was not assigned to a particular community and was made to feel where he travelled that he had no right to claim the rank of presbyter.[15] It was only when he settled down at Nola that his position in the church was clear. Writing about the situation in the early and medieval church Cyrille Vogel expresses the opinion that where the link of the presbyter to a particular church was dissolved he simply resumed the position of a layperson.[16] Vogel might be stating the case too strongly, since it seems that on admission to another presbyterium the candidate did not again receive the laying-on of hands. However, he has shown that the office of presbyter, like that of bishop, was not considered as a reality in itself but rather as an assignation to a church. Without this assignation, the office-holder had no functions to perform.

This early church practice is markedly different from later practices

[14]See B. Kleinheyer, *Die Priesterweihe im Römischen Ritus: eine liturgiehistorische Studie* (Trier: Paulinus, 1962), pp. 49-53; H. B. Porter, *The Ordination Rites of the Ancient Western Churches* (London: SPCK, 1967), pp. 49-51; C. Vogel, "Titre d'Ordination et Lien du Presbytère à la Communauté Locale," *La Maison-Dieu* 115 (1973): 70-85.

[15]See *Letters of Paulinus of Nola*, translated by P. G. Walsh, Ancient Christian Writers 35 (Westminster, Md.: Newman, 1966), Letter 5, 7-14, pp. 59-64. Compare Letter 1,10 (p. 37) and Letter 2,2 (p. 39).

[16]C. Vogel, "Laica Communione Contentus. Le Retour du Presbytre au Rang des Laics," *Revue des Sciences Religieuses* 47 (1973): 56-122.

of absolute ordinations, that is to say of ordinations without assignment to a particular community, or even from what came to be the established practice of ordaining men for churches without seeking the voice of the people. Ignorance of the teaching of Augustine on the permanency of order is often adduced as the reason why the medieval church doubted the validity of certain types of ordination or envisaged the possibility of degradation to the lay state.[17] It is assumed that Augustine's teaching as interpreted by scholastic theology is correct.

Augustine's position however deserves more careful attention. He argued in the first place against the rebaptism practiced by the Donatists and against any desire to rebaptize the Donatists themselves if they were reconciled to the Church. His argument is based on his understanding of the rite of baptism.[18] Despite their schism, the Donatists rightly invoked the Trinity and the name of Christ and rightly practiced baptismal immersion. Since therefore they possessed the true *verbum fidei* they possessed the sacrament of the Lord's Body and of unity in the Spirit, even though they did not in Augustine's view possess the reality signified by the sacrament. Augustine's reverence for the word and the sacrament meant that he did not wish to see the rite repeated, even if it was performed and given outside the unity of the Church. Once a person had been given the sacrament, it could not be given again, but reunion with the community of faith and charity brought with it the life of the Spirit signified in the sacrament. In speaking of this view, he used the metaphor of the emperor's mark on a soldier.

He extended his argument to the case of those who received the laying-on of hands, conceding that the Donatists possessed not only the sacrament of baptism but through the laying-on of hands the *ius dandi*.[19] Consequently, if their ministers were ever admitted to ministry within the unity of the Catholic Church they were not to receive again the laying-on of hands. The metaphor of the emperor's mark could be used in this case also. However, this cannot lead to the conclusion that Augustine in any way envisaged the laying-on of hands for office outside the context of assignation to a community. In the first place, his

[17]See H. Cowdrey, "The Dissemination of Augustine's Doctrine of Holy Orders During the Late Patristic Age," *Journal of Theological Studies* 20 (1969): 448-481; N. M. Häring, "The Augustinian Axiom: Nulli Sacramento Injuria Facienda Est," *Medieval Studies* 16 (1954): 87-117.

[18]Augustine, "On Baptism Against the Donatists," in M. Dods, ed., *The Works of Aurelius Augustine*, vol. 3 (Edinburgh: T. & T. Clark, 1872), pp. 1-228.

[19]Ibid., Bk V, XXII, 30; Dods, pp. 140f.

only reason for accepting either baptism or ordination among the Donatists was his concession that they possessed right doctrine on the Trinity and on the name of Christ, and invoked these correctly in their community rites. In the second place, what he said of baptism needs to be applied equally to ordination; namely, that while one may possess the sacrament outside the unity of the true Church, one does not possess the reality signified. In other words, while a bishop or presbyter might duly communicate the sacrament in a schismatic community, he does not participate in the full unity that is signified by this sacrament, whether it be baptism or the laying-on of hands. The same is true of persons who receive these sacraments. There is nothing in Augustine's teaching to justify the idea that a person may lay claim to the exercise of ministerial functions outside the context of a community of faith. The one legitimate conclusion that can be drawn from Augustine's teaching is that in the celebration of sacraments, the faithful do not have to be worried about the faith or worthiness of the minister, since the rites themselves are adequate guarantee of what is signified and celebrated. This, however, does not mean that he was indifferent to the qualities of church ministers or that he thought in terms of sacramental powers which could be functional outside the context of a faith community and its celebration.

Contrasting Patristic Views of the Episcopacy

Given the relation of the episcopal office to the community, and its rather obscure historical relation to the church of the apostles, it is not surprising to find that there were rather divergent views among some Fathers of the Church on the nature of the office. Ideas held about its origins, its relation to the apostles, and the charism of the office-holder can serve to clarify the questions about office which are important today.

The respective positions of Cyprian of Carthage and Augustine of Hippo can serve as one example of divergency. Their different attitudes to the episcopacy appear in the different ways in which they interpret the biblical text, Matt 16:18. Neither writer was aware of the exegetical distinction which needs to be made between the twelve and the twelve apostles. In these words of Christ to Peter, Cyprian found the origin of the episcopacy. The words are addressed, according to him, not merely to Peter but to all the apostles.[20] Since the bishops are for him the direct successors of the apostles, the power and authority which Christ

---

[20]*St. Cyprien: Correspondance,* ed. L. Bayard (Paris, 1961), pp. 84f., Letter 33,1.

gave to the apostles are now vested in the bishops. There is no sign here of the distinction between apostle and bishop which is found in the writings of Irenaeus. Cyprian did indeed follow the tradition of calling for the election of the bishop by the people, but his understanding of this text meant that in describing the power of the office he placed more emphasis on the transmission of powers than on the candidate's recognition by the people.

Augustine interpreted this same text as an address to the faith of the community, or indeed to the community itself. He wrote:

> Jesus meant: Upon this rock I will build the faith which you profess. Because you said to me, you are the Christ, the Son of the living God, I will build my Church on you . . . In a virtually unique way Peter represented the entire Church. In his capacity as representative of the whole Church, these words were fittingly addressed to him: I will give you the keys of the kingdom of heaven. It was not one man, but the whole Christ, which received these keys. Peter's prominence was acknowledged inasmuch as he stood for the one, universal Church when the Lord said to him, "I will give you" the power that was given to all.[21]

Since it is to the whole Christ that the power of the Son belongs, this interpretation of the text places the office of bishop in much closer relation to the community than does that of Cyprian. The bishop in this case is one who serves the faith of the community and exercises a power which is a power of the Church rather than his own as officeholder. The office does not carry its justification within itself in virtue of a commissioning received from Christ, but its authority derives from what Christ has given to the whole Church.

The juridical perception of authority which we find in Cyprian[22] can also be contrasted with a more spiritual conception, of which Basil of Caeserea may serve as an example.[23] Basil based his ideas and images of authority in the Church on his sense of the presence of the Holy Spirit in the community. The gift and charism of the Spirit lie at the

[21]Augustine, *Sermon 295*. On both authors, see Y. Congar, *L'Ecclésiologie du Haut Moyen-Age* (Paris:Cerf, 1968), pp. 138-151. See also A. M. La Bonnardière, "Tu es Petrus: La Péricope Matt 16, 13-23 dans l'Oeuvre de Saint Augustin," *Irénikon* 34 (1961): 451-499.

[22]See A. Beck, *Römisches Recht bei Tertullian und Cyprian* (Halle, 1930).

[23]See P. J. Fedwick, *The Church and the Charisma of Leadership in Basil of Caeserea* (Toronto: Toronto University Press, 1979).

root of all ecclesial power. The possession of the charisms needed to lead the Church in faith had to be ascertained prior to the laying-on of hands and appointment to office. From one point of view, the laying-on of hands can be seen as an invocation of the Spirit who gives the gifts, but from another point of view it is a recognition of gifts already possessed and the placement of a charismatic person in a position of church leadership.

Curiously enough, the persuasion that charisms which precede ordination give the necessary power of leadership is the reason why Basil was one of those most influential in leading to a clericalization of office and ministry. His very conviction that bishops and other ministers had to be richly endowed with the Spirit made him look for candidates primarily in the ranks of ascetical brotherhoods who followed a strict rule of life. He feared that choosing candidates elsewhere might run the risk of having leaders who sought only the prestige, the power, and the gain of office. By a strange twist, therefore, the very emphasis on the need for the charisms of the Spirit and a virtuous life meant that candidature could be reserved to certain types of person who had led a distinctive style of life. Church orders and canonical literature from the *Apostolic Tradition* onwards are the most obvious evidence for this gradual clericalization of ministry in the Church.[24]

Episcopal Image

Given this desire to make spiritual authority the basis of official authority, a number of other factors in church piety can be seen to have contributed to the assimilation by the episcopacy of the qualities and role of the apostle, so that apostle and bishop became practically identical. One of the leading factors was probably the cult of the saints.

In Rome, the cult of the great apostles Peter and Paul bolstered the persuasion that they remained continually present in the church as its protectors and guardians. This presence was in turn associated with the office of bishop. Appealing to the cult and to the presence of the apostles, Leo the Great could describe the ordination of the bishop of Rome as a kind of repetition of the Lord's words to Peter in Matt 16:16ff.[25]

---

[24]See A. Faivre, *La Naissance.*

[25]*Sermon* 94, 2-3, ed. Sources Chrêtiennes 200 (Paris: Cerf, 1973), pp. 257-260. On the influence of cult on the image of the Bishop of Rome, see Ch. Pietri, *Roma Christiana: Recherches sur l'Eglise de Rome, son Organisation, sa Politique, son Idéologie de Militiade à Sixte III* (Rome: Ecole Française de Rome, 1976), pp. 311-440.

Hagiography, particularly the lives of great bishops, contributed largely to this identification between apostle and bishop, a comparison which indeed extended to one between the bishop and Christ. A very good example of this is the *Life of Martin of Tours* by Sulpicius Severus.[26] Martin seems to have become through this biography and through legend not only the ideal saint but also the ideal bishop for the church of Gaul. In the *Life*, holiness, evangelization, the foundation of monasteries, thaumaturgy, martyrdom, at least by aspiration, and suffering for Christ's name, all converge to present the image of the ideal apostolic bishop who is in all things configured to Christ.[27] The account of Martin's election to the episcopacy is very instructive, since in a single narrative it brings together so many elements which belong to the figure and role of the bishop in the Church.[28] While the choice of Martin as bishop is clearly ascribed to popular choice, the motive for this choice is ascetical. Martin was the people's ideal because in his life of evangelical poverty and conformity to Christ in all things, including his opposition to the powers of this world, he was seen by them as a truly apostolic man. Severus describes the opposition to Martin's election as a kind of Satanic opposition, and he does not hesitate to draw the parallel between Martin and Christ before his accusers. The account also includes a divine judgment or intervention in favor of Martin, overcoming opposition and confirming the people's choice, through a kind of "sortes biblicae" in the random choice of a biblical passage which is taken as a sign of the divine will.[29]

Gallican ordination rites testify that the people played their part in the choice of bishops, as they also testify to a mixed image of the episcopacy and its power.[30] Alongside the figure of the apostolic missionary there is the more domestic image of the bishop and elder of the Pastoral Letters. There is thus a blend between the image of the householder whose authority rests in the good esteem and respect in which he is held by all, and the image of the missionary bishop whose ministry is "in the power of signs and wonders" and "in the demonstration of

[26]*Sulpice Sévère: Vie de Saint Martin de Tours.* Introduction, text and translation by J. Fontaine. Sources Chrétiennes nn. 133, 134, 135 (Paris: Cerf 1967-1969).

[27]See the commentary by Fontaine, *Sulpice Sévère*, vol. 1, pp. 155-158.

[28]See the commentary on this episode by Fontaine, *Sulpice Sévère*, vol. 2, pp. 641-661.

[29]This is confirmed by reference to other hagiographies in Ph. Rousseau, "The Spiritual Authority of the 'Monk-Bishop.' Eastern Elements in some Western Hagiography of the Fourth and Fifth Centuries," *Journal of Theological Studies* 22 (1971): 380-419.

[30]Porter, *The Ordination Rites*, pp. 40-47.

the Spirit and power."[31] These images coincide quite well with the details and images of Martin's life as recounted by Severus.

As in the case of Basil in the east, so in the case of Martin in the west the bishop is not only a pastor but an ascetic and founder of monasteries as well. Indeed, the two things are made to go intimately together, so that the spiritual power of the ascetical life as it flourished under a canonical rule was integrated into the image and reality of episcopal power. On the one hand, this served to put outstanding holiness at the service of the Church in the pastoral ministry; but on the other hand it contributed to the clericalization of church office, since it set expectations about episcopal life-style and restricted the choice of suitable bishops to the ranks of ascetics, or at least to the ranks of those whose life-style resembled that of ascetics in such matters as celibacy and poverty of possessions.

The "Claves Ecclesiae"[32]

The convergence of juridical notions of power with images of spiritual, apostolic and pastoral authority is well expressed in the growing popularity of the image of the *Claves Ecclesiae*. The text of Matt 16:18 came to be more consistently applied to the origin of the episcopacy. The keys of the Church served as an image whereby to describe the kind of power which a bishop possessed and the nature of his office. The use of this text and image actually occurs in texts where writers are describing the *sacerdotium* which it had become customary, in the wake of Cyprian, to predicate of bishops. Two well known examples of this usage are the writings of The Venerable Bede and of Saint Isidore of Seville.[33] For them, the fact that the *sacerdotium* of the New Testament is conferred by these words of Jesus is proof that it is different from the priesthood of the Old Testament. In the Old Testament, consecration conferred on its recipients the priesthood of Aaron. In the New Testament, that which is conferred is the power of the keys and it is this which constitutes the New Testament priesthood. This is the power to teach or preach the gospel, for it is the gospel which is the foundation of that living sacrifice which is served by the priests of the New Testament.

Later on, the power of the keys was used to describe the power of the

---

[31]Porter, *The Ordination Rites*, p. 44.

[32]Congar, *L'Ecclésiologie*, pp. 141-151.

[33]Isidore of Seville, *De Ecclesiasticis Officiis* V,5 (PL 83, 781-782). Bede, *In Matt* III, XVII (PL 92, 83).

bishop to excommunicate and to reconcile. This is in line with the idea
that teaching builds up the living sacrifice of the faithful. Keeping the
community pure in faith and in life through a process of excommunication and reconciliation is but the extension of the original exercise of
the keys, which is to teach. It is only a further step in this same
direction to associate the Eucharist with this same power, for it too
belongs to the celebration of the living sacrifice of the faithful. Whatever then must be said about the juridical turn given to the definition of
the power of the keys in later centuries, the early developments of this
image are not confined to the juridical but describe the pastoral office
of bishop in such a way as to demonstrate the unity of his various
responsiblities, while still keeping the foundation of the teaching office.

Presbyterium

This paper has been addressed primarily to the question of the episcopacy. The story of the presbyterate shows the same kind of fluctua-
tion, pluriformity, and even ambiguity. There is a common origin to
the episcopacy and presbyterate in the need of local churches to be
guided in the true faith and to be organized in keeping with its tenets.
When the episcopacy became the task of one individual person, the
presbyterium continued to exist as a group of respected persons which
guaranteed the elements of a collegiate form of leadership, even though
the functions of its members are ill-defined in history.[34] In due time, the
pressures of local need and the new dignity of the bishop combined to
make of the presbyter a "priest of the second rank," or in other words a
kind of low-ranking bishop. For the purposes of this essay it is here
sufficient to note that the same kind of questions arise in the case of the
presbyter as arise in the case of the bishop. When a person is appointed
to the task of presbyter, whether in its early or in its later history, what
place do personal holiness and charism have in his choice, what is the
part of the community, and what is the precise significance of the
laying-on of hands or other form of official appointment? One would
also have to ask whether clericalization, or the setting apart of persons
by distinctive life-style and status, has any legitimate part in the preparation, choice and service of the ordained.[35]

---

[34]See A. Vilela, *La Condition Collégiale des Prêtres au IIIe Siècle* (Paris: Beauchesne, 1971).

[35]What I have concentrated on in this essay is the relation of office to charism and to
community. The study would need to be completed by an examination of the non-
theological factors in development, such as is done by Schillebeeckx, *Ministry*.

CLARIFYING TERMS

The history of church office which has been outlined is by no means complete. The intention has been simply to indicate that doctrinal, theological and disciplinary questions cannot be resolved by a simple appeal to the early history of the Church. What we get is the picture of a community in growth, where practical issues of church government were settled in different ways, for different reasons, and by no means according to a clear set of criteria. Along with this practical pluriformity, there is also a pluriformity of ways in which choices or decisions were motivated, and in which what had already been done was given speculative or scriptural justification.

Is it possible to find a set of terms which can help to clarify the questions at stake? Words such as charism, power, authority, leadership, are commonly used, but their meaning is not always well defined. Some clarification can be offered by using these terms in ways that have been adopted by religious sociology, without necessarily subscribing to the theoretical explanations of religious phenomena given by sociologists.[36]

By *power* we may understand the gift and capacity to bring about, influence, sustain or change a human community, or the actual doing of these things. Since we are here dealing with the Church, such activities refer to its life and mission, and power is something which we believe originates in its authentic forms in Christ and in the Spirit. One also has to be attentive in the life of the Church to the inauthentic forms of power.

Authority can stand for institutionalized or formalized power. It is power aggregated to social structures and directed to specific ends. In the Church we usually think of episcopal authority, but inasmuch as the power exercised by others is aggregated to office or institution it too can be defined as authority.

Legitimacy can best be defined in the form of a question. When authority is assumed, or that is to say when power is affected to office,

---

[36]A number of recent studies make an appeal to sociology of religion in describing the development of office in the early church. See B. Holmberg, *Paul and Power: The Structure of Authority in the Primitive Church as Reflected in the Pauline Epistles* (Lund: C.W.K. Gleerup, 1978); H. C. Kee, *Christian Origins in Sociological Perspective* (Philadelphia: Westminster, 1980); A. J. Malherbe, *Social Aspects of Early Christianity* (Baton Rouge: Louisiana University Press, 1977); J. H. Schütz, *Paul and the Anatomy of Apostolic Authority* (London: Cambridge University Press, 1975); G. Theissen, *Sociology of Early Palestinian Christianity* (Philadelphia: Fortress, 1978).

it can be asked whether this form of institutionalization is in keeping with tradition and with the origins and end of the society. Hence, in ecclesiology there are questions not only about fact but about the legitimacy of the episcopal and other offices. The issue of legitimacy can also be raised with regard to power not attached to office. Thus the word *charism* may be seen as a word which expresses the legitimacy of actions performed in the ecclesial community, since it indicates that these actions are accepted as gifts of the Holy Spirit which serve the good of the community.[37]

Leadership exists where power alone, or power associated with authority, is recognized in the society and obeyed by the members. In the Church we can talk about a crisis in leadership when the legitimacy of the office is acknowledged but the office-holder fails to command a following.

Appointment is the action whereby a person is installed in office. This may be done by commissioning or through some appropriate form of ritual. In ecclesiology, it is possible to distinguish between assignation to office through ordination and assignation through commissioning, and of course the varieties of commissioning are many.

Using these five terms, it is possible to clarify what was going on during the period that office in the Church found its structure and development, and by the same token to see the issues which are at stake in all contemporary development. At a time when it was clear that the *power* of the apostle was in the preaching of the Word and that his *authority* rested on his vision of the risen Lord and on his personal call, the *power* and *authority* of the bishop remained clearly distinct from the apostolic. If, of course, the polysemy of the term "apostle" and the role of the twelve in the New Testament are well understood there is little risk of confusing the bishop with the apostle in such a way as to so define his office. It was only when texts such as Matt 16:18 were used to *legitimize* the *power* and *authority* of the bishop that the merger between the figure of the apostle and the figure of the bishop was open to juridical determination. Parallel to this development was the tendency to use Pauline images of *power* to describe the *authority* of the bishop, thus readily leading to the idea that it is with *appointment* to office that one is commissioned to the tasks which in fact derive from the grace of the Spirit and the sense of personal call.

The exact relationship between *power*, *authority* and *appointment*,

---

[37]Schütz, *Paul and the Anatomy*, p. 252.

especially when this takes on the form of the laying-on of hands, in fact remains unclear in early church history. Put rather roughly, it is a question of whether *power* precedes *appointment* and the conferring of *authority*, or whether *power* and *appointment* are simply taken as identical and attributed quite simply to the effects of ordination. From the historical data, however, there is good reason to say that *power* derives from the charism of the Spirit and *leadership* from the people's recognition. In this case, *appointment*, and in particular the laying-on of hands, is in a formal sense the conferring of *authority* through an aggregation of *power* to social and sacramental structures of community. When *power* and *authority* are simply taken as synonymous, then the prior disposition and ability of the candidate is only a desirable disposition for office and not in any way integral to the role or pertinent to the sacrament whereby the office-holder is appointed. The more juridically the office is conceived, the more easily *power* and *authority* are confused into one notion. The more charismatically it is conceived, the more readily the place of ordination can be seen as an action of the Church or the particular community which is a sacramental recognition of a *power* already possessed, with the conferring of the kind of *authority* that this brings with it, so that the office-holder can better serve the community and its mission through the use of his *powers* in the appropriate social and sacramental context.

This necessarily raises questions about the *legitimacy* of accession to office. The historical data indicate that there is more to this than maintaining the line of connection with the apostolic church, or a proper relationship to the college of bishops. The role of the community in recognizing *power* and *leadership* is intrinsic to the whole process, and has to be kept if the Church is to be faithful to its authentic tradition and to the meaning which the episcopacy has for the life of christian communities. This can be overlooked only if there is too hasty an identity established between the bishop and the apostles, and so between a commissioning given by Christ to the apostles and a similar commission passed on by them to the bishops.

OTHER OFFICES

Before passing on from these clarifications to futher theological reflection, a word should be added about ecclesial offices which are not part of the history of the sacrament of order. It is not possible here to go very fully into the matter, but some few remarks are essential to our question.[38]

In the western church, offices distinct from those of the ordained are inevitably associated with the history of minor orders. Even in the east, it is difficult to discuss these offices without noting the trends of clericalization. However, offices such as that of reader/teacher, psalmist, almoner, or exorcist, have an earlier history which does not admit of this confusion between task and status. We do not, however, go very far into the pages of history before realizing that the story of such offices becomes by and large the story of the clericalization of ministries which of their nature require no special appointment but belong to any of the baptized who have the particular charism needed for the task. The question then is whether some ministries do, according to their nature or to the circumstances of time and place, need the authority of official appointment, and whether this can be given without yielding to the temptation of clericalization.

In distinguishing between official and unofficial ministry, as in distinguishing between the ministry of the ordained and that of the baptized, lines cannot always be clearly drawn. The fact that the laying-on of hands has been reserved from the third century to the ordained as a matter of ecclesial principle does not of itself explain the distinction. More light can be thrown on the matter by looking to the connection between the ministry of the ordained and the Eucharist. It has been already observed that the presidency of the community and the presidency of the Eucharist naturally went together, and that this is the fundamental reason why the bishop is the ordinary minister of the Eucharist. Interestingly, it can also be said of presbyters and deacons that their part in the life of the community was given a corresponding part in the ministry of the Eucharist and that the former is the reason for the latter. On the other hand, the history of ordination rites, beginning with the *Apostolic Tradition*, indicates that it was increasingly the eucharistic ministry of the ordained that was highlighted in the ritual.

It was because he was head of the community that the bishop was president of the Eucharist. It was because they represented the collegiate character of church government that presbyters were first given special places in the eucharistic assembly. It was because of their service of tables that deacons assumed the service of the eucharistic table. The role of each of these ministers in the Eucharist is the primary

---

[38]See Power, *Gifts That Differ*, pp. 59-87.

sacramentalization of their role in the community. Ultimately, this is the sense behind the statement of the Second Vatican Council that through the laying-on of hands a person is ordained to the threefold ministry of word, sacrament and government.

When offices are instituted for the service of the community that belong to the laity simply in virtue of baptism and charism, there is no special eucharistic ministry attached to the office which would distinguish the person from the rest of the baptized. If this principle is correct, one can immediately see the ambiguity of special commissioning ceremonies for acolytes, readers, and ministers of communion. On the one hand, one has to ask whether there is any service in the life of the community to which this special ministry corresponds. On the other hand, one has to ask whether these ministries do not belong of their very nature to all the baptized and consequently whether such a form of appointment does not necessarily clericalize them.

THEOLOGICAL REFLECTIONS ON THE SACRAMENT OF ORDER

From these clarifications, it is possible to proceed to a further theological reflection on sacrament and ecclesial office. A test of theology is whether or not it can supply some criteria whereby to assess the legitimacy of office and to reckon with the development of new forms of office, which must nonetheless within discontinuity keep apostolic continuity.

Starting these reflections not in the early pages of history but at the point of ordination, it is possible to appeal to Karl Rahner's understanding of sacrament as "the Church's actualization in Word of itself as the fundamental sacrament or as the presence of God's invincible salvific activity in Jesus Christ."[39] While the sacraments are too often viewed as actions relating to individuals, they are in fact in the first place actions of the Church and expressions of the Church's reality. It is only as manifestations of the Church, as celebrations of the Church as sacrament of the Word, that they bring God's grace to those who take part in them. This principle is true of the sacrament of order as it is true of any other sacrament. In looking therefore to the sacrament of

---

[39]Rahner, *Open Questions*, p. 12. Schillebeeckx, *Ministry*, p. 68, of ordering ministry states "the self-understanding of the Christian churches as the 'community' of God is the all-embracing principle," and of ordination as a sacrament "it is the liturgical and sacramental expression of the sense of the community that what happens in the *ecclesia* is a gift of God's Spirit and not an expression of the autonomy of the church."

order, one has to enquire what it is that it signifies about the nature and life of the Church before one can ask what it means for the ordained.

In this sacrament, by invoking the Holy Spirit and the memory of Christ's own service over its office-holders, the Church expresses the sense of its continuity with the apostolic church. In the unity of the one saving faith in Jesus as Lord, in the catholic communion of all the churches which profess the same faith, it keeps both its sense of apostolic identity and its awareness of living in constant dependence on the gratuity of God's outpouring of gifts and ministries. Consequently, the office-holder, through the service of supervision and presidency, represents back to the Church that which in the faith of the ordination ceremony it has expressed about itself.

There have been in the course of time two misuses of the notion of sacramental efficacy in relation to the sacrament of order. The first comes from the idea that the grace of good ministry is given with ordination, and leads to unreal expectations regarding the holiness, gifts and perseverance which are expected from ordination. This can be counteracted only through an awareness that from one point of view, as confirmed by history, ordination is a recognition of the gifts and spiritual authority of the person whom the community deems fit for leadership. The second misuse of this notion comes from the idea that *power* and *authority*, as defined above, are synonymous and that they both come with ordination, or at least with the jurisdiction given subsequent to ordination. However, when it is realized that the Spirit gives gifts freely and that these gifts constitute the power on which the Church depends for its existence and fidelity to Christ's name, then ordination is better understood as a sacramental and formal institution of social authority which aggregates the freely given power of the Spirit to the sacramental and institutional structures of the Church.

The stress on the efficacy of order and of the actions of the ordained, which allows for a notion that is independent of priestly worthiness or community acceptance, is probably due to a misreading of what Augustine had to say about baptism and the *ius dandi*. Augustine was more interested in the nature of sacramental actions than he was in any particular power of the ordained. He was talking of a ritual celebrated in a community which, whatever its schismatic intent, gave right expression to the faith and duly invoked God's name. In this case, the principle of efficacy was applicable whether or not the minister was ordained. When the same principle was later used in reference to the celebration of the Eucharist or to the sacrament of reconciliation, it was stretched to mean that a power given in ordination could be exercised independently of the minister's worthiness of or any reference to community. Indeed, in time the sacrament of order was taken to consist essentially in the conferring of such power. However, it may be suggested that the applicability of the principle of ritual efficacy is the same for the Eucharist as it is for baptism, because in both cases it is the nature of the ritual which is at issue. On those odd occasions, therefore, which even history seems to attestify,[40] when someone who has not received the laying-on of hands presides at the Eucharist, the principle of sacramental efficacy applies in the same way as in baptism. But it is important to add immediately, that as in the case of baptism so in the case of the Eucharist the proper minister is the leader or president of the community of faith. This is not an arbitrary fittingness but one that goes with the sacramental structure of the whole ecclesial mystery. Were the position, indeed, to become such that one who had not received the laying-on of hands were to assume the regular presidency of the Eucharist it could be asked whether it is any longer a case of a "non-ordained" person so presiding. *Ordination* is a broader notion than that of laying-on of hands and there may be other, if unusual, forms of appointment to the office of leader and so to the sacramental roles that go with this office.[41]

This last point is particularly important today in face of the phenomenon of grass roots or basic Christian communities. New structures of leadership and new ways of promoting people to this responsibility have in fact emerged in these communities. The situation, however, remains anomalous in respect to what has become canonically established and there is marked hesitation on the part of the institutions of the Church to recognize this new situation in a fully formal way. What is done is that the celebration of the Eucharist is denied to these leaders, but provision is made for the celebration of the sacraments of baptism, communion, and marriage, as well as for the burial of the dead, through acts of jurisdiction. This is strangely in line with certain historical practices whereby jurisdiction over a church was con-

---

[40]See G. Otranto, "Nonne et laici sacerdotes sumus? (Tertullian, Exhort. Cast. 7,3)," *Vetera Christianorum* 8 (1971): 27-47.

[41]C. Vogel makes the case from history that ordination and laying-on of hands are not to be strictly identified, and that a mandate is more fundamental for office than the laying-on of hands. See C. Vogel, "Chirotonie et Chirotésie: Importance et Relativité du Geste de l'Imposition des Mains dans la Collation des Ordres," *Irénikon* 45 (1972): 7-71, 207-238. This is reprinted in *Ordinations Inconsistantes et Caractère Inamissible* (Torino: Bottega d'Erasmo, 1978), pp. 69-116.

ferred without ordination, even to the point that there could be a
theory which said that a person becomes the bishop of Rome on election rather than by ordination. In both cases there is an undue separation between the sacramental structure of the Church and authority or
jurisdiction, and, in the case of the basic Christian communities, an
attempt to supply by jurisdictional fiat what ought to be recognized
as dependent on the charismatic and sacramentally recognized role
of leaders.[42]

It is now possible to give a summary statement of the meaning of
ordination in the Church. Power to lead the people in Word and Spirit
is given through charisms. When these gifts and services are recognized
by the community and aggregated into the life of the Body through the
sacrament of ordination, the person ordained is given a formal authority within the community. The legitimacy of this process is not re-
ducible to the question of due rite and authoritative approval, but
includes those procedures which have to do with acceptance by the
particular community from which or to which one is ordained. As a
sacrament, the rite symbolizes that all power in the Church is from
Christ and the Spirit and that it can be duly exercised only when
acknowledged as such. Through this sacrament, the Church continues
to live in the faith of the apostles, and in the historical awareness of
God's advent into history which leads to hope for the coming kingdom.
Because of the relation of order to Eucharist, the sacrament further
signifies that all charism, power and authority in the Church finds
ultimate meaning and purpose in the mystery of the unity of the Spirit,
of the Lord's Body and Blood. Expressions such as "in the power of
Christ," "in the name of the Church," or "in the power of the Spirit,"
when used to designate the action of the president of the Eucharist, are
tensive symbols which serve to indicate the manifold relations of the
Church to its source and origins.

ECCLESIASTICAL LAW

It is still required that an office-holder in the Church, bishop or
priest, receive jurisdiction from a higher authority and that he exercise
his office according to the due prescriptions of law. While this need not

---

[42]Schillebeeckx, *Ministry*, pp. 76-80, discusses leadership in these communities as an
alternative practice which has a diagnostic and dynamic effect on the life of the Church.
Eventually, such practice comes to the point where it postulates official recognition by
the greater Church.

be questioned, it is not always clear how it fits into a theology of the Church. The question formulated some time ago by Rudolf Sohm must still be heard: how does the system of ecclesiastical law which prevails in the Catholic Church, with its emphasis on the authority of the office-holder and the hierarchy of law, relate to "Urchristianity" when the charism of teaching prevailed and all other forms of organization could be seen as variant expressions of this charism and ministry?[43] In Sohm's notion of charismatic organization, the organization exists only for the sake of the teaching and the teaching is that of the Master.

As earlier references in this essay indicate, Sohm's is not a simplistic view of the early church as far as the historical data are concerned. Since, however, it cannot account on the mere basis of data for the authoritative teaching and rule which obtain within the Catholic tradition it assumes this to be an aberration. Leaving aside the question of the abuses of authority, which cannot be denied, can a satisfactory explanation be given for the need of authoritative structure and ecclesiastical law?

Some insights from sociologists are helpful. As N. Luhmann, for example, writes, "the dominant structures of a social system (. . . values . . . contingency formulas and dogmatic systems) are institutionalized to the extent that they can be successfully translated on the level of behavior patterns, roles and collectively binding specific actions . . ."[44] In this context, he points to the important role of interpretation, which explains why teaching authority has been so central to the Catholic concept of office: "a dogmatic system may then arise to control and coordinate those interpretations which sanctifies particular concepts, key interpretations and combinations of ideas, and at the same time, by generalizing them, gives them sufficient flexibility to deal with events in the world, its own texts and religious experiences."[45]

From this kind of insight it can be seen how teaching and values or meaning, which at a more basic level can be expressed in general and in symbolic terms, need to be translated into terms which regulate practice and behavior. Systems of authority have to evolve which do this.

---

[43]See Y. Congar, "R. Sohm Nous Interroge Encore," *Revue des Sciences Philosophiques et Théologiques* 57 (1973): 263-294.

[44]N. Luhmann, "Institutionalized Religion in the Perspective of Functional Sociology," *Concilium* 91 (New York: Seabury, 1974), p. 54.

[45]Ibid.

However, they retain their basis in what is more fundamental and have to change in virtue of both needs and fidelity to the values and meanings which are at the core of the social group. While the members of the Church are expected to act according to the legislation and practical norms which are established, they can at the same time continue to submit these to a critique which comes from an interpretation of the more basic expressions or symbols of communal belief and origin. In this sense, while the authority of an office-holder in the Church is factually regulated by the existing provisions of law, these provisions are subject to a critique based on what is expressed in a more general and symbolic manner in the sacrament of ordination. The provisions, in other words, translate into practice what is expressed in the sacrament, but they are subordinate to that more fundamental expression which can serve as a constant critique of the legislative provisions.

To Sohm's question it is then possible to concede that teaching is indeed the major charism of service and that it is the basis for all ecclesial self-expression in both sacrament and the provisions of formal authority. The historical data have indicated that the charism of teaching evolved in a form which enabled teachers to claim the authority to interpret and supervise gospel beliefs. This kind of teaching authority was linked with presidency of the Eucharist, and so evolved into what is now known as the sacrament of order. The association of community leadership and sacramental presidency with the teaching office and charism is vital, since this combination of services expresses the foundation of the Church in the Word of God, its dependence on the gifts of the Spirit, and its own nature as a living sacrifice of obedience to the gospel.

This model is loose enough not to canonize definitively any particular form of church government, and so to allow in time for the integration of other forms and indeed for some plurality in forms at any given time. The model is one which allows for a movement from charismatic teaching to ritual expression of apostolic authority within the Eucharist, and finally to specific provisions of social organization through law. This is not to say that the exact historical sequence was in that order, but what is emphasized is the relationship between all the elements which go to constitute authority and its usage in the Church.

CRITERIA

From all that has preceded, it is possible to list certain criteria which can be of use in assessing the development of office in the Church, the procedures followed in appointing to official ministry, and the making of laws which govern the practical exercise of authority. These criteria are not attached to any particular form or structure of office, but of their nature allow for plurality.

First of all, it can be said that while office has its historical origins in the apostolic church, social and cultural factors play an important part in determining the development and exercise of power in the Church. The exact types of leadership or juridical forms of authority do not have the consistency that can be attributed to the general qualities or responsibilities of ministry, or to the symbols which express its meaning. Appeal to the symbols and narratives of the New Testament may continue to transform office and its exercise in the life of the Church.

Secondly, the ordination rite signifies that the Church and its ministry remain rooted in the apostolic church and dependent on the gifts of the Spirit. Like any ritual, it can receive distorted interpretation or be put to ideological use. It can also in time embody non-theological elements, more the result of accretion than of authentic development. Hence, it is necessary for the Church to constantly reconsider its use of ordination and the conditions under which ministers are ordained, lest it be ideologies rather than the gospel which govern the process.

Thirdly, "the ordained ministry is authoritative only in and through the community to which it belongs," and "only if the authority of the minister finds genuine acknowledgment in the communion of the community can this authority be protected from the distortion of domination."[46] This includes some form of participation of the community in the choice, ordination, and reception of the candidate. Naturally, one cannot expect the procedures to be identical at all times and in all places, but the principle as such is important. Room also has to be allowed for the sending of a minister from one community to another, and in this case some procedures for the action of the sending community and of the receiving community are necessary.

Fourthly, of the social and juridical structures which govern the exercise of authority it has to be asked whether they genuinely serve the reality and interest of the community. Another aspect of this is whether they promote the growth of the whole body as one which serves, acts and worships as an organism endowed with many gifts and services.

Fifthly, the community into which a person is ordained has to be a

---

[46]Faith and Order, *One Baptism*, p. 34.

eucharistic community, however this is realized in practice. Only in the Church as Eucharist is its true nature expressed and the true nature of the gifts of the Spirit made manifest. Conversely, every community of faith has an innate right to a ministry of the Eucharist and discipline ought to be such as to serve that right, not impede it.

Sixthly, the process of appointment, ordination and governance needs to be such as to express the true catholicity of every community, that is to say, its communion in the one apostolic faith with other churches.

Seventhly, any procedure which separates jurisdictional and sacramental powers and authority, or which substitutes juridical authorization for sacramental ordination, is suspect. This is particularly important today, as already noted, for the growth of office in basic Christian communities.

NON-CLERICAL OFFICES

These criteria apply in the first place to the ordained ministry. Some application to the offices of the baptized is also possible. Despite the canonical provisions made since Vatican II concerning the ministries of the baptized in the eucharistic assembly and the aspects of office which go with that, it would seem that any specific consideration of offices for the baptized has to do with non-eucharistic ministries. The ministries of acolyte, reader, usher, communion, and the like, which pertain to the assembly, belong of their nature to all the baptized and do not need the authority of special commissioning.[47]

There are, however, some cases in which the power that goes with charism may well be supplemented for the good of the Church by the kind of formal authority that goes with office. What exact path this development will follow is not at this moment clear, but one thinks of the kinds of office envisaged by the Decree on the Apostolate of the Laity of Vatican II[48] and of the different types of pastoral or teaching office that have been recognized within the last fifteen years by local episcopacies. Beyond what is common to all the baptized, these offices because of their formal recognition carry a specific authority.

Prior, however, to any specific rulings about offices confided formally to the baptized, church law ought to recognize the juridical

---

[47]Power, *Gifts That Differ*, pp. 133-148.
[48]*Apostolicam Actuositatem*, 24; Flannery, pp. 789-790.

element present in the sacrament of baptism and applicable to the rights of all members of the Church. All the baptized have some rightful part in ordering the life of the community and hitherto not enough canonical provision has been made to recognize this. It would be a distortion to legislate for special offices if this were not based on a recognition of a general responsibility, which allows for use of any charism or gift which can serve the community.

When one does allow for special offices, as in the case of ordination, one can look for a twofold basis. There has to be a basis in the present, in the personal call and charism of the individual and in the recognition of this person by the community. There also has to be basis in the past, in the relation of the present to the apostolic tradition. In other words, it can be asked whether offices that are newly instituted serve the nature of the Church and fidelity to the apostolic faith, according to the circumstances and needs of the present moment and place. On this twofold basis, canonical regulation can provide for the translation into practical norms of what already exists by the grace of the Spirit in the life of the community.

CONCLUSION

These criteria have been deliberately stated in rather general terms, so that they may be suited to a plurality of church experience. The need for change in church office is urgent, and for this reason a theology which relates charism, sacrament and authority is important. Within the vision given by this relationship, it becomes possible to take different social and cultural situations into account. Since some help has been sought in this essay from sociology, it is not inappropriate to conclude with the words of a sociologist of religion, as he reflects on the present situation of authority in the Church:

> . . . When the Church is felt as an "organization," it has no hope of focusing the identification which is an essential condition for the transmission of its values. It seems that religious motivation can only be transmitted within social relations of a "community" rather than a "society" type, but no "ideology of community" can in the long run conceal the societal character of the dominant social relations in the Church. This means that one of the main problems of church organization in the future will be to encourage, and give ecclesiastical status to, social units of the group type, precisely because they conflict with the dominant

principles of church organization deriving from canon law . . .
It is not destruction, but growing complexity and diversity, of
ecclesiastical organization, a deliberate mixing of formal and
informal structural elements, which seems to offer the greatest
hopes for the future of the Church as a religious organization.[49]

[49]F.-X. Kaufmann, "The Church as a Religious Organization," *Concilium* 91 (New York: Seabury, 1974), p. 81.

LAY PARTICIPATION
IN THE APOSTOLATE OF THE HIERARCHY

EDWARD J. KILMARTIN, S.J.
University of Notre Dame

The Second Vatican Council's dogmatic constitution *Lumen Gentium* grounded the laity's responsibility for the mission of the Church on baptism. It also taught that the normal sphere of the ministry of the laity is the secular as opposed to the inner ecclesiastical life of the Church. Correspondingly, the ministry of the ordained was based on ordination and its exercise was viewed as primarily related to the ecclesiastical domain. But the constitution did not preclude the appointment of laity, by way of exception, to some pastoral ministries traditionally reserved to those in Holy Orders. Still the limits of lay incorporation into the apostolate of the hierarchy were not set. For, despite the attention given to this subject, the council was not able to develop those elements of a theology of the laity which are a prerequisite for this. In the post-conciliar period the pressing need for such a theology has become apparent due to the changing pastoral situation.

LAY PARTICIPATION IN PASTORAL MINISTRY

During the last fifteen years appointments of laity to a variety of pastoral ministries at the diocesan and parish levels have significantly increased within the Roman Church. Many bishops in the U.S.A. and elsewhere are allowing laity to serve as assistant pastors where the priest is overburdened. Especially in dioceses where the number of parishes is completely disproportionate to the number of priests and new vocations, the hierarchy has taken a further step. The instances of laity being appointed on a permanent basis to act as leaders of parishes has risen dramatically. In the wake of the women's movement some bishops have recognized the anomaly of the practice of priests acting as vicars for religious communities of women and have commissioned religious women for this office.

In these various roles the laity exercise either or both teaching and decision-making functions. But can they be formally recognized by the

Church as sharing in a pastoral authority tantamount to that attributed to the ordained in the exercise of similar ministries? Can they, to use traditional ecclesiastical language, exercise the power of jurisdiction?

THE MEANING OF POWER OF JURISDICTION

The term "power of jurisdiction" has undergone several changes of meaning in the history of its ecclesiastical usage.[1] In the course of this development it came to embrace both the pastoral powers of teaching and governing exercised by the hierarchy. At the First Vatican Council, for example, it served as the governing notion under which all the characteristic functions of the pope were gathered. In its dogmatic consititution *Pastor Aeternus,* the primacy of jurisdiction—the supreme form of episcopal power of jurisdiction attributed to Peter and his successors, the popes—is said to include the supreme power over the whole Church in matters of discipline and government as well as "the supreme power of teaching."[2] The term "power of jurisdiction" was also used at Vatican I and up through most of the 20th century in official documents to describe the share of bishops and priests in the teaching and governing ministries of the Church.

A shift of meaning of the term after Vatican II is exemplified in the *Schema Canonum Libri I, De Normis Generalibus,* part of the post conciliar project intended to replace the old Code of Canon Law. This draft makes power of ruling (*potestas regiminis*) a synonym for power of jurisdiction in canon 97. This amounts to a contraction of the traditional meaning of the latter term. A similar use is found in the previous canon of the same draft. Evidently referring to such cases as lay assistant pastor and lay judge on marriage tribunals, canon 96 states that, in the exercise of the power of ruling, laity can have that share which papal authority concedes for particular reasons. The second draft of the new code, *Schema Codicis Iuris Canonici* (1980), retains the content on these two canons in canon 126:

> Those are capable of the power of ruling, which indeed is in the
> Church by divine institution and is also called power of jurisdiction, according to the norm of the precepts of law, who are

[1]G. Alberigo, "La Jurisdiction: Remarques sur un terme ambigu," *Irenikon* 49 (1976): 168-180.

[2]H. Denziger, and A. Schönmetzer, eds. *Enchiridion Symbolorum: Definitionum et declarationum de rebus fidei et morum* (Herder: 36th ed. 1965), 3053-3065.

marked by a holy order; in the exercise of this same power, insofar as it is not based on the same holy order, the Christian laity can have that share which the supreme authority of the Church concedes to them for particular reasons.

This canon deserves careful analysis from the viewpoint of the theology of Church and papal authority which it supports. While this lies outside the scope of this present study, it may be noted that some German speaking canonists have raised serious objections against the content of the second part as it appears in Canon 96 of the first draft of the new Code. The principal one is based on Vatican II's teaching that ordination is the source of the power of jurisdiction. As will be seen in some detail, no Vatican commission has given a satisfactory theological explanation why this teaching of the council does not exclude lay participation in the exercise of the power of ruling. However for now it suffices to say that the meaning given to power of jurisdiction in the two drafts of the new Code is too narrow to define the scope of the question addressed here.

Still the term may be employed in accord with the broader meaning suggested by the old Code of Canon Law, canon 118, which excludes laity from the exercise of this power. This essay is concerned with the capacity of the laity to share in the exercise of the power of ruling as part of a more complex theological problem. A precise demarcation between the exercise of the powers of ruling and teaching seems too artificial. The one inevitably includes elements of the other in varying degrees. Therefore the issue under consideration can be formulated in this way: Can the laity be co-opted into forms of the pastoral ministry which involve the exercise of the power of jurisdiction, understood to include various modes of participation in the pastoral power of teaching and governing? Employed in this way the meaning of power of jurisdiction corresponds to a usage found in much of the post-conciliar theological and canonical literature which treats this subject.

The issue of lay capacity for leadership in the celebration of certain sacraments is related to the above question. Vatican II teaches that the power of order and jurisdiction are complementary aspects of the one holy power bestowed in ordination. On the other hand, as already mentioned, the Pontifical Commission for the Revision of the Code of Canon Law finds no difficulty with the concept of the laity exercising power of ruling in a limited way. One may, therefore, ask: To what extent can the laity share in the exercise of the power of order, i.e., act as leaders of sacramental celebrations? Is this to be confined to emergency baptisms or can it be widened to embrace other sacraments for which the power of order, received in ordination, is traditionally required for validity? This topic is not explicitly treated here. Nevertheless from the following discussion it can be concluded that Catholic theology is still struggling to produce a commonly acceptable explanation of the relationship between power of order and power of jurisdiction. To this extent it indicates the need for a more profound analysis of this relationship before any theoretical conclusions can be drawn regarding the scope of lay capacity for liturgical leadership.

Ambiguities in the Teaching of Vatican II

The limits of lay participation in the apostolate of the hierarchy might seem to be set, as far as the exercise of the power of jurisdiction is concerned, by Vatican II. It grounds the pastoral power of teaching and governing on the sacrament of order. The canonical mission given by competent authorities only has the effect of enabling the ordained to exercise this power freely. Moreover *Lumen Gentium* 10, on the basis of the holy power conferred in ordination, states that the ministries of the ordained and laity differ "in essence and not only in degree" (*essentia et non gradu tantum*). This qualification excludes the opinion that the hierarchical ministry is simply an intensification of the laity's or that the lay ministry as such is merely an inferior degree of that exercised by the hierarchy. This is brought out by the words "not only in degree."

The use of the phrase "in essence" is, perhaps unfortunate. It could be interpreted to mean that the laity are not only absolutely excluded from even a limited share in the exercise of the pastoral power of teaching and governing but also have an inferior degree of responsibility for the mission of the Church. However, the discussions preceding the formulation of this passage and the immediate context itself do not favor the imposition of either interpretation.[3] The phrase simply describes a new kind of ministry, mission and authority of the ordained which is radically different from that of the laity because it is established by Christ and the Spirit.

---

[3]H. Schütte, *Amt, Ordination und Sukzession: im Verständnis evangelischen und katholischen Exegeten und Dogmatiker der Gegenwart sowie in Dokumenten ökumenische Gespräche* (Dusseldorf: Patmos, 1974), pp. 353-356, provides a summary of negative reactions of Orthodox theologians to *Lumen Gentium* 10 and responses of Catholic theologians.

This distinction indicates that a functional differentiation exists between the ministries of the ordained and laity. *Lumen Gentium* 10 also points out that the difference has a personal dimension attributable to the sacrament of order. The hierarchical ministry is given to definite persons who alone can fulfill its full scope, as Vatican II states here and elsewhere. Consequently there are certain kinds of concrete ministry which are reserved to the ordained. According to *Lumen Gentium* and other passages of Vatican II, these include the leadership of the Eucharist, administration of sacraments such as confirmation, penance and ordination, along with certain forms of the exercise of the power of teaching and governing.

On the other hand *Lumen Gentium* 33 concedes that the laity can be called to "more immediate cooperation in the apostolate of the hierarchy," and be appointed to "some ecclesiastical offices with a view to a spiritual end." Since the laity are compared with those "who helped the apostle Paul," the prophetic ministry comes to mind. Other ministries, however, are not excluded. *Lumen Gentium* does not elaborate on the extent to which the laity can share in the ruling office of Christ within the inner life of the Church. *Lumen Gentium* 36, which expatiates on the laity's share in this office, merely describes it as exercised in the world. *Apostolicam Actuositatem* 24 makes some general suggestions about lay cooperation in teaching, liturgy and care of souls.

The inclusion of laity in "some ecclesiastical offices" which pertain to the spiritual sphere provides a remedy for the popular mystique which has surrounded clerical activity. It implies that a special efficacy cannot be awarded to such ministries simply because they are exercised by the ordained. Still a difficulty arises from *Lumen Gentium*'s teaching about the pastoral ministry of the word, one which it implies is open to the laity.[4] This constitution emphasizes that the ordained "nourish the Church by the word and grace of God in the name of Christ" (11) and are consecrated "in order to preach the gospel" (28). The laity are also considered to have a share in the prophetic office of Christ. But this is explicitly distinguished from that of the hierarchy "who teach in his [=Christ] name and power" (35). Nevertheless a correct interpretation of this passage must take into account the context which focuses exclusively on the laity's ministry of the word in the world. A theological

---

[4]G. Rambaldi, "Notae circa sacerdotium et ministerium sacerdotale in Vatican II et in synodo episcoporum a. 1971," *Periodica* 63 (1974): 537-542, lists texts of Vatican II which point to an essential difference between the ministry of the hierarchy and laity not only in the celebration of sacraments but also in the preaching of the word.

interpretation of the distinctive efficacy of the prophetic ministry of the ordained vis-à-vis the laity, where both exercise it on the basis of a canonical mission, is not intended.

THE ECCLESIOLOGIES OF VATICAN II

The theological problem of lay capacity to exercise power of jurisdiction must be approached from a theology of Church. Ministries of the Church must be consistent with the nature of the Church, or more precisely, derived from the nature of the Chruch. The way in which one conceives the nature of the Church determines whether a particular form of ministry is acceptable. For example, the following description of the Church contains a theology based on the orientation of Vatican II which excludes forms of public ministry unregulated by the hierarchy: The Church is the new People of God living a hierarchically ordered existence in the service of the kingly rule of God proclaimed and initiated in its final phase through Jesus Christ. Likewise, beginning with this description, a systematic theology of Church could be constructed which excludes all forms of lay exercise of the pastoral power of teaching and governing. Klaus Mörsdorf provides an instance of this.[5]

The normative value of this ecclesiology depends on its power of synthesis. Where possible it must also be evaluated from the practice of the Church. If it rejects a style of ministry which has proved that it can contribute to the building up of the Church, its weakness is demonstrated. For such a ministry must be consistent with the nature of the Church. At the present time sufficient data, drawn from the practice of the Catholic Church, is not available to support one or other ecclesiology and its conclusions regarding lay participation in the exercise of the power of teaching and ruling. Nevertheless this does not preclude an opinion about the relative merits of ecclesiologies which are open or closed to the experiment.

This essay is confined to Roman Catholic responses to this problem and, more precisely, with opinions based on Vatican II's teaching about the Church. However this council does not present a tightly knit, systematic theology of the Church. Rather, several ecclesiologies are

---

[5]In "Das konziliare Verständnis vom Wesen der Kirche in der nachkonziliaren Gestaltung der kirchlichen Rechtsordnung," *Archiv für katholisches Kirchenrecht* 144 (1975): 390, the above description of Vatican II's teaching about the nature of Church serves as point of departure for the discussion of lay participation in pastoral power of jurisdiction.

intertwined without being integrated and sysnthesized. They can be described as juridical, christomonistic communion, and trinitarian ecclesiologies. An overview of the main characteristics of these theologies and their implications furnishes an important conclusion. To the extent that they lead to different results, it would be incorrect to attempt to identify one or other resulting view about lay ministry with the implicit teaching of the council. Any other opinion about the theoretical possibility and extent of lay participation in the apostolate of the hierarchy must take into account the intrinsic merits of these ecclesiologies as well as the relevant pastoral practice.

Juridical Ecclesiology

From the latter part of the nineteenth century through the first three decades of the present one, Catholic ecclesiologists generally approached their subject from an apologetic standpoint. They were preoccupied with proving that Christ founded the Church as a society equipped with legislative, executive and coercive powers, and hierarchically structured to include, by divine right, a distinction between the governed and governors.

Several influences played a role in this orientation. Scholarly research bent on proving that Christ did not institute the Church or promoting the thesis that the Church of the Spirit is opposed to the Church of Law can be mentioned. But there were also the new political theories employed by the European states to gain domination over the Church. The concrete need to defend the rights of the Church against the claims of these states seems to be the main cause for the juridical orientation in official ecclesiology. In Roman documents, with minor exceptions, the emphasis was placed primarily on the Church conceived as a distinct, visible society, autonomous with respect to the state and possessing in itself, by divine right, all the powers required to obtain its supernatural end.

This juridical outlook naturally concentrates on what Jesus did for the Church during his earthly life. It tends to neglect what the Risen Lord is now doing for the Church. Among others the Gregorian University professor Sabastian Tromp recognized this weakness. His more dogmatic approach to ecclesiology contributed to Pius XII's attempt to redress the imbalance in his encyclical letter *Mystici Corporis*. In this document the Pope reintroduces the aspect of grace and charisms into the reality of the social body by insisting that Christ is both founder and ever present foundation of the Church-society. The Church, he observes, is called the Body of Christ because Christ is head both as founder and as one who actively supports his Body, communicating to it his gifts.[6]

Nevertheless the methodological approach of *Mystici Corporis* to the theology of Church is defective. Essentially it corresponds to that of the older scholastic theology which moves from the prevailing official teaching of the Church to seek clarification and support of it from the sources of Scripture and Tradition. Hence a predominantly juridical ecclesiology emerges. The results would have been different if the newer method of theologizing, recommended for seminary training in Vatican II's *Optatam Totius* 16, had been employed. This latter approach begins first with the relevant data of Scripture and then investigates how this material has been interpreted in changing historical contexts. In this way a more realistic evaluation of the partial syntheses achieved in the various historically determined official teachings is attainable.

In keeping with the older method the Pope does not begin with the New Testament and patristic concept of the Body of Christ in order to describe the intrinsic relation between the visible and spiritual dimensions of the Church. Rather, the point of departure is the universal Roman Catholic Church viewed as a society of members gathered under the hierarchy which possesses the twofold power of order and jurisdiction.

If the Church is defined in terms of the Pauline concept of the Body of Christ, the way is open to a clearer recognition that the local episcopal church is truly Church in the full sense. The responsiblity of each local church and all its members for the sustaining and building up of the whole spiritual edifice comes to the foreground. If the Mystical Body is defined in terms of the universal Roman Catholic Church, a juridical concept is dominant. The Church takes on the appearance of a society organized along the lines of a constitutional monarchy subdivided pragmatically into dioceses with the pope as visible head. The bishops, as his vicars, depend on him for the power of jurisdiction. Thus the ecclesiological reality of the local church is obscured, to say nothing of those churches which do not submit to the primacy of jurisdiction of the pope. As a consequence the sacramental-liturgical life, which finds place in the local church, is neglected when the grounds of episcopal and presbyteral authority is raised.

In the logic of this universalist juridical ecclesiology the power of order, which pertains to the sacramental life of the local church, has its

---

[6]*Acta Apostolicae Sedis* 35 (1943): 217-218.

source in the liturgy. The bishop receives the power to ordain others in the liturgy of episcopal ordination. He confers a power of order in the ordination rites of the various degrees of the hierarchy. According to their measure of incorporation into the clerical state, the candidates obtain the capacity to act as leaders of the Eucharist and to administer other sacraments. But the ordination rite does not confer the power to teach and govern. This latter power derives from the visible head of the Church, the pope. He bestows it on bishops by an act of his will. They, in turn, as his vicars communicate it to priests by a similar juridical act.

Because of his approach to the relationship of Church to Mystical Body, Pius XII retained this key aspect of juridical ecclesiology: the distinction between the sources of power of order and jurisdiction.[7] In *Mystici Corporis* he accepts the theory of contemporary Catholic theology that power of jurisdiction is immediately bestowed on bishops by the pope.[8] He also makes his own the theological opinion that the power of jurisdiction of the pope, though ordered to the episcopal office, can exist independently of it.

At the time it was commonly taught by Catholic theologians that a lay person is truly pope after canonical election, acceptance of the election and promise to receive episcopal ordination.[9] Although unable to celebrate the sacraments for which ordination is a requirement, he could

[7]As a result the integration between the spiritual church and the church of law is only partially achieved in *Mystici Corporis*. In the old church this integration was obtained because the relationship between eclesiastical law and Spirit was interpreted in terms of the dependence of law on the sacrament of ordination which confers the Spirit. The authority of the official ministry had its basis in the sacrament of order. K. Mörsdorf argues that R. Sohm's thesis, i.e., canon law is contradictory to the Church of the Spirit, can only be refuted on the basis of the intrinsic unity between the sacrament of order and power of jurisdiction ("Kanonische Recht als theologische Disziplin," *Archiv für katholisches Kirchenrecht* 145 [1976]: 45-58).

[8]*Acta Apostolicae Sedis* 35 (1943): 211-212. With an eye to this text, as well as others, the *nota praevia* 2 d, linked to *Lumen Gentium* 22, states that recent papal documents dealing with episcopal jurisdiction should not be understood to refer to the bestowal of the power of jurisdiction by the pope. They should be read to mean a granting of the freedom to exercise powers received through episcopal ordination. This amounts to a correction of earlier papal teaching.

[9]Vatican II's teaching that the power of jurisdiction is a complementary aspect of the one holy power received in ordination renders this opinion obsolete. The apostolic constitution *Romano Pontifici eligendo*, promulgated by Paul VI on October 1, 1975, affirms the logical consequence. The one who is elected becomes bishop of Rome, pope and head of the college of bishops after his acceptance and reception of episcopal consecration (*una cum consecratione episcopali*) (*Acta Apostolicae Sedis* 67 [1975]: 609-645, espec. no.35).

exercise papal jurisdiction which includes the highest form of the power of the magisterium, i.e., proclaim infallible doctrinal teaching. This explanation was given by Pius XII as late as October 5, 1957, in his address to the Second World Conference on the Lay Apostolate.[10] However this same address rejects the theory that a lay person can be subject of the "power of order and jurisdiction" through a canonical mission. The Pope reasons that this power is linked "to the reception of the sacrament of order, in its diverse degrees."[11] It is noteworthy that he speaks of power of order *and* jurisdiction. It is not explicitly stated that, prescinding from the lay pope, a lay person cannot share in the power of jurisdiction as distinguished from the power of order.

This somewhat ambiguous statement of Pius XII may be traced to a tenet of classical juridical ecclesiology which allows that a lay person, who is ordered to some grade of the clerical state, has sufficient juridical status to be awarded a share in the power of jurisdiction. But if the laity in first tonsure can exercise this power, the theoretical possibility exists for those not destined to be incorporated into the clerical state. This possibility can only be excluded if it can be shown that, according to divine law, it is only fitting for one who is ordered to or shares in the clerical state to exercise power of jurisdiction.[12]

The Code of Canon Law, canon 118, excludes laity from a share in the exercise of the power of jurisdiction. But this canon does not provide an adequate theological basis within a juridical ecclesiology to limit the exercise of papal primacy in this regard. Theoretically the pope could act against the law. As we have already seen, the *Schema Codicis Iuris Canonici* accepts this possibility. The argument on which it is based was worked out by the Pontifical Commission for the Revision of the Code of Canon Law. It does not include a consideration of divine law. Rather it appeals to the opinions of older influential canonists and a questionable reading of a text of Vatican II. This argument and the resulting negative criticism are treated in the next section.

CHRISTOMONISTIC COMMUNION ECCLESIOLOGY

In a juridical ecclesiology pride of place is given to concepts of visible

---

[10]*Acta Apostolicae Sedis* 49 (1957): 924.

[11]Ibid.: 925.

[12]This is the opinion of H. Heimerl, *Kirche, Klerus und Laien* (Vienna: Herder, 1961), pp. 74-75.

society and its structures of government. In a communion ecclesiology the members, their relationship to Christ and to one another, come to the foreground. The dogmatic constitution *Lumen Gentium* contains elements of a juridical ecclesiology, but it also includes aspects of the more recently rediscovered patristic communion ecclesiology. The Church is described as "constituted and organized as a society in the present world, which is governed by the successor of Peter and by the bishops in communion with him" (8), and as a "hierarchically constituted society" (20). Still other texts indicate that the notion of communion provides the key concept for a theology of the Church. From this latter point of view the Church is, in the first place, a community consisting of baptized believers who have a common life in Christ and their measure of spiritual gifts to share with one another. The ordering of chapters II and III of *Lumen Gentium* point in this direction. A consideration of the People of God as a whole comes before the treatment of the ministerial role of the hierarchy.

Elements of a communion ecclesiology were introduced into *Lumen Gentium* as the result of a compromise worked out in the course of the preliminary deliberations. But the desired integration with a more juridically conceived notion of the Church was not attained. This was due in great part to the failure to draw out the implications of the mission of the Holy Spirit to the Church. As a result the communion ecclesiology of Vatican II, and *Lumen Gentium* in particular, provides only a weak orientation toward a Trinitarian ecclesiology wherein the unity of Father, Son and Spirit is understood not only as the source but also the model of the unity of the Church.

The communion ecclesiology of Vatican II can be described as christomonistic. In other words, it is Christocentric along the lines of the teaching of the apostle Paul who speaks of our communion with God and with one another as grounded on our union with the Risen Lord. *Lumen Gentium* 40-42 offers a good example of this. The marginal references to the Holy Spirit do not offset the description of the present economy of grace which takes the form: Christ, Church-People of God.

Within the perspective of this ecclesiology a number of German Catholic canonists and theologians have been pursuing the task of redefining the constitutional structure of the Church. Klaus Mörsdorf, the most influential leader of this movement, thinks that doctrinal recomposition of order and jurisdiction, which this work entails, can be accomplished without significant modifications of the concrete ordinances in vigor within the Roman Catholic Church and in accord with principles laid down by Vatican II.[13]

A review of the position of the school of Mörsdorf serves two purposes. It provides a systematic outline of the dominant christomonistic communion ecclesiology of Vatican II and the conclusions which logically follow regarding lay participation in pastoral office. Likewise it shows the weaknesses inherent in an undifferentiated appeal to the teaching of the council to support a position on lay capacity for power of jurisdiction which is inconsistent with a christomonistic ecclesiology. This synthesis can be made in nine steps.

1. The universal Church is a communion of local episcopal churches. Each one is a true realization of the Church of Christ with corresponding rights and duties vis-à-vis all other episcopal churches.

2. Each church is a unique "complex reality" (LG 8) in which the visible and juridical components are inseparable from the spiritual elements. Thus the Church actualizes and builds itself up as sacrament of salvation through its several forms of preaching the word and the seven sacraments.

3. At the basis of all ministries of the Church is a sacrament: "The sacramental nature and organic structure of the priestly community is brought into operation through the sacraments" (LG 11). One is incorporated into the ministry of all Christians through baptism and into various degrees of the hierarchy through ordination (LG 11). This sacramental distinction founds the concepts of laity and clergy. Therefore the dividing line between the two is the diaconate. Paul VI

---

[13]"Das konziliare Verständnis," 387-401; "Das Weihesakrament in seiner Tragweite für den Verfassungsrechtlichen Aufbau der Kirche," *Ephemerides theologicae Lovanienses* 52 (1976): 193-204. K. Peters supports Mörsdorf's thesis with a systematic presentation of the twofold representative role of the ordained ("Die doppelte Repräsentation als verfassungsrechtliches Strukturelement der Kirche," *Trierer theologische Zeitschrift* 86 [1977]: 228-234). W. Aymann employs Mörsdorf's understanding of the relation between *ordo* and *jurisdictio* to exclude lay judges on marriage courts ("Laien als kirchliche Richter?" *Archiv für katholisches Kirchenrecht* 144 [1975]: 3-20). On the other hand J. Neumann finds that it supports the ordination of women. The practice of allowing women to exercise the pastoral ministry apart from the administration of certain sacraments both sets up a false dichotomy between the ministry of word and sacrament and, de facto, separates the power of order from that of jurisdiction. He concludes that since the Church needs the ministry of women the anomalous situation should be rectified by incorporating women through ordination into the ministerial priesthood ("Wort und Sakrament nicht spalten!" *Orientierung* 40 [1976]: 86-87; "Über die gewandelte Rolle der Frau in unserer Gesellschaft," *Theologische Quartalschrift* 156 [1976]: 126-128).

affirmed this by suppressing minor orders and the subdiaconate in the *motu proprio*, *"Ministeria Quaedam"* of 1972.[14] Vatican II itself rejects the idea that religious as such pertain to an intermediate state (*Lumen Gentium* 43).

4. *Lumen Gentium* attributes to the laity a share in the "priestly, prophetic and kingly office of Christ" (31). But it adds that "their secular character is proper and peculiar to the laity" (31). Hence their normal involvement in the Church's mission consists in the witness of a life of faith.

5. The clergy's special role in the inner ecclesiastical life of the Church is grounded on the sacrament of ordination (LG 10). A canonical mission, even when included in the rite of ordination, is a different process. It does not confer the holy power but rather determines the sphere in which it can be freely exercised (LG 22; *nota praevia* 2b).

6. The holy power conferred in ordination has the complementary aspects which are traditionally described as a power of teaching, governing, and leadership of the liturgy of the sacraments. Since the power of jurisdiction is a complementary aspect of the one holy power it cannot be bestowed on laity by a juridical act, even of the pope in the exercise of his plenary power. In short, a role of pastoral leadership with true jurisdictional authority cannot be assigned to the laity within the hierarchically structured People of God, for this type of ministry is based on the sacrament of order.

7. The christological dimension of Church, as described in Vatican II, provides support for the foregoing conclusion regarding lay capacity to exercise power of jurisdiction. The council teaches that the Church is hierarchically structured to reveal its mystery: Christ, the invisible head of the Church. Since the hierarchical structure is grounded on the sacrament of ordination, only through this sacrament does one become a sacramental representative of Christ the head. On the other hand, the hierarchical structure itself supposes different degrees of representation of Christ. Within the college of bishops Christ is symbolically rendered present and active by the pope. In this context only he is the one, unique representative of Christ. The bishop fulfills this function within the presbyterium of the local church and in the diocese at large. Presbyters and deacons represent Christ the head within the scope of a canonical mission received from competent authorities.

---

[14]*Acta Apostolicae Sedis* 64 (1972): 529-534.

Moreover because the Church is "one complex reality" (LG 8) in which the juridical and spiritual spheres are intrinsically related, those who act as heads of the Church must also be the ones who sacramentally represent Christ, the head of the Church. Consequently this unipersonal structure militates against the incorporation of the laity into a pastoral charge with true jurisdictional authority. The attempt to bestow on the laity a measure of such authority is not in accord with the Catholic concept of hierarchical authority. It removes the sacramental basis which is required by the nature of the Church.

8. Within the communion of churches, corresponding to the unipersonal structure, the pope is head in the fullest sense. He has supreme power, limited only by divine law, natural law, and respect for the statutes of the Church and Tradition. Beyond this the plenary power is conditioned by the fact that the Church is a communion. It is a collegial power, exercised properly when account is taken of the coresponsibility of the whole college of bishops and, indeed, of the whole body of the faithful for the mission of the Church. However the pope does not merely have the last responsiblity; he has the chief responsibility. Hence the coresponsibility of the rest of the hierarchy and other members of the Church does not imply that the principle of majority decision holds.

Within the local diocese the bishop is head in the full sense. His jurisdictional power, being derived from ordination, is limited by the demands of the economy of salvation which is discerned in concrete cases in the light of faith. But in the economy of salvation jurisdictional power is exercised collegially. Therefore the bishop is limited in practice by the particular cases which the pope reserves to himself or to another authority. Presbyters and deacons are limited by the degree of incorporation into the sacrament of order and the scope of their canonical mission.

9. The bishop must take account of the coresponsibility of all members of the diocese for the mission of the Church. He is pastor of a living organism which is being built up to the extent that each member assumes an active role. Hence he is responsible for supporting other members of the diocese in ministries which correspond to their gifts and for encouraging the flowering of their charisms. Moreover the principle of collegiality should be honored in the diocese. But the responsiblity of all for the mission of the Church does not imply that decision-making should be modeled on the democratic form of secular government. The bishop alone has the chief responsiblity for the diocese. As Vatican II teaches, the bishop is the reason why the local church can consider itself

as church in which and from which the one Catholic Church exists. He is literally the visible principle and visible basis of the unity of the local church and of its comuntion with other churches in the one Catholic Church.

Presbyters, and to a lesser degree deacons, can be given a limited share in the decision-making process within the diocese in virtue of ordination. This does not apply to the laity. Therefore the pastoral councils which include laity along with priests and deacons can, as such, exercise only a consultative function. Unlike the priests' senate, such councils cannot be given a share in the exercise of the power of jurisdiction.

The school of Mörsdorf has developed a coherent theological explanation for the exclusion of laity from the exercise of power of jurisdiction, based on Vatican II. The Congregation for the Doctrine of the Faith has indicated some support for the same position but not with sufficient clarity. Its *Declaration on the Question of the Ordination of Women to the Ministerial Priesthood*, October 15, 1976, affirms that it is only "the Holy Spirit given in ordination, who grants participation in the ruling power of the supreme pastor Christ."[15] But this is rendered somewhat ambivalent by a previous statement in the same passage: "The pastoral charge in the Church is normally linked to the sacrament of order." The word "normally" may indicate the inability of the congregation to settle the question about lay capacity for the exercise of the power of jurisdiction.

The official commentary on the *Declaration*, issued by the same congregation, is more forthright, at least as far as women are concerned. It judges that the historical instances of the exercise of power of jurisdiction by some abbesses were an abuse based on an incorrect understanding of the relationship between jurisdiction and the holy power received in ordination. However its further remark on this relationship, applicable to both lay women and lay men, renders the above observation somewhat ambiguous: "The Second Vatican Council has tried to determine better the relationship between the two; the council's doctrinal vision will doubtless have effects on discipline."[16]

It is not immediately evident what the congregation intends to convey by this last statement. The members are certainly aware of the approach to the question of lay participation in the exercise of the

---

[15]No.35 (*Origins* 6 [1977]: 523).
[16]No.35 (ibid.: 529).

power of jurisdiction already taken by the Pontifical Commission for the Revision of the Code of Canon Law. The *motu proprio "Causas Matrimoniales,"* of 1971, allows a layman to be one of the three judges in marriages cases.[17] The theoretical grounds for this decision was supplied by the Pontifical Commission for the Revision of the Code of Canon Law. This commission argued from the authority of classical canonists who held that the pope, exercising his plenary power, could make a layman competent to act as judge with power of jurisdiction. It also appealed to the implications of Lumen Gentium 33 which, as has been seen, concedes the possibility of laity being appointed to certain ecclesiastical offices.[18]

However it is not clear that the Congregation for the Doctrine of the Faith would find the argument based on the opinions of some canonists convincing, especially since they worked out of a juridical ecclesiology. It is even less likely that this congregation would merely appeal to the implications of *Lumen Gentium* 33. There are no indications in the preliminary discussions of this conciliar text that the council intended to include ministries linked to the exercise of the power of jurisdiction.[19] The failure of the congregation simply to accept the position of the Pontifical Commission is probably due to the latter's inability to reconcile it with Vatican II's teaching that the power of jurisdiction is bestowed or ontologically grounded in ordination.

The foregoing considerations may indicate that a pluralistic approach exists in modern Roman commissions on the question of the layman's capacity for the exercise of power of jurisdiction. This would not be surprising since the same kind of pluralism is reflected elsewhere on jurisdictional issues.[20] But all Roman commissions display the same hesitancy on the capacity of lay women for jurisdictional authority. The official commentary on the *Declaration* of the Congregation for

---

[17]*Acta Apostolicae Sedis* 63 (1971): 441-446, espec. no. V, 1-2.

[18]Pontificia Commissio Codici Iuris Canonici Recognoscendo, *Communicationes* 2 (1970): 188-189. The study commission *"De sacra hierarchia"* agrees that lay judges exercise "jurisdictional power of governing" (*Communicationes* 31 [1971]: 187).

[19]W. Aymann provides a negative assessment of the arguments of the commission ("Laien als kirchliche Richter?" 11-15).

[20]The different approaches of the Congregation for Sacraments and Worship and the Congregation for the Doctrine of the Faith to the authoritative role of episcopal conferences in the matter of approval of the new vernacular translations of liturgical texts are presented in B. Kleinheyer, "Formulae sacramentales sacrorum ordinum: zu Mitteilungen der Kongregation für Sakramente und Gottesdienst," *Zeitschrift für katholische Theologie* 100 (1978): 620-624.

the Doctrine of the Faith, commenting on the exercise of jursidiction by abbesses, seems to imply that women are incapable of jurisdictional authority. The study document of the Pastoral Commission of the Congregation for Evangelization of Peoples, *The Role of Women in the Church*, treats the question gingerly. It recognizes that women can be engaged in decision-making roles with the pastoral ministry. But it states that such activities are not to be considered "ministries in the strict sense."[21] The same document recommends that religious women placed in charge of parishes be awarded an official commissioning of a juridical type. But it offers no reflections on the juridical implications of such appointments.[22]

The cautious approach to the problem of lay women sharing in the exercise of the power of jurisdiction is probably based, in part, on Vatican II's presentation of the christological aspect of the hierarchical ministry. If one who exercises power of jurisdiction acts *in persona Christi*, the question is raised about the need for a symbolic correspondence between the male Christ and his representative. The *Declaration* of the Congregation for the Doctrine of the Faith, mentioned above, uses the argument of symbolic correspondence to exclude women from ordination to the presbyterate.[23]

This is no place for a detailed analysis of this argument. However it may be noted that a certain confusion exists in the *Declaration*, as well as other documents of the magisterium, over the levels of signification of the activity of the hierarchical ministry. What is ultimately signified is often presented as though it was immediately and directly signified. As a matter of fact the activity of the hierarchy denotes, directly signifies, aspects of the life of faith of the community. It connotes, indirectly signifies, for the eyes of faith the grounds of the life of faith: the active presence of Christ in the power of the Spirit. From this point of view it is not immediately evident why a symbolic correspondence must exist between those who exercise the pastoral office of the Church and Christ to the extent that only males may be ordained or be included in a limited exercise of the power of jurisdiction.[24]

The requirement of symbolic correspondence between the ordained

---

[21]*Crux Special* (October 4, 1976) 2, no. IV.

[22]Ibid., 3-4, no. V.

[23]Nos. 24-27 (Origins 6 [1977]: 522).

[24]24. E.J. Kilmartin, "Bishop and Presbyter as Representatives of the Church and Christ," in L. & A. Swidler, eds. *Women Priests: A Catholic Commentary on the Vatican Declaration* (New York: Paulist, 1977), pp. 295-302.

minister and the male Christ runs into more difficulty when one begins to transcend a christomonistic view of ordained ministry. If the role of the Holy Spirit is introduced into the theology of ordained ministry more space is given for a consideration of the possibility of ordaining women. Correspondingly, some theological grounds are also provided for the justification of awarding to lay persons, male and female, a measure of the exercise of the power of jurisdiction.

TRINITARIAN ECCLESIOLOGY

Vatican II uses the concept of "holy power" to distinguish the clergy from the laity. The power, bestowed or ontologically grounded in ordination, radically equips the ordained to represent Christ who, through them, exercises leadership in the community in the roles of teacher, shepherd and priest (LG 10; 21). The ordained, therfore, can be said to share in the threefold office of Christ or, more pregnantly, in the "office of the unique mediator, Christ" (LG 28).

This latter expression, however, is open to a misunderstanding which can be overcome by a consideration of Vatican II's teaching about the role of the Holy Spirit in the establishment of the ordained ministry and its activity. In the literal sense the ordained do not share in the once-for-all mediatorship role of Christ. This cannot be the meaning of the statement: "On the level of their ministry sharing in the office of the unique Mediator, Christ." The corrective is found in *Lumen Gentium*'s teaching that the ordained share in this office through the Holy Spirit who is bestowed in ordination. It is through the action of the Spirit that the ordained become sacramental representatives of Christ the head (LG 21). Hence it is more accurate to say that the ordained share in the power of the Spirit whose mission to the Church originates from the priestly act of Christ and is ordered to the priestly work of Christ. Thereby one guards against the danger of giving the impression that Christ's work was not sufficient to redeem the human race and, at the same time, avoids an overdrawn identification of the hierarchy with Christ.

The introduction of pneumatology into the theology of ordained ministry serves as a corrective to the more christomonistic concept of ordained ministry which emerged in scholastic theology. In its extreme form this theology describes the ordained minister as an *alter Christus* who functions along the lines of a platonic concept of symbol wherein the historical appearance, detached from a communitarian relation, serves as transparency for supra-mundane realities. This relationship to

Christ is then proved from biblical statements about Christ's promise to be with the apostles and their successors and the implications of the image of the Church as a body of which Christ is the head.

To a certain extent Vatican II contains elements of this theology. At least it is not sufficiently transcended. The attempt is made to integrate the role of the Holy Spirit into the christological dimension of Church. Sometimes, however, the Spirit is described merely as conserver of what Christ did for his Church: "The Holy Spirit preserves unfailingly that form of government which was set up by Christ the Lord in his Church" (LG 27). This is offset by other texts which attribute a more active role to the Spirit. But the result is not sufficient to justify the conclusion that Vatican II moves beyond a fundamentally christomonistic understanding of ordained ministry.

The influence of the older scholastic approach can be detected in the tendency to describe the Spirit as one who facilitates the sharing of the ordained in "Christ's Spirit," i.e., in the Risen Lord as distinguished from the Holy Spirit. This christological shortcircuit, the appropriation of the activity of the Holy Spirit under that of Christ the head, probably accounts for the lack of sensitivity to the "over against" dimension of ordained ministry. On the basis of the teaching of Vatican II, many commentators simply arrange the ordained ministry on the side of Christ over against the Church in the exercise of the threefold office. This undifferentiated way of speaking, however, needs to be qualified. The ordained ministry certainly does not stand over against the Spirit-filled Church! One can say that the ordained, in the exercise of their ministry, stand over against the world of humanity, both inside and outside the Church, in need of the gospel. But so can any Christian. This qualification is needed lest the impression be given that the ordained alone have the task of shouldering the real responsibility for carrying on the mission of the Church.

As is well known, Vatican II never made the attempt to show how the ministries of the laity and ordained derive from the mystery of the Spirit-filled Church and are ordered to one another without the one simply being under the control of the other. Without the integration of pneumatology into a theology of Church and its ministries a satisfactory explanation of the qualitatively equal responsiblity of all baptized for the mission of the Church cannot be given. Likewise the spiritual capacity of the laity, based on their charisms, for any exercise of pastoral leadership remains questonable. Thus within the christomonistic option, which P.J. Cordes identifies with the teaching of Vatican II, no possibility exists for lay participation in the decision-making process. In his generally excellent study of Vatican II's *Presbyterorum Ordinis* he concludes that, according to the teaching of the council, a sharp distinction must be made between a priests' senate and a diocesan pastoral council in the matter of juridical competence. Since the latter contains lay people, it cannot have a deliberative vote. This is based on the "differentiated spiritual capacity for consultation."[25]

A different picture is presented from the standpoint of a pneumatological ecclesiology which situates the Holy Spirit, as principle of unity and source of all spiritual activity, between Christ the head and the Church. If all baptized share in the same Spirit who unites the Church to Christ and bestows ministries on individuals which are consistent with their natural gifts, what prevents the baptized lay person from being called by the Church to some measure of the exercise of the power of jurisdiction?

Roman Catholic theology, insofar as it tends to favor lay sharing in the exercise of power of jurisdiction, generally does so on the basis of the implications of the pneumatological approach to ministries of the Church. It has no quarrel with the intention behind the teaching that the hierarchical priesthood acts *in persona Christi*. This expression has a sacramental meaning, when correctly understood. It stresses the fact that Christ himself, in relation to the human minister, is the first actor, as *Lumen Gentium* 21 affirms. But it recognizes that the introduction of the theology of the Holy Spirit blurs, to a certain extent, the clear cut differentiation between ministries open to the ordained and laity which is attainable from a christomonistic standpoint. Some aspects of this pneumatological approach to the problem can be treated under the headings: (1) Mission of the Holy Spirit to the Church; (2) Church, Image of the Trinity.

1. Mission of the Holy Spirit to the Church

The first chapter of *Lumen Gentium* outlines the traditional belief in the Spirit's personal mission to the Church and activity in all aspects of the life of the Church. It makes its own the Trinitarian vision of Irenaeus who speaks of the Church as "a people brought into unity from the unity of the Father, Son and Holy Spirit" (LG 4). As a consequence of the mission of the Spirit, the constitution concludes that full incorporation into the Church-society involves possesssion of

---

[25]*Sendung zum Dienst: Exegetische-historische und systematische Studien zum Konzilsdekret "Vom Dienst und Leben der Priester,"* Frankfurter theologische Studien 9 (Frankfurt a. M.: J. Knecht, 1972), p. 305.

the Spirit. The faithful are said to be "fully incorporated into the Church-society, who having the Spirit of Christ, accept the integral organization of it and the means of salvation instituted in it" (LG 14). The Church can, therefore, be described as fully constituted as sacrament of salvation through the mission of the Holy Spirit:

> Rising from the dead (Rom 6:9) he sent his life-giving Spirit upon the disciples and through him set up his Body which is the Church as the universal sacrament of salvation. . . . The promised and hoped for salvation . . . is carried forward in the sending of the Holy Spirit and through him continues in the Church (LG 48).

This last statement implies that the Spirit is not merely a conserver of what Christ did for his Church. The Spirit appears to function as a kind of co-institutor. As such the Spirit's role is not confined to the primordial Pentecostal event. This is brought out in another passage of *Lumen Gentium*:

> Just as the nature assumed by the Word is at his service as a living organism of salvation which is indissolubly united to him, likewise the social structures of the Church serve the Spirit of Christ who vivifies it, in building up the Body (Eph 4:5) (LG 8).

Working with divine freedom, the Spirit initiates changes which correspond to the new needs of the Church. But can it be expected that the Spirit will inspire the inclusion of laity into ministries with some measure of the exercise of power of jurisdiction? In the christomonistic perspective the option is closed. The question is not so easily settled from the viewpoint of pneumatological ecclesiology.

This latter ecclesiology is particularly sensitive to the ecclesial dimension of ordained ministry. It reacts against a concept of hierarchical ministry which tends to overdraw its position vis-à-vis the rest of the community. Nevertheless it clearly distinguishes the ordained from the laity. The latter are not able to assume a pastoral authority which embraces the full scope of the permanent ministry of leadership in the Church. On the other hand it recalls that through ordination the candidate is incorporated into a ministry of the Church: placed in a permanent relationship to the Church as leader, and given the support of the spirit to organize and bring to fruition the share which other members have in the ministry of the Church.

The ordained is expected to mediate the active presence of Christ in the Spirit. But this takes place through fidelity to the apostolic faith. As successor of the apostles in the ministry of the Church, the ordained has the mission of handing on the apostolic faith which the Church as a whole possesses. To the extent that this task is fulfilled the ordained stands with the Spirit-filled apostolic Church over against the world, i.e., humanity both inside and outside the Church, in need of the gospel. The ordained thus represents both the apostolic Church and Christ who works through the Spirit in this ministry.

On the other hand since the Church as a whole succeeds the apostles, a baptized believer is also capable of standing with the Church over against all those in need of the gospel, who may include the ordained. The laity who are faithful to the inspirations of the Spirit have spiritual authority. They represent both the Church and Christ who works through the Spirit in their ministry. Vatican II affirmed this by recalling that the baptized have the vocation to exercise personal responsibility in the mission of the Church in accord with their gifts. The responsibility of the laity has its limitations. They may not take up the full scope of the ministry of the ordained. But it is not immediately apparent why the laity should be disqualified, in principle, from any share in the exercise of the power of jurisdiction.

The exclusion of the laity from the exercise of this power is consistent with a monarchical model of Church-society derived from the secular sphere. However the laity are not absolutely excluded in this model. For the will of the highest authority can prevail as long as the source of jursidiction is distinguished from that of the power of order. On the basis of this concept of Church-society and source of power of jurisdiction, some twelfth century decretists concluded that the clergy could award a share in the right of election of bishop to lay persons.[26] The theological grounds for this conclusion are not available to modern Catholic theology which identifies ordination as the source of power of jurisdiction.

On the other hand within the more Spirit orientated ecclesiology of the early church, the laity's active cooperation in the decision-making process within the Church is not adequately explained in terms of the modern understanding of consultation as distinguished from deliberative vote, with its juridical overtones. At that time the laity's participation in ecclesiastical processes, including election of officials and councils, was not understood to be comparable to the role of ordinary

---

[26]H. Müller, *Der Anteil der Laien an der Bischofswahl: Ein Beitrag zur Geschichte der Kanonistik von Gratian bis Gregor IX*, Kanonistische Studien und Texte 29 (Amsterdam: B.R. Gruner, 1977), pp. 209-210.

citizens in secular political activities.[27] The Christian laity's greater involvement was due to the unique constitutional situation of the people and office in the Church. The designation *laikos* contained the idea that the baptized Christian is a member of the people called forth by God in the Spirit with a dignity that demands inclusion in the decisive matters of Christian public life. This precludes the type of opposition between laity and clergy in matters of decision-making which is envisioned in the later radically secularized understanding of ecclesiastical jurisdiction.

In the past the Catholic Church has awarded limited exercise of the power of jurisdiction to the laity, albeit on faulty theological grounds.[28] In the post-conciliar period various examples of the tendency in this direction can be found. While the theological basis has not been completely worked out, it is partially grounded on Vatican II's teaching about the responsiblity of the baptized for the mission of the Church.

From this viewpoint two kinds of jurisdiction found in the practice of the Church could be distinguished on a sacramental basis. One is grounded on ordination, the other on baptism. U. Mosiek takes this position and concludes that Mörsdorf's thesis is too narrowly conceived. He argues from past and present practice, and the implications of the theology of baptism, that the laity are capable, through a canonical mission, of undertaking tasks of the hierarchical apostolate with true jurisdictional authority.[29]

By itself the argument from past practice is always fraught with difficulties. A practice which has a long history can be in accord with the Christian economy of salvation even though it originates from a faulty theological outlook. On the other hand it can be contrary to this economy. The lesson of history is clear in this regard. The Congregation for the Doctrine of the Faith, in its commentary on the *Declaration* mentioned above, surely merits assent when it judges that the theological justification for granting abbesses power of jurisdiction was defective. But it should not receive the same support insofar as it seems to imply, perhaps unwittingly, that there are no possible grounds which could justify the practice. Correspondingly, the rediscovery that the

---

[27]J. Speigl, "Zum Problem der Teilnahme von Laien an den Konzilien in kirchlichen Altertum," *Annuarium Historiae Conciliorum* 10 (1978): 243.

[28]U. Mosiek surveys the past and present practice of awarding forms of jurisdictional authority to laity ("Der Laien als Jurisdiktionsträger?" *Österreichisches Archiv für Kirchenrecht* 25 [1974]: 3-15).

[29]Ibid.: 14-15.

power of jurisdiction of the ordained is grounded on ordination does not necessarily entail the conclusion that a limited share in the exercise of this power could not be awarded to the laity. The rediscovery of the source of the power of jurisdiction of the ordained excludes the notion that a canonical mission confers this power. Likewise a canonical mission given to the laity to exercise this power cannot be the source of it. The source must be baptism. Although this is a new idea, it can find support in the patristic concept of *laikos*.

2. The Church, Image of the Trinity

According to the Christian economy of salvation, the Father is the primordial source of the saving missions of the Son and the Holy Spirit. Through this twofold mission humankind is gathered into the unity of the Father through the Son in the Spirit. Therefore the unity of the divine Trinity brings into being the unity of the People of God. But how is this unity concretely effected?

The Father enters into the world in a decisive way through the Son in the Incarnation. It is the Son, come in the flesh, who communicates the revelation of the Father's love and draws those who hear into union with the Father. But he does this in the power of the Spirit who works through his ministry (Luke 4:14). In the time of the Church the same Spirit bestows the gift of faith and works through the believing disciples, in accord with their gifts, to gather humankind into the unity of the Father through the Son. Through the gift of faith and their particular charisms the members of the Church are enabled to mediate, to one another and those called to the Church, the Holy Spirit who acts through their faithful witness to the gospel.

In recent times this insight has led to the rediscovery of the old patristic understanding of the Church as a people called to live a style of life like that of the Trinity. In the Trinity unity and multiplicity are bound together in the dynamic union of divine life. Likewise the members of the Church, in the power of the Spirit, are enabled to live in communion with Christ and with one another. This communion, or dynamic personal union. is realized through the action of the Spirit who fashions the life of the Church after that of the Trinity by the gifts he bestows on particular churches and individuals. Because this is the nature of the Church, it is being built up to the extent that it displays the characteristics of unity and multiplicity in all dimensions of its life, including its social structures. Thereby it also fulfills its essential mission. In the measure that the Church strives to be a more perfect image of the life of the Trinity, it reveals the mystery of the Trinity, the source of its life, to the world.

In this purview an organic, synodal model should be realized in the relationships between the local episcopal churches within the one universal Church: one in which the spiritual authority and rights and duties of each church with respect to the others are recognized in theory and practice.

Lumen Gentium 26 explicitly affirms the ecclesial reality of the local church: "The Church of Christ is really present in all legitimately organized local groups of the faithful." The source of this gathering in different geographical localities is said to be the Spirit: "For these are, in fact, in their own localities, the new people called by God in the power of the Holy Spirit" (ibid.). How the Spirit works to bring into being and maintain these churches is explained in *Lumen Gentium* 12: "Allotting his gifts according as he wills (1 Cor 12:11), he also distributes special graces among the faithful of every rank. By these gifts he makes them fit and ready to undertake various tasks and offices for the renewal and building of the Church." At the same time the constitution recognizes that each church has special charisms which can contribute to the building up of the whole communion of churches: "In virtue of this catholicity each part contributes its own gifts to other parts and to the whole Church, so that the whole and each of its parts are strengthened by the common sharing of all things and by the common effort to attain to fullness of unity" (LG 13). To the extent that each church recognizes itself as an acting subject in the economy of salvation, is faithful to the inspirations of the Spirit, accepts its responsiblity for the mission of the Church and its dependence on other churches, all are being built up "together for a habitation of God in the Spirit" (Eph 2:22).

One important application of the Trinitarian ecclesiology to the relationship between local churches is worth noting. This theology supports the notion that regional churches, made up of local episcopal churches, are capable of a collegial act. The bishops of these churches can come to a decision in which the wills of the co-members of the episcopal college are integrated into the collegial will. A collegial act of this kind, made in the power of the Spirit, is fully separated from the wills of the individual members and constitutes an instance of mediation between the bishop of Rome and diocesan bishops. Our main concern, however, is with the application of Trinitarian ecclesiology to the laity's role in the Church. To what extent does it support lay participation in power of jurisdiction?

The author of the Epistle to the Ephesians describes the Church as built "upon the foundation of the apostles and prophets, Jesus Christ himself being the chief cornerstone" (2:20). Corresponding to this perspective the Church has traditionally recognized the authority of its official ministers who receive a special bestowal of the Spirit through ordination in apostolic succession. On the other hand it has also recognized that laity exercise a ministry with an authority based on their personal life of faith and special gifts of the spirit. The conclusion can, therefore, be drawn that a dynamic interplay should exist between these ministries; that the adjective *solus* should not be applied to anyone in the Church. Everyone lives from others and for others. Even though Christ himself does not receive divine life through the Spirit acting in the ministries of the Church, he also depends on these ministries for the growth of his Body, the Church.

No member of Christ's Body can be said to exist totally "for others." What holds among the members of the Church are such relations as pope and college of bishops, episcopal conferences and local bishops, bishops and presbyters, ordained ministers and laity—where the *and* indicates a relationship of mutual dependence. All the members of the Church have a personal responsibility for the mission of the Church.

The relationship between the hierarchy and the laity is such that the ordained ministers have the task not only of ordering but of fostering the development of the different charisms of the laity. Through this pastoral ministry the bishop, as chief instrument of the construction of the living temple of God, serves the local church in the best way. This responsiblity requires of him a variety of forms of recognition of the ministries of individuals which does not, a priori, seem to exclude the awarding to a lay person some measure of the exercise of the power of jurisdiction.

The prudent judgement of the local bishop should be a sufficient basis for the awarding of the exercise of this power to the gifted lay person for his or her pastoral ministry. The *Schema Codicis Iuris Canonici* reserves such appointments to the "supreme authority of the Church." While this authority is exercised by "both the Roman Pontiff and the College of Bishops" (Schema, 277), in practice the pope would make such decisions or delegate others to do so. In any case, whether the new Code retains this restriction in its final form or grants local bishops the right to freedom of action, the significance of the canonical mission remains the same. It does not involve the bestowal of the spiritual gifts on which the spiritual authority of the lay minister rests. As in the case of the canonical mission given to the ordained, it provides the juridical basis for the free exercise of these gifts in the public forum and so contributes to the acceptance of this ministry by the community.

CONCLUSION

An analogy exists between the official Catholic theological approach to the differentiation of the pastoral ministry of bishop and presbyter and that of the ordained and laity. Vatican II was not able to offer any precise demarcation between the powers received in ordination by bishop and presbyter. The old problem of what a bishop can do that a presbyter is absolutely incapable of doing was left unanswered. The sacramental relationship between the two offices could not be clarified because of the inability to overcome two divergent views of the origin of these grades of the sacrament of order. One opinion held that the two offices were instituted by Christ; another maintained that the distinction has an ecclesiastical source, based on jurisdictional considerations.[30]

Similarly, lay capacity for a limited share in the exercise of the power of jurisdiction could neither be affirmed nor denied. The council was unable to offer a satisfactory formulation of the ecclesiological basis of the relationship between the ministry of the baptized and the ordained. The predominantly christomonistic orientation in its theology of the hierarchical or ministerial priesthood prevented the council from pursuing this question. As a result it did not show how the ministry of the laity and ordained grow out of the mystery of the priestly People of God and are ordered to one another, without the one being simply under the control of the other.

The tentative, marginal attempts of Vatican II to transcend christomonism were only partially successful. But they offer a challenge to Catholic theology to rethink its understanding of the ministry of the Church. It goes without saying that the practical implications of Trinitarian ecclesiology have not been fully explored and implemented at

---

[30]This question is discussed fully in H. Müller, *Zum Verhältnis zwischen Episcopat und Presbyterat in zweiten vaticanischen Konzil: Eine rechtstheologische Untersuchung,* Weiner Beiträge zur Theologie 35 (Vienna: Herder, 1971).

all levels of the life of the Church.[31] Still the direction which Catholic theology must take in its reflection on the differentiation of ministries of the ordained and laity has been established by the Spirit orientated communion ecclesiology which was placed alongside the juridical and christomonistic ecclesiology in *Lumen Gentium*. In theory and practice the Catholic Church can settle for no less than the unfolding of the understanding of the Church which is implied in the succinct statement of *Unitatis Reintegratio* 2: "The supreme model and principle of this mystery [= the unity of the Church] is the unity, in the Trinity of Persons, of the Father and the Son and the Holy Spirit."

---

[31]This theme was the subject of an international colloquium held under the direction of G. Alberigo at Bologna, April 8-12, 1980. For reports of the proceedings, cf. "Ekklesiologie: trinitarisch, nicht nur christologisch," *Herder Korrespondenz* 34 (1980): 220-222; J. Grootaens, "Dynamisme et prospective de l'ecclesiologie de Vatican II," *Irenikon* 53 (1980): 196-208; B.C. Butler & J. Tillard, "The Pope and the Bishops," *The Tablet* (October 11, 1980): 987-989.

DETERMINING THE "VALIDITY" OF ORDERS
AND THE MEANING OF "VALIDITY"

HARRY MCSORLEY
St. Michael's College
University of Toronto

There are several ways to approach this complex topic. One might examine the current Code or the proposed new Code and *Lex Ecclesiae Fundamentalis* to see what they say about the conditions for validity on the part of the minister and the recipient of the sacrament of orders. Interesting and important as this approach may be, it should be undertaken by one more skilled in canonistics than the present writer.

Another approach would be an investigation of the history of the question to see how and in what sense "validity" of orders or something comparable to it has been determined in the past. Clearly, unless one were to confine oneself to a limited period, such an undertaking would require a monograph of colossal proportions that would have to take into account not only the vast range of relevant source materials, but also the many efforts of scholars to interpret those materials with more or less historical and philological sensitivity.

Other angles of attack might prove more fruitful than the eclectic one I have followed. In view of the magnitude of the topic and the several possible avenues to it, modesty of ambition is required of me and liberty, I trust, is allowed me to undertake a less than thorough investigation. I shall begin by rehearsing the general state of the question in Catholic theology and canon law on the eve of the Second Vatican Council. After noting some important new turns taken by Vatican II, I shall in part III review some recent ecumenical statements, as well as work by individual scholars which seem to point to a newer and more satisfactory state of the question concerning what the Church does—and what it means—when it determines the "validity" of orders.

I. CRITERIA FOR VALIDITY OF ORDERS ON THE EVE OF VATICAN II

At the beginning of his impressive study of Leo XIII's declaration of the invalidity of Anglican orders, John Jay Hughes offers a succinct statement of what he calls "the traditional[1] standards of validity. . . . still generally accepted in Roman Catholic theology" for the validity of ordination:

> Before the Church extends her recognition to an ordination, she looks for the following qualities in the minister of ordination: The intention of doing what the Church does, the use of a sufficient sacramental form of ordination accompanied by the laying on of hands as the visible sign or matter, and the possession of the requisite "character." General standards of what is a sufficient form of ordination have never been established, and the number of forms accepted as valid by the Church is very large. Possession of the requisite "character" means that the minister of holy orders must be in the apostolic succession: he must have inherited his ministerial commission from a bishop able (in theory) to trace his descent through other bishops back to the apostles. In cases where one or more of these requirements is not fulfilled the Church is unable to recognize the orders of the ministers concerned as technically valid.[2]

Hughes brackets the requirements for validity which involve the subject or recipient of the sacrament because, as he correctly notes, "these are not in dispute in the controversy over Anglican orders. . . ."[3]

---

[1]As will become clear in the course of this essay, this "tradition" is hardly universal and not nearly as long-standing as other traditions of the Church.

[2]J. J. Hughes, *Stewards of the Lord: A Reappraisal of Anglican Orders* (London: Sheed and Ward, 1970), pp. 2-3.

[3]Ibid., p. 4, n. 6. Hughes could not have foreseen the controversy that has arisen over precisely one of the requirements for validity on the part of rhe recipient—masculinity! Important and lively as the debate over ordination of women is, it suffices to note here that the official Roman Catholic policy, restated if not reinforced by the Congregation for the Doctrine of the Faith in January, 1977, sees masculinity as a requirement for valid ordination. As long as this policy prevails it is difficult to see how the Catholic Church could recognize as valid the ordained ministries of other churches if these include women. Pope Paul VI, writing to the Archbishop of Canterbury November 30, 1975 and March 23, 1976, said, however, that although ordination of women by Anglicans presents a "grave, new obstacle" to restoration of unity, "obstacles do not destroy mutual commitment to a search for reconciliation." *Catholic Mind* 75 (1977): 62-63. The same attitude was expressed already by the Faith and Order Commission of the World Council of Churches; see *One Baptism, One Eucharist and a Mutually Recognized Ministry: Three Agreed Statements*, Faith and Order Paper No. 73 (Geneva: World Council of Churches, 1974), p. 49, para. 69. An unpublished "provisional text" on ministry prepared in June, 1980 comments that, while "an increasing number of churches have decided to

The above criteria are not without their problems. One that Hughes points to "is that the existing concept of apostolic succession leads to recognition of the validity of orders possessed by eccentric *episcopi vagantes,*" while regarding the Archbishop of Canterbury as a layman.[4]

The anomalies arising from the pre-Vatican II tradition's criteria for validity, says Hughes (and the demands of ecumenism, a renewed sacramental theology and the ecclesiology of Vatican II, I would add) have occasioned some recent efforts by Catholic theologians "to reappraise the whole notion of sacramental validity."[5] However, in his able critique of the bull, *Apostolicae Curae* of 1896, which declared Anglican ordinations "absolutely null and utterly void" because of alleged defects of form and intention, Hughes deliberately chooses to use the pre-Vatican II criteria for determining validity of orders. He thus seeks to establish an *a fortiori* argument: if a conservative critique of the bull is sound, how much more so will be one based on the newer approaches to validity.[6]

As far as determining the validity of ordination in churches deriving from the continental Reformation is concerned:

> A simplified expression of the traditional Roman Catholic outlook is that those who preside at the eucharist do so in virtue of being ordained by a bishop who stands in succession to the apostles. . . . Without such ordination a man can make no claim to a valid eucharistic Ministry. Now, at the time of the Reformation in Germany, the bishops did not ordain Ministers that professed to follow Martin Luther; and so it came about that priests who had adopted Lutheran beliefs ordained other men to preside at the eucharist, thus perpetuating a presbyteral succession. . . . Thus the Lutheran eucharistic Ministry would

---

ordain women, the majority hold that the unbroken tradition of the Church in this regard should not be changed today" (p. 9, para. 17). Para. 51 of the same document (p. 22) maintains a hopeful attitude but does not discount the "obstacles" that ordination of women "could raise."—Concerning the other crucial requirement for validity on the part of the minister and the recipient, that of intention, see J. M. Tillard, "Sacramental Questions: The Intentions of Minister and Recipient," *Concilium* 31 (1968): 117-133.

[4]Hughes, p. 2, n. 3.

[5]Ibid., p. 3, n. 4. Some of these will be considered in part III below.

[6]Ibid. H. M. Legrand, "Bulletin d'Ecclésiologie: Le Ministère ordonée dans le dialogue oecuménique," *Revue des Sciences Philosophiques et Théologiques* 60 (1976): 660 rightly notes, however, that the criteria of the pre-Vatican II period support the validity of the orders of the *episcopus vagans,* while the newer criteria do not.

seem to be deficient in what Catholics have hitherto regarded as essential elements.[7]

The question of determining the validity of orders arises, under the pre-Vatican II criteria, not only when the Roman Catholic Church asesses the ministries of other churches. It is also a question put to Roman Catholic ordinations—and to all of them. For, as Karl Rahner asks:

> How does any priest know he has been validly ordained? If he allows this validity to depend totally and solely on an unbroken chain of valid ordinations (understanding validity in its usual sense), starting with the ordination of the bishop ordaining him all the way back to the apostles, and if he thinks about the conditions for validity as they are usually understood (among them the *intentio interna*; in the Middle Ages, perhaps, a quite specific *traditio instrumentorum* and very many other conditions that once belonged or still belong to validity) then such a priest would have to say that he has at most a moral probability that his orders are valid and we would have to trust that in the good providence of God there were not too many invalid ordinations, even though this endless chain of ordinations could very easily be broken without anyone noticing. Is such a concept of validity really meaningful? Does it correspond to the nature of the reality involved? Is it worthy of God? I think not.[8]

A further point should be mentioned in describing the pre-Vatican II tradition of the criteria for determining valid orders: a determination that certain orders were invalid was regularly accompanied by the conclusion—rather, the assumption—that nothing happened *sacramentally* when an invalidly ordained person "attempted" to offer the Eucharist. A "spiritual communion" in which the *res sacramenti* (grace) is imparted could be made by those who received such a non-sacrament in good faith. While conceding that there is a "spiritual reception of the sacrament itself" in such cases, such a modern sacramental theologian as Schillebeeckx is on record as saying that the

---

[7]*Lutherans and Catholics in Dialogue IV: Eucharist and Ministry* (Washington: U.S.C.C., 1970) p. 23, n. 36. Henceforth cited as *LC*.

[8]K. Rahner, *Vorfragen zu einem ökumenischen Amtsverständnis*, Quaestiones Disputatae, 65 (Freiburg: Herder, 1974), p. 41. A summary of his argument can be found in "Open Questions in Dogma Considered by the Institutional Church as Definitively Answered," *Journal of Ecumenical Studies* [*JES*] 15 (1978): 217-218.

Protestant communion service "is not even partly a valid sacrament."[9] Such reasoning, widespread in Catholic theology since the Reformation, was completely abandoned by the Second Vatican Council, as we shall see in the next part.

Related to the preceding point, finally, is this one: what does it *mean* to say that certain orders are "invalid"? This was among the least-discussed questions of canon law or sacramental theology on the eve of Vatican II. It is my hope that part III of this essay will offer some help toward a satisfactory answer to that question.

II. Some Vatican II Teachings Related to the Question of the Validity of Orders

A. *The Broader Understanding of "Church"*

Lumen gentium's rejection of the view that Protestants, Anglicans and other Christians are "outside the Church" (cf. nos. 8 and 15) provided the basis not only for the dramatic new teaching on ecumenism that was spelled out in *Unitatis Redintegratio*. It is also laden with implications for determining the validity of orders. The Cyprianic tradition about the nullity of ordinations performed "outside the Church" that co-existed through the twelfth century with the Augustinian view which held them to be "valid" but ineffective caused Peter Lombard to lament: "Hanc quaestionem perplexam ac pene insolubilem faciunt doctorum verba, qui plurimum dissentire videntur."[10] The Cyprianic view causes far less perplexity for Roman Catholic theology now that Protestants, Anglicans and other Christians are no longer seen as outside the Church! For if it is by faith and baptism that a person is incorporated into Christ and into a real, albeit imperfect communion with the Roman Catholic Church (UR 3), then the Cyprianic strictures against ordinations by "heretics" or "schismatics" simply do not apply to those who believe in Christ and are baptized.

More positively, the teaching of UR 3 that Protestants and Anglicans belong by faith and baptism to the one Church of Christ implies that they have or are capable of having a Christian Eucharist through a

---

[9]E. Schillebeeckx, *Christ, the Sacrament of Encounter With God* (New York: Sheed and Ward, 1963), p. 194.

[10]*Sententiae* IV, d. 25, par. 3: PL 192, 907.

[11]"Towards an Ecumenical Understanding of the Sacraments," *JES* 3 (1966): 73.

Christian ministry. Many theologians have seen the force of J. van Beeck's argument: "Where the Church is, there is sacrament."[11] And, of course, where there is sacrament, there must be a "valid" minister of it. K. McDonnell has called this the "ecclesiological way" of validating ministry, as distinct from the "ritual way."[12]

J. Hamer's commentary on selected passages of UR rightly cautions against reading into the texts something the council did not intend.[13] Anticipating this caution, McDonnell speaks for many contemporary Catholic theologians when he writes: "Whether the fathers of the council intended this theological deduction or not . . . it is not theologically possible to postulate a true manifestation of the Church with a false or non-ministry."[14] Hamer makes it clear that Vatican II deliberately called the Protestant churches "ecclesial communities", not "churches." He adds, however, that this does not "shut the door" to the case for ecclesiological validation we are discussing. In fact, he explicitly invited such theologizing as long as one does not invoke "the authority of the Decree." Moreover, he concludes, "the theological language of Vatican II does not allow us to conclude to the validity of the ministries of the Protestant communities."[15]

One has to agree with K. Lehmann, however, that the distinction between "churches" and "ecclesial communities" is really not "effectively significant"

> because in both cases an analogous, true ecclesial reality is described. . . . It is difficult to see how one can attribute to the non-Catholic churches—including the churches of the Reformation—a genuinely ecclesial status if one does not to a certain degree and analogously come to recognize their ministries. . . . One cannot, in my opinion, carry through in principle the recognition of the salvific action of these churches if one does not at the same time in some form attribute to the ministries which carry out this salvific service a kind of positive value and thus also a certain "validity".[16]

---

[12]"Ways of Validating Ministry," *JES* 7 (1970): 254-263.
[13]"Vatican II and Protestant Ministries," *Catholic Mind* 70 (1972): 27-32.
[14]McDonnell, p. 256.
[15]Hamer, pp. 30-31.
[16]"Zur Frage der ökumenischen Anerkennung der kirchlichen Ämter: Versuch zur Ortsbestimmung des gegenwärtigen Problemstandes," in A. Völker, K. Lehmann, H. Dombois, *Ordination Heute*, Kirche zwischen Planen und Hoffen 5 (Kassel: J. Stauda, 1972), pp. 54-77, esp. p. 73.

B. *A "Defect" of Orders does not mean there is no Eucharist*

Article 22 of UR states:

> Although the ecclesial communities separated from us lack the fullness of unity with us which flows from baptism, and although we believe they have not preserved the genuine and integral substance of the eucharistic mystery, especially because of a defect of orders, nevertheless when they commemorate the Lord's Supper, they profess that it signifies life in communion with Christ and await his coming in glory.

Two things can be noted. (1) The Decree does not call Protestant and Anglican orders "invalid," "null," or "void." It says, rather, that there is a "defect of orders" or, as the *Relatio* puts it, an "essential deficiency"—but not an "absentia" or "carentia" of orders. (2) The Decree does not say that because of this defect or deficiency these communities *do not have* the Eucharist or that their Eucharists are invalid, as 152 bishops wanted the text to say. Replying to this objection, and to another raised by thirteen bishops who claimed that, in the absence of orders there is neither the full nor a partial reality of the Eucharist, but only a non-efficacious sign, the Secretariat for Christian Unity stated: "We believe they have not preserved the full reality of the eucharistic mystery, especially because of a defect of the sacrament of orders. . . ." Elsewhere I have suggested that the fullness of the eucharistic mystery that is lacking is *not* that of the presence of the body and blood of Christ, as the 152-plus bishops mentioned above would have the text say, but of something else that is nonetheless integral to the eucharistic mystery, namely the full expression of church unity by a minister who stands in an ordered relationship to the bishop, whose episcopacy, as van Beeck has said, is "the canon and touchstone of all . . . church order."[17]

C. *The Possibility of Ordination of Presbyters by Presbyters is Left Open*

As is well-known, the Vatican II documents combine old insights with new. As at Trent, so also at Vatican II, the old *opinio Hieronymi* was respected. This position sees the distinction between presbyter and

---

[17]H. McSorley, "Protestant Eucharistic Reality and Lack of Orders," *The Ecumenist* 5 (1967): 68-75, esp. pp. 70-75. The phrase from van Beeck is in *JES* 3 (1966): 96.

bishops as one of church law rather than as a disposition of the Lord.[18] A consequence of this opinion is that there are certain circumstances and conditions under which presbyters may validly ordain others to the presbyterate.[19]

Drawing attention to this possibility does not have as its function the setting up of another line of succession parallel to that of the succession of bishops. It serves rather to help demonstrate that all is not as fixed and as clear as the pre-Vatican II tradition's criteria for validity might suggest. In fact, it did serve this function rather well in the official dialogue on ministry between Lutherans and Roman Catholics in the United States. In view of the already noted commitment of K. Lehmann to "ecclesiological validation" we are not surprised when he says the concept of presbyteral succession is "hardly necessary" for an ecumenical agreement. But he does see it as a "genuine point of approach" to the ecumenical problem of recognizing other ministries, because it helps shatter the easy certitude of those who, using the pre-Vatican II criteria, have unhesitatingly called Protestant ministries invalid because they have not been "rite ordinatus" in the usual pre-Vatican II Catholic sense.[20]

D. *Recognition of the "True Sacrament" of Orders in Orthodox Churches*

A frequently expressed wish of bishops at Vatican II was that the council's text be pastoral rather than juridical in language and tone. We have already seen how the council abandoned the category of "invalidity" in speaking about Protestant and Anglican orders. In fact, it is only rarely, and often only in an improper sense that the council uses the categories "valid" and "invalid." In keeping with this, the council declares concerning the "Eastern Churches" (Orthodox): "Although these Churches are separated from us, they possess *true sacraments*, above all—by apostolic succession—the priesthood and the Eucharist, whereby they are still joined to us in a very close relationship."[21]

---

[18]See H. McSorley, "Recognition of a Presbyteral Succession?" *Concilium* 4 (1972): 23-32 and G. Fahrnberger, "Episkopat und Presbyterat in den Diskussionen des Konzils von Trient," *Catholica* 30 (1976): 119-152.

[19]K. Rahner, in H. Vorgrimler, ed., *Commentary on the Documents of Vatican II*, I (New York: Herder and Herder, 1966), pp. 194-195.

[20]"Zur Frage," p. 67.

[21]UR 15, my emphasis. See P. Timko, "Vatican II and the Validity of Orthodox Orders," *Diakonia* 10 (1975): 168-172.

In contrast to the three previous points, this text does not represent a new departure with its recognition of "true priesthood" among the Orthodox. It expresses, rather, the prevailing and longstanding Roman Catholic attitude toward Orthodox orders. At the same time, it suggests a sometimes forgotten strength of the Augustinian view of determining the "validity" of orders. In contrast to the Cyprianic view upheld by Cardinal Humbert, the man who excommunicated Patriarch Michael Cerularius of Constantinople in 1054, it was the theory originating with St. Augustine that prevented Western canonists and theologians from declaring invalid the orders of the entire East after 1054.[22]

III. POST-VATICAN II DEVELOPMENTS AND THE NEWER STATE OF THE QUESTION FOR DETERMINING THE "VALIDITY" OF ORDERS

A. The Question of Validity of Orders in Selected Ecumenical Dialogues

It is no accident that much of the recent re-thinking of the question of determining the validity of orders has been done in the context of ecumenical dialogues. Indeed, this question has become an increasingly prominent item on the agendas of bi- and multi-lateral dialogues ever since the Third Assembly of the World Council of Churches declared at New Delhi in 1961 that "biblical, theological and historical studies must be continued" in order to arrive at "a ministry accepted by all," which is one of the integral elements of "the unity which the Lord wills for his Church on earth here and now."[23]

A study of the development of thought about "validity" of orders, or "recognition of ministries" in the various plans of union as well as in the national and international bi- and multi-lateral dialogues would be quite voluminous. For this reason I feel justified in making a selection, with no claim that it is the best selection for this purpose.

[22]P. Grelot, "Réflexions Générales Autour du Thème du Symposium: Le Ministre de l'Eucharistie," in *Ministères et Célébration de l'Eucharistie*, Studia Anselmiana 61 (Rome: Ed. Anselmiana, 1973), pp. 38-45. This symposium volume is henceforth cited as *Ministères*. The section of Grelot's long essay just mentioned contains a critique of C. Vogel, "Laica communione contentus: Le retour du presbytre au rang des Laïcs," *Revue des Sciences Religieuses* 47 (1973): 66-122.

[23]"Report on the Section on Unity," para. 1, 2, 17 in L. Vischer, ed., *A Documentary History of the Faith and Order Movement* (St. Louis: Bethany, 1963), pp. 144-145, 149-150. For earlier Faith and Order statements dealing with the question of validity of ministry see ibid., pp. 37-38 (Lausanne, 1927) and pp. 55-56 (Edinburgh, 1937).

1. *Faith and Order*

a. Already at the Faith and Order Conference in Edinburgh in 1937 the need was felt to clarify the confusing way different churches used the terms "validity" and "invalidity" with reference to the sacraments and ordinations of other churches.[24]

b. Great as were the achievements of the Fourth World Conference on Faith and Order at Montreal in 1963 on such questions as Scripture and Tradition and on the nature of sacraments, especially with regard to the sacrificial dimension of the Eucharist, insufficient background preparation prevented any real headway being made on the question of the ordained ministry.[25]

c. At the Bristol meeting of the Faith and Order Commission in 1967 a report on the Holy Eucharist was accepted containing an appendix on intercommunion in which it was stated that "if the problems of unity and intercommunion are to be clarified, there is need for" a study "to consider the importance of mutual canonical (formal) recognition for sacramental intercommunion and to decide whether such recognition be sufficient in and by itself to secure the theological reality of unity and consequent possibility of sacramental sharing."[26]

In calling for an inquiry on the nature and necessity of the ordained ministry in general and episcopacy in particular, Bristol requested the "Catholic" churches to ask themselves "whether the ministries of non-episcopal churches—quite apart from their possession of apostolic succession or their lack of it—do not in fact contain elements of value (such as charismatic or extraordinary ministries) and if so, of what value such elements may be."[27]

"Protestant" churches, for their part, were requested to reconsider "the value of the commonly accepted ministry of the Early Church and of Pre-Reformation times."[28] All churches, moreover, should ask themselves, among other things, whether "the principle of 'economy'" can be applied to ministries otherwise rejected.[29]

---

[24]Vischer, pp. 55-56.

[25]P. C. Rodger and L. Vischer, eds., *The Fourth World Conference on Faith and Order: Montreal, 1963* (New York: Association Press, 1964); cf. pp. 25-28 and pp. 61-69.

[26]*New Directions in Faith and Order: Bristol, 1967*, Faith and Order Paper No. 50 (Geneva: WCC, 1968), p. 67.

[27]Ibid.

[28]Ibid., p. 68.

[29]Ibid.

Bristol also approved an outline for a study on ordination which contained the following questions relevant to our inquiry:

1) Can orders continue "valid" when schism or heresy occurs? Why or why not?

2) Does the power to ordain continue to be a bishop's apart from the church (i.e. when he is in schism, or an *episcopus vagans*)? If so, why? If not, why not?[30]

Noteworthy is the fact that Bristol uses two different vocabularies related to our question. The appendix on intercommunion speaks of "mutual canonical (formal) recognition" of ministries and raises the question whether recognition in and of itself suffices "to secure the reality of unity" and thus open the way for eucharistic sharing. The outline for further study of the ministry, on the other hand, uses the "traditional" terms, "valid" and "power to ordain" and poses the classical problems of the schismatic, heretical, or *vagans* bishop—without alluding to the unclarity surrounding the term "valid" that Edinburgh had noted thirty years previously. It can be said here, by way of anticipation, that the long and complex development of the Faith and Order study on ministry, after taking note of some of the problems connected with the "traditional" terms, has effectively moved away from those categories (though not entirely) and toward the category of "recognition"—without, however, following up the question posed by Bristol: does recognition *of itself* suffice to secure unity?

d. In chapter VII, "Mutual Acceptance of Ministry," of the Study Report on "The Ordained Ministry" presented to the Louvain meeting of the Faith and Order Commission in 1971, we read that "the Second Vatican Council has made new thinking on the ministry both possible and necessary in the Roman Catholic Church."[31] One major change in Roman Catholic thought, and in the thought of theologians of other churches, the Report points out, is the new tendency to interpret episcopal succession as the effective sign of, but not as coextensive with the apostolic succession of the whole Church. A number of points are offered to support this interpretation. These include: (1) the lack of New Testament.information on how church leaders were appointed and also concerning the question: who presided at the Eucharist? (2) the plural forms of organization in the New Testament communi-

30Ibid., p. 146.

31*Faith and Order: Louvain, 1971*, Faith and Order Paper No. 59 (Geneva: WCC, 1971), p. 97.

ties; (3) lack of evidence that the Ignatian bishop at the beginning of the second century was the universal pattern in the Church; (4) further lack of evidence that the authority of bishops to ordain priests was absolute—there is, in fact, evidence that priests did ordain priests; (5) the distinction between "valid" and "licit" ordination as it has been used in recent centuries cannot be found in the primitive church, even though there was a concern for maintaining "order" (*taxis*) in the Church from the time of the New Testament; (6) unclarity about the meaning of the term "power" as attributed to the ordained minister from ancient times.[32]

The Report sees these data as implying that there is more than one way to "validate" ministries. Besides the ordinary "ritual validation" the Report also lists "ecclesiological" and "charismatic validation".[33]

In its response to the Report, Committee III of the Commission recommended its publication along with its own brief comments. While stating that the Report provides "a promising basis . . . for progress towards mutual recognition of ministry," the Committee requested that the document as a whole be further developed.[34]

e. The Marseilles consultation held in September, 1972 took up the task of further development of the Louvain document by reworking and expanding it. For our purposes, three points are significant in the Marseilles draft. First, while allowing the Louvain references to "validation" of ministry to remain in section III/C/5, the concept of "recognition" of ministries becomes dominant in section VI/A-D.[35]

Second, in response to a specific request from Louvain, Marseilles offers a helpful distinction of four different "degrees and modes of mutual recognition" of ministries. (1) "The least degree", and one that is accorded by virtually every church involved in the ecumenical movement, is "mutual respect." (2) The next degree "is reached when

---

[32]Ibid., pp. 97-98. If these arguments seem similar to those used in *LC* (see above n. 7) this is no coincidence; two Roman Catholic members from that dialogue participated in the 1970 consultation at Cartigny which prepared the draft for Louvain.

[33]Ibid., p. 99. If these categories recall those developed by McDonnell in the article cited in n. 12 above, it is because he was a member of the Cartigny drafting team.

[34]Ibid., p. 221. Louvain, p. 89 seems to be responding to a question asked by Bristol when it states flatly, albeit less than juridically, that in view of the relation of the ordained person to the community "there is no place for detached ministers." Like Bristol, Louvain also thinks "ecclesia supplet" or "economy" might be helpful in the quest for mutual acceptance of ministries.

[35]"The Ordained Ministry in Ecumenical Perspective," *Study Encounter* 8/4 (1972): 1-22.

the ecclesial nature of the other church is acknowledged; then the ministry, though it may not be without defects, cannot be declared to be without any spiritual significance. . . . [I]t just lacks the fullness which is promised to the apostolic ministry." (3) "Still another stage is reached when the ministry of the other church is officially acknowledged as the apostolic ministry given by Christ." Full communion would result if there were no other barriers. (4) The final stage is the "mutual recognition of the communities, implying the mutual recognition of the ministry."[36]

The second degree of recognition described above corresponds to the position Vatican II has taken with regard to Anglican and Protestant ministries, while the third stage represents the Vatican II stance toward the Orthodox ministries. It would seem that this four-fold distinction conforms much more to Christian experience than the two-fold determination, "valid"/"invalid."

Third, in order to achieve mutual recognition of ministries, says Marseilles, "different things are required of different churches."

a) Churches which have preserved the episcopal succession have to recognize the real content of the ordained ministry that exists in churches that do not have an episcopal succession. In spite of the mutual separation . . . God . . . gives to the communities that lack the episcopal succession but that live in a succession of apostolic faith, a ministry of word and sacraments the value of which is attested by its fruits.

b) The churches without episcopal succession have to recognize that, while they may not lack a succession in the apostolic faith, they do not have the fullness of the *sign* of apostolic succession. If full visible unity is to be achieved, the fullness of the sign of apostolic succession ought to be recovered.[37]

The argument in (a) is a direct appeal to Christian experience rather

[36]Marseilles, pp. 19-20, VI/B.

[37]Ibid., p. 21, VI/C, 1 (a) and (b). I omit citing steps 2 (a) and (b) because even though they are retained in the next stage of the Faith and Order study at Accra, they disappear in the present proposed re-drafting of Accra. See Accra, para. 105-106 for substantially the same points, although para. 106 is couched in less imperative language. The present stage of the draft also omits the *possibility*, envisioned by both Marseilles, p. 21 VI/C/2(b) and Accra, p. 106, that the churches with episcopal succession might recognize not only ministries standing in a non-episcopal succession but also some that, claiming neither episcopal nor presbyteral succession, intend simply to "maintain a succession in the apostolic faith."

than to the deductive argument of ecclesiological recognition/valida-
tion. To be sure, the latter argument is invoked in the "second stage" of
recognition cited above.

f. Revised by still another consultation held in Geneva in late 1973,
the Marseilles document underwent further modification by the Faith
and Order Committee at its 1974 meeting in Accra, Ghana. This statement was published along with statements on baptism and the eucharist.[38] The Accra statement contains no mention of "validity" nor does
it deal with such problems as the *episcopus vagans* or ordinations
conferred by heretics. A "recognition" of the special ministry by the
Church is required "of which a form is already found in Apostolic
times (for example, II Timothy 1: 6f.) and which later became commonly known as ordination."[39]

A constant affirmation from Louvain through Marseilles is continued: on the one hand it is affirmed that, "although ordination of
ministers by bishops was the almost universal practice in the Church
very early," it is said on the other hand that "the episcopate is being
seen increasingly as an effective" or "pre-eminent sign" but not as
"identical with the apostolicity of the whole Church."[40] A consequence
of this is that: "In particular situations . . . a ministry may emerge
which, because of its authenticity, is accepted by the particular community and receives only afterwards a form of official recognition."[41]
Here we have a position similar to that of Rahner, which will be
outlined below, one that involves a basic sacramental validity spring-
ing from the sacramental nature of the Church—an ecclesiological
validation—as distinct from official public recognition, or canonical
validation. This passage, perhaps unfortunately, is missing from the
proposed current modification of the text.[42]

Accra says there are "certain pre-conditions and expectations regarding the ordinand [that] are indispensable, while others are not."
"Among the basic requirements" are: (1) a call from the Lord; (2) the
ability to commit oneself to the task for which one is called and

[38]*One Baptism, One Eucharist and a Mutually Recognized Ministry*, Faith and Order
Paper No. 73 (Geneva: WCC, 1975).

[39]Accra, p. 33, para. 16.

[40]Ibid., p. 37, para. 32 and 34; p. 39, para. 37.

[41]Ibid., p. 39, para. 36.

[42]"Ministry": Provisional text for submission to the Faith and Order Standing Committee, January 1981; final draft from meeting of June 3-7, 1980. Cited henceforth as
1980 Text.

ordained; (3) appropriate theological education.[43] Nothing is said about the status of a person who is ordained without fulfilling these "indispensable" conditions. The avoidance of such canonical terms as "validity" or "legitimacy" seems almost deliberate. It can reasonably be countered, however, that this is a theological document aimed at mutual recognition of ministries, not a draft of church discipline for a united Church of the future. The spirit of the document, moreover, allows one to see it as well within the range of likelihood that the bishop—or whoever exercises the function of *episkope*[44]—can declare an ordination "invalid" or "not recognized" if any of the basic conditions are lacking.

g. At the Nairobi Assembly in December, 1975 the member churches were asked to study the three agreed statements emanating from Accra and to submit their replies to the Faith and Order Commission by December 31, 1976. The unusually heavy response from over 90 member churches, plus responses from seventeen Roman Catholic theological faculties solicited by the Secretariate for Promoting Christian Unity and various other responses, was evaluated in June, 1977 by a large consultation. A draft report was sent to the Faith and Order Steering Committee which met the following month to revise and publish the report.[45]

The Response to the Churches says nothing about the determination of validity nor about the demise of that term. Presumably this was deemed a matter of great concern by the responding churches and theological faculties. One may also presume the respondents were basically satisfied with the way the question of mutual recognition of ministries was treated, for the only reference to that section had to do with the point that "different ways toward recognition, moving at varying speeds, are to be expected."[46]

In presenting the Response to the Central Committee of the World Council of Churches in August, 1977, Lukas Vischer, director of the Faith and Order Commission, noted that the three texts, "especially

---

[43]Accra, pp. 42-43, para. 50-56.

[44]Accra, p. 36, para. 26. The 1980 Text collapses this entire, rather unsatisfactory section on conditions for ordination into a single short paragraph (p. 20, para. 42) which, while still entitled "The Conditions for Ordination," is clearly not intended to be a statement of church discipline.

[45]*Towards an Ecumenical Consensus on Baptism, the Eucharist and the Ministry: A Response to the Churches,* Faith and Order Paper No. 84 (Geneva: WCC, 1977), pp. 2-19, esp. pp. 10-12.

[46]Ibid., p. 12, 4 c).

the one on the ministry, had still too much the character of theological essays" and they did not specify clearly enough the decisions the churches were being invited to make. "They seemed to call rather for an expression of theological opinion."[47]

h. The most recent stage of the process available to me is a mimeographed copy of a provisional text prepared in June, 1980 for submission to the Faith and Order Standing Committee in January of 1981.[49] Significantly shorter than the Accra statement (52 paragraphs versus 106), it omits, as was mentioned earlier, the four-fold degrees of mutual recognition outlined by Marseilles and Accra, as well as the sentence expressing the thought that ministerial reality can be present prior to "official recognition" of it. Some new sections show the clear influence—sometimes verbatim—of the Consultation on Church Union's revised chapter on ministry drawn up in January, 1980.[50]

A surprising proposed alteration is the re-introduction of the terms "valid" and "invalid." To be sure, the sense of the Accra statement is not changed, nor is the heavy weight of "recognition" language diminished. With Accra, the 1980 Text notes that churches without episcopacy, including those engaged in union negotiations, are expressing "willingness to accept episcopal succession as a sign[51] of the apostolicity of the life of the whole Church." In contrast to Accra's statement that the only thing unacceptable with regard to episcopal succession is the view that "episcopal succession is identical with . . . the apostolicity of the whole Church,"[52] the 1980 Text says non-episcopal churches "cannot accept any suggestion that the ministry exercised in their own tradition should be *invalid* until the moment that it enters into an existing line of episcopal succession."[53] Again, in speaking of the meaning of ordination, the 1980 Text says: "It is clear that churches have different practices of ordination and that it would be wrong to single out one of those as exclusively *valid*."[54] The ambiguity sur-

---

[47]Ibid., p. 27.

[48]Ibid., pp. 29-30.

[49]See n. 42 above.

[50]Cf. the 1980 Text, pp. 12-14, para. 23-28 on the "personal," "collegial" and "communal" principles for exercising ordained ministry and the functions of bishops, presbyters and deacons; and, *In Quest of a Church of Christ Uniting: An Emerging Theological Consensus* (Princeton: COCU, 1980) pp. 39-46, chap. VII, para. 19-65.

[51]The earlier Faith and Order adjectives "pre-eminent" or "effective" have disappeared.

[52]Accra, p. 39, para. 37.

[53]1980 Text, p. 17, para. 35; my emphasis.

[54]Ibid., p. 18, para. 36; my emphasis.

rounding these terms, already noted at Edinburgh, has still been left standing, however.

Accra and the 1980 Text each underscore that in churches lacking the historic episcopate, "Ordination . . . is always done . . . by persons in whom the Church recognizes the authority to transmit the ministerial commission."[55] Is not this ecclesial manner of speaking about the authority to ordain preferable to the *potestas ordinandi* which has proved to be so misleading since its inception with the Scholastics?

For both Accra and the 1980 Text resumption of the ministry after a leave of absence "requires no ordination . . . in recognition of the God-given charism of ministry."[56] Many Roman Catholic theologians would see here the basic intent of the Tridentine doctrine of the indelible character.

2. *The Lutheran-Roman Catholic Dialogue in the United States*

In this dialogue a representative group of Roman Catholic theologians, including two bishops, underwent a theological conversion that led them to abandon the view most of them held at the start of the dialogue, namely that Lutheran orders were invalid.[57]

In the light of fresh study of biblical and other historical sources and as a result of a fuller theological appreciation of the sacraments, of apostolicity and of apostolic succession than had obtained in Catholic theology from the 16th century to the early part of the 20th, the Catholic participants stated: "Our traditional objections to the Lutheran eucharistic Ministry were seen to be of less force today, and reasons emerged for a positive reappraisal."[58] They concluded:

> The historical and theological reflections made above move us to doubt whether Roman Catholics should continue to question the eucharistic presence of the Lord in the midst of the Lutherans when they meet to celebrate the Lord's supper. And so we make the following statement:
>
> As Roman Catholic theologians, we acknowledge in the spirit of Vatican II that the Lutheran communities with which we have been in dialogue are truly Christian churches, possessing the elements of holiness and truth that mark them as organs of

---

[55]Cf. Accra, p. 39, para. 35; and 1980 Text, p. 17, para. 34.
[56]Cf. Accra, p. 45, para. 62; and 1980 Text, p. 21, para. 45.
[57]This view is described in the quotation above at n. 7.
[58]*LC*, p. 24, n. 37.

grace and salvation. Furthermore, in our study we have found serious defects in the arguments customarily used against the validity of the eucharistic Ministry of the Lutheran churches. In fact, we see no persuasive reason to deny the possibility of the Roman Catholic church recognizing the validity of this Ministry. Accordingly we ask the authorities of the Roman Catholic church whether the ecumenical urgency flowing from Christ's will for unity may not dictate that the Roman Catholic church recognize the validity of the Lutheran Ministry and, correspondingly, the presence of the body and blood of Christ in the eucharistic celebrations of the Lutheran churches.[59]

This dialogue, a process of long and sustained effort, is a case study in determining the validity of orders. More than the Faith and Order dialogues, it operates in categories quite familiar to Roman Catholics, for the simple reason that the statement just cited is found in a section of the report written by Roman Catholics for Roman Catholics. The first sentence of the citation contains a "soft" version of the argument for ecclesiological validation: the Lutheran communities are "truly Christian churches." For some, though not all of the members of the Catholic team, this already implied that the ministers of those churches were true or valid ministers, however deficient their ministries might be judged to be because of lack of episcopal ordination.

The second sentence contains a different argument: reasons traditionally advanced against the validity of Lutheran orders have all been found wanting—including the objection that ordination by a bishop "in apostolic succession" is an absolute condition for conferral of valid orders. Since the Catholic team could find no persuasive reasons against recognizing the validity of Lutheran orders, in view of the urgency arising out of Christ's will for unity among his followers, there was no alternative than to ask the Roman Catholic authorities to recognize the validity of those orders.

Widely discussed in Europe as well as in North America, and by the Faith and Order Commision, *LC* found positive reception among such theologians as Walter Kasper[60] and Heinz Schütte.[61] In a doctoral dis-

---

[59]*LC*, p. 31, n. 54.

[60]"Zur Frage der Anerkennung der Ämter in den lutherischen Kirchen," *Theologische Quartalschrift* 151 (1971): 97-109.

[61]*Amt, Ordination und Sukzession* (Düsseldorf: Patmos, 1974), pp. 359-370. Schütte's only reservation about *LC* is that it says "zu wenig" about episcopal succession when, in *LC,* p. 27, n. 44, it calls it a "valuable" sign of apostolicity. However he overlooks, p. 33,

sertation accepted by the School of Canon Law of the Catholic University of America, an Episcopalian canonist saw in the Catholic proposal of *LC* the possible beginning of a basic reorientation of the Western theological and canonical traditions.[62] *LC*'s influence is discernible in the 1971 Malta Report of the Lutheran/Roman Catholic International Commission, which also recommended mutual recognition of ministries.[63] The statement also influenced the controversial "Memorandum" of the several German university ecumenical institutes.[64] Because the latter document seemed to be long on assertion and short on argument, it drew the fire of the German Catholic Bishops' *Glaubenskommission.*[65]

---

n. 57, where it is called "the effective" sign of unity and a "pre-eminent way" of retaining apostolic ministry. For a reply to the criticism made by a Study Committee of the Catholic Theological Society of America (*CTSA Proceedings* 27 [1972]: 191-202) that *LC* did not make sufficiently clear the grounds for recognition of Lutheran orders and that it should have decided the question whether recognition by the Catholic Church would constitute validity or confirm existing validity (a critique recently endorsed by Carl Peter), see H. McSorley, "Roman Catholic Recognition of Protestant Ministries," *Ecumenical Trends* 10 (1981): 97-100. I shall also address the second part of this critique in terms of Rahner's position toward the end of this essay.

[62]L. M. Knox, *The Ecclesial Dimension of Valid Orders,* Canon Law Studies No. 477 (Washington: Catholic University of America, 1971).

[63]"Report of the Joint Lutheran/Roman Catholic Study Commission on 'The Gospel and the Church'," *Lutheran World* 19 (1972): 266-270, nn. 47-64. For reasons other than that of a *defectum ordinis* (see text above at n. 17) Roman Catholic Eucharists can also be said to "suffer from imperfections," says the Malta Report. Catholic Eucharists "will become the perfect sign of unity of the Church only when all those who through baptism have been invited in principle to the table of the Lord and are able in reality to participate" (p. 271).

[64]*Reform und Anerkennung kirchlichen Ämter:* Ein Memorandum der Arbeitsgemeinschaft ökumenischen Universitätsinstitute (Munich: Kaiser; Mainz: Grünewald, 1973).

[65]Rahner's *Vorfragen* (n. 8 above) arose in the context of this inner-German controversy. He does not oppose the conclusion of the *Memorandum* with regard to mutual recognition of ministries, but he has it in mind when he writes on p. 22 that theological "changes of consciousness" are made possible not when a new, different consciousness is simply declared to be self-evident, but when, starting from the official or standard existing consciousness, one seeks to actualize the already-present tendencies to such a change. This applies especially to the Church, he adds, for which a historical continuity of consciousness is necessary and essential. H. M. Legrand's critique of Rahner, mentioned below in n. 101, fails to appreciate Rahner's pastorally sensitive method of inquiry.

On p. 20 Rahner is also critical of the excessively brief critique of the *Memorandum* made by the German bishops' doctrinal commission and the impression it gives of being

3. *The Anglican-Roman Catholic International Commission*

The 1973 Canterbury Statement on "Ministry and Ordination" of the Anglican-Roman Catholic International Commission did not discuss directly the question of validity of orders or even the judgment of *Apostolicae Curae*. But these questions were addressed unmistakably, though indirectly. By reaching an "agreement on the nature of Ministry" the commission correctly saw that the verdict of 1896 had to be seen in the light of the new theological context expressed in this statement as well as in the earlier Windsor statement on the Eucharist.[66] In the *Elucidations* concerning the Canterbury statement published in January, 1979, the commission explicitly "calls for a reappraisal" of *Apostolicae Curae*'s "verdict on Anglican orders."[67]

4. *Orthodox-Roman Catholic Dialogue in the United States*

It was noted above in section II/D that the Roman Catholic Church at Vatican II officially recognized the "true priesthood" of the Orthodox churches. On the other hand, mainly because the Orthodox have yet to deal with the matter in a council, "the Orthodox Church has not yet made an official statement about its understanding of the ecclesial status of the Roman Catholic Church and its relation to the Orthodox Church."[68]

To be sure, such an eminent Orthodox spokesman as the Ecumenical Patriarch Demetrios of Constantinople could count it as a "basic fact" that "we have the same sacraments," including "the same priesthood in an uninterrupted apostolic ordination . . ." from which he drew the conclusion that "we must explore together through . . . dialogue the ways to our unity in Christ."[69] This statement by such a representative Orthodox leader is sufficient to make us skeptical when

---

too satisfied with the present state of theological awareness, which it too easily assumes to be dogmatically binding. The commission, he says, also misses the positive ecumenical possibilities opened up by its own admission that the New Testament is too unclear about the nature of ministry to draw many firm conclusions from it.

[66]"Ministry and Ordination," in *Anglican-Roman Catholic International Commission —The Three Agreed Statements* (London: CTS/SPCK, 1978), p. 24, n. 17.

[67]*Anglican-Roman Catholic International Commission—Eucharistic Doctrine/ Ministry and Ordination: Elucidations* (London: SPCK/CTS, 1979), p. 16.

[68]E. Kilmartin, *Toward Reunion: The Orthodox and Roman Catholic Churches* (New York: Paulist, 1979), p. 44.

[69]"Speech of His Holiness Patriarch Demetrios to Cardinal Jan Willebrands and a Catholic Delegation in Constantinople, Nov. 30, 1977," in Kilmartin, p. 112.

we hear such uncritical generalizations as: "the Orthodox" don't believe any sacraments but their own are valid.

At its 14th meeting in May, 1976, the Orthodox-Roman Catholic meeting in the United States issued two Joint Statements: one on "The Pastoral Office" and one on "The Principle of Economy."[70] Both are related to our theme.

In the first document, the Roman Catholic participants acknowledge a "weakness of western theology of priesthood" since the Middle Ages in allowing the pastoral office to be dissociated from its ecclesial context and thus giving rise to "absolute ordinations." Vatican II's stress on the collegial nature of each order is seen as a corrective that leads to more harmony with the Orthodox view.[71] No reference is made to "validity." In its place we find "recognition": "Bishops and presbyters can only represent Christ as bishops and presbyters when they exercise the pastoral office of the Church. Therefore the Church can recognize an ordination only which involves a bishop with a pastoral office and a candidate with a concrete title of service."[72] Here is a firm, clear stand against both *ministri vagantes* and persons ordained "absolutely." Whatever such ministers do, whatever some people think they are doing, the Church simply does not recognize them. When one reads the history of the conflicting theories and practices concerning reordinations, one is pleased, if not astonished, at the unanimous agreement that "the ordained is claimed permanently for the service of the Church and so cannot be reordained."[73]

The Statement says "Ordination in apostolic succession is required for the bestowal of the pastoral office."[74] No distinction is made between episcopal succession and apostolic succession, nor is any effort made to say whether this is an absolute requirement. The document thus seems not to have dealt with the significant questions that the Lutheran-Catholic dialogue, Faith and Order, and other dialogues had to face. This is understandable given the fact that this dialogue is between two episcopal churches. Moreover, even as it stands—that is, precisely because it does not specify that ordination *must* be by a *bishop*—this statement is open to harmonization with other agreed statements on ministry.

[70]Texts in Kilmartin, pp. 79-85 and 85-88.
[71]Ibid., p. 81, I.
[72]Ibid., p. 83, II/7.
[73]Ibid., p. 83, II/8 (a).
[74]Ibid., p. 82, II/5.

Patriarch Demetrios stated as a "fact" that "Roman Catholics and Orthodox have the same priesthood." The U.S. dialogue doesn't deny that, but simply says it is looking "for criteria leading to" the goal of "mutual recognition of ministries."[75]

The Joint Statement on "The Principle of Economy" is important for our theme for two reasons. (1) It shows Orthodox theologians using the categories "valid" and "invalid" with the same ease as their Roman Catholic colleagues—again, however, without defining these terms! (2) It demonstrates that in view of the wealth of meanings the term "economy" has had over the centuries, and the contradictory opinions concerning its possible applications, it is impossible at the present stage of development to appeal facilely to this principle to solve the problem of recognition of ministries.

Some recent presentations of economy have indeed contended that "from the point of view of strictness" (akribeia) "all non-Orthodox sacraments . . . are null and void but that the Orthodox Church can, by economy, treat non-Orthodox sacraments as valid."[76] However, "these recent interpretations do not, in the judgment of the Consultation, do justice to the genuine whole tradition underlying the concept and practice of economy. . . . Nor can the application of economy make something invalid to be valid, or what is valid to be invalid."[77]

The Statement on "The Pastoral Office" spoke of a search for "criteria" for mutual recognition of ministries. The Statement on "Economy," on the other hand, is less intellectualistic. It says "economy" involves "the exercise of spiritual discernment." The dialogue partners "hope and pray, therefore, that our churches can come to discern in each other the same faith, that they can come to recognize each other as sister churches celebrating the same sacraments, and thus enter into full communion."[78] The fact that Patriarch Demetrios and

---

[75]Ibid., p. 84, III/4.

[76]Ibid., pp. 87-88, n. 9 (b).

[77]Ibid., p. 88, n. 10. For a survey of recent work on "economy" see the paper presented at the dialogue by M. Fahey, "Ecclesiastical 'Economy' and Mutual Recognition of Faith: A Roman Catholic Perspective," Diakonia 11 (1976): 204-223. To his fine bibliography one could add Y. Congar, "Propos en vue d'une théologie de l'Economie' dans la tradition latine," Irenikon 45 (1972): 155-206 and some of the studies listed by C. Vogel, "Rata Sacerdotia: Position de Léon Ier (406-461) sur les Ordinations Conferées Irregulièrement," Revue de Droit Canonique 25 (1975): 22, n. 8.

[78]Kilmartin, p. 88, n. 10.

many Orthodox before him[79] have already been able to make such a discernment is an indication that recognition of Roman Catholic—and other—orders as "valid" is not in principle a problem for the Orthodox churches, and that this will increasingly be the case as more and more Orthodox come to appreciate the breadth and depth of their tradition.

B. The Validity of Orders in Recent Historical and Theological Scholarship

In section A of this part, we have, of course, been dealing with a great deal of scholarship, without which the several statements on ministry we have surveyed would not have been possible. Here I simply wish to bring forward, again without pretense at a complete dossier, a few insights and findings from recent scholarship that contribute to a newer state of the question concerning the determination of the "validity" of orders. The first point figures so prominently in ecumenical statements that I state it here with utter brevity and without references.

1. One can speak today of an ecumenical exegetical consensus that the New Testament evidence indicates that the primitive church had pluriform structures of ministry, and that while ordination indeed has roots in the New Testament, there is no evidence that *only* the Apostles or ordained persons presided at the Eucharist. Nor, it must be added, is there any evidence that *every* Christian was authorized so to preside.

2. Historical research has recovered long-overlooked facts showing that while ordination by bishops was the *almost* universal norm in the pre-Reformation church—so that, by the end of the Middle Ages the bishop could be called, significantly, the "ordinary" minister of ordination[80]—there are possible examples of unordained "charismatic"

[79]See the illuminating study by Francis J. Thomson, "Economy: An Examination of the Various Theories of Economy Held Within the Orthodox Church With Special Reference to the Economical Recognition of the Validity of Non-Orthodox Sacraments," *Journal of Theological Studies* 16 (1975): 368-420; 417-418: "This examination of the canons shows that in general the Church in both East and West has accepted the validity of baptism conferred in the name of the Trinity. At most times it has probably also accepted the validity of ordinations within the unbroken Apostolic Succession." Vogel's claim in "*Rata Sacerdotia*," p. 22, n. 8, that the application of the principle of economy to recognition of ministries for the Orthodox requires as "an essential . . . condition" that the "pseudo-bishop" or priest pass over from heterodoxy to orthodoxy is far too sweeping if this means the ministers in question must join the Orthodox Church. In the face of the plural, if not confused understanding of "economy" by Orthodox theologians and canonists as demonstrated by Thomson and the U.S. Orthodox-Roman Catholic statement discussed above, Vogel's view is one-sided. He makes the same claim in "Le ministre charismatique de l'Eucharistie," in *Ministères*, pp. 207-208 and n. 22.

[80]DS 1326, Decree for the Armenians.

leaders of the Eucharist[81] and certain examples of presbyteral rather than episcopal ordinations of priests.[82] Moreover, the theory connected with the practice of ordinion of priests by presbyters, associated with the name of St. Jerome, was known and respected in the medieval church and was defended at Trent by many speakers, especially by those from the "Italian party." During the divisive debate of the final period of the council on the obligation of bishops to reside in their dioceses, the "Spanish party" wanted to say this duty arose out of divine law, but the other side argued that to say this would involve an implicit condemnation of St. Jerome and a host of Catholic teachers.

[81]See the dossier collected by C. Vogel in the essay cited at the end of n. 79, pp. 191-207. He omits consideration of Did. 10: 7; 14-15 on which see McDonnell, pp. 246-247. Vogel grants that there is evidence, rare but real, of "charismatic" ministers of the eucharist prior to the third century. Although Schütte, pp. 323-326 is justifiably skeptical of a supposed "charismatic" church order at Corinth in the time of Paul, he is sympathetic to the growing Catholic theological opinion that unordained Christian laity can lead a sacramental Eucharist in case of need when no priest is available. For a sound theological, pastoral and juridical reflection on this possibility, and for the distinction between a faithful, reverent lay celebration and "sauvages" celebrations of anarchical groups seeking to demonstrate their independence of the official ministry or even their rejection of ordination, see P. Grelot (n. 22 above), pp. 77-93.

[82]McDonnell, pp. 231-244. For more detail see H. Schütte (n. 61 above), pp. 330-349. The view of William of Auxerre that Schütte, p. 347 cites from L. Ott's *Das Weihesakrament* is indicative that Counter-Reformation Catholic efforts to absolutize the necessity of bishops for valid ordinations does not have very deep roots in the Catholic tradition. If there were only three priests left in the world, William argues, one of them would have to consecrate one of the others as bishop and the other as archbishop, not because of the dignity of the office, but by reason of the special situation of need which justifies an exception to the rule. C. Vagaggini, "Possibilità e Limiti del Riconoscimento dei Ministeri Non Cattolici: Riflessioni a partire dalla prassi della 'economia' e dalla dottrina del 'carattere'," in: *Ministères*, p. 274, sees that the requirement that a priest be ordained by a bishop is of ecclesiastical—not divine—law. But he gives no source for his conviction that this is an *invalidating* condition. G. Fahrnberger, *Bischofsamt und Priestertum in den Diskussionen des Konzils von Trient. Eine rechtstheologische Untersuchung* (Wien, 1970), pp. 125-126 and n. 34 is convinced that Trent did not settle the question whether a priest who ordains without papal delegation does so invalidly or only illicitly. Vagaggini's position is influenced in part at least by his uncritical reception of the excessive seventeenth century view of J. Morin, which in turn was derived from the doctrine of the medieval Bologna school, which allowed popes to deprive bishops of the power to confirm and priests of the power to baptize (p. 272). Vagaggini ignores the devastating critique of Morin by L. Saltet, *Les réordinations* (Paris: Gabalda, 1907), pp. 372-374, and F. J. Thomson, pp. 414-415, both of whose works he otherwise cites. Vagaggini, pp. 303-305, nonetheless holds that "invalidly" ordained Protestant clergy— and even Christian laity—can, under certain circumstances, celebrate true, sacramental Eucharists by virtue of the principle, "Deus supplet."

The future Pope Urban VII, for example—John Baptist Castagna, Archbishop of Rossano—argued eloquently and at length that in view of the contrary opinion of Jerome, it would be inappropriate for the council to exclude his view by transforming the other opinion, which he personally found congenial, into a "canon of faith." One does not draw up a canon of faith, he argued, on a matter that is "at least disputable" by Catholics. He rejected the argument that Trent should make such a definition because "the heretics" assert the opposite and use it to justify their ordinations. "The heretics have said many things which are true," he contended. "And if Luther or Calvin . . . should say bishops were not immediately instituted *jure divino* . . . we should not condemn many theologians and all professors of canon law along with two heretics . . . Not everything Luther says should be condemned by the council."[83]

3. There is growing consensus in the ecumenical discussions and in the literature that apostolic succession is not confined to episcopal succession. Instead of being understood as coextensive with apostolic succession, the historic episcopate is being increasingly seen as an ancient, eminent, continuingly viable and effective sign of the apostolic succession of the whole Church in the apostolic faith, life, teaching, mission and witness. The immediate implication of this historically and theologically more defensible understanding of episcopal succession is that ordinations are not *ipso facto* invalid if they take place, for sufficient reason, outside the normal pattern of episcopal ordination. Episcopal churches can then look more positively on the ordinations of non-episcopal churches and do not need to "re-ordain" ministers of non-episcopal churches as a condition for restoration of full communion.[84] This changed attitude has had the reciprocal effect of an increasing willingness on the part of non-episcopal churches to recover episcopacy.

[83]*Concilium Tridentinum* 9. 54, lines 25-39. For the Reformers' use of Jerome see McSorley, *Concilium* 4 (1972): 23-32.

[84]In plans of union where non-episcopal churches prepare to enter into communion with episcopal churches, ordination by bishops is to be the norm *after* reconciliation has been achieved. In the reconciliation service, however, where laying on of hands occurs, it is explicitly stated that this "is not regarded as an act of ordination or re-ordination . . . since the uniting churches recognize that the ministers of all these churches have already been ordained": *A Plan of Union for the Church of Christ Uniting* (Princeton: COCU, 1970), p. 84, n. 9. In the *Canadian Plan of Union* (Toronto: The General Committee on Union, 1973) the same understanding obtains and the mutual laying of hands "on the shoulders" removes any ambiguity about what is happening; cf. p. 80, n. 273, and p. 84, nn. 292-293.

From the point of view of sacramental theology, David Power sees the shift from concern with episcopal succession to emphasis on the apostolic succession of the Church as a gain. Episcopacy, he points out, is one of a complexity of signs, and its meaning must relate to these, above all to the "central sign" of "keeping memorial of Jesus Christ." This sign is not dependent on other signs such as the episcopal succession, but other signs depend on it "for their meaning and reality." Accepting the Accra statement's view of the significance of episcopacy as adequate, Power notes:

> In that document [episcopacy] is accepted as an element which belongs to the totality of the church's sacramental structures. This, however, does not mean that its absence would deprive whatever sacramental structures are kept intact (and particularly those of keeping memorial of Jesus Christ) of meaning and ontic content. *Wherever a sign genuinely expresses some meaning, the corresponding reality is made present.*[85]

We have referred frequently to the ecclesiological way of validating sacraments. Here is an argument for "validation" drawn from reflection on the nature of the sacramental sign in accord with the traditional principles that sacraments "cause" grace *by signifying* it.

4. Virtually all the recent literature and dialogues concerning ordained ministry underscore the point that ordination, like all the sacraments, is a sacrament *of the Church*. This new emphasis on the ecclesial context of orders has important implications for determining the "validity" of orders:

a. Ecclesiality or ecclesial reality does not depend on the ministry for its existence; it is the other way around.[86]

b. The ecclesiological way of validating ministry follows from this: where there is an actual manifestation of true ecclesiality there must be at least the possibility of true sacraments and true ministry of sacraments.

c. The ecclesial emphasis shifts the focus away from the "powers" and the "character" conferred by ordination, which gave rise historically to an individualistic sense of the priesthood and a "metaphysical

---

[85]D. N. Power, "A Note on the Question of Apostolic Succession," in *Baptême, Eucharistie, Ministère*, Studia Anselmiana 74 (Rome, 1977), pp. 249-250. My emphasis.

[86]For a study of Congar's own development on this point see J. M. Courtie, *Theology* 82 (1977): 110-117.

clericalism."[87] Whereas the individualistic view of ordination gave rise to fears about the horrible desecrations that could be performed by *ministri vagantes*, the ecclesial view, stressing that ministers are ordained in, by and for the Church, renders virtually meaningless (and "invalid"!) any exercise of the ordained ministry in defiance of the community.

5. A number of things have been pointed out about the very concept of "validity" which require us henceforth to use the term with circumspection.

a. The terms "valid" and "invalid" are of relatively late origin in the christian vocabulary. They are seldom used of the sacraments in the pre-Tridentine period even in the West, and they are not even found among the canonists until the end of the 13th century.[88] The dominant comparable terminology for canonists and theologians prior to that time in the West was that which was "in use from the time of Cyprian, Augustine and Leo I."[89] Moreover, it is only with the pontificate of Benedict XIV (1740-1758) that the papal magisterium fully appropriates the terms.[90]

b. To equate the later terms "valid"/"invalid" (whose meaning has hardly been constant from the Scholastic period to our own) with earlier language such as *ratum, irritum, akyros* is a widely committed anachronism that leads to distortion of the sense of ancient texts. The otherwise often impressive work of R. Sohm and C. Vogel has suffered in this respect.[91]

---

[87]See P. Fransen, "Orders and Ordination," *Sacramentum Mundi* 4 (New York: Herder and Herder, 1969) pp. 324-325; C. Vagaggini, 260-268; H. M. Legrand, "The 'Indelible' Character and the Theology of Ministry," *Concilium* 4 (1972), esp. pp. 60-62.

[88] P. M. Gy, "La notion de validité sacramentelle avant le Concile de Trente," *Revue de Droit Canonique* 28 (1978): 193-195.

[89]J. Gurrieri, "Sacramental Validity: The Origins and Use of a Vocabulary," THE JURIST 41 (1981): 32; and 27, n. 19.

[90]Ibid., pp. 51-56.

[91]Despite the criticism to which his own study is open, A.Schebler, *Die Reordinationen in der 'altkatholischen' Kirche* (Bonn, 1936), p. 303, has convincingly demonstrated against Sohm that the determination that an extra-ecclesial or inner-ecclesial uncanonical ordination is "irritum" does not of itself say anything about the value of that ordination (*kein Werturteil*), since the term can mean absolute nothingness as well as *practical* nullity or lack of effectiveness. Its real meaning must be derived from the context in each particular case. For a similar criticism of Vogel see Vagaggini pp. 255, 271-272. For the same point see K. Mörsdorf, "Die Entwicklung der Zweigliedrigkeit der kirchlichen Hierarchie," *Munchener theologische Zeistschrift* 3 (1952): 1-16; J. Gilchrist, "'Simoniaca Haeresis' and the Problem of Orders from Leo IX to Gratian," in S.

c. Even the ancient Roman law use of "valid," which underlaid the emerging canonical vocabulary,[92] had a wide range of meaning. As the Roman law specialist, Max Kaser, points out:

> There was scarcely any area of private law which the classical [lawyers] developed so poorly as the ineffectiveness of legal acts. There is no fixed terminology for the multiple forms of legal ineffectiveness. The approximately 30 expressions in the sources —among which "nullum, nullius momenti, inutile (non ratum), inane, imperfectum, vitiosum, non valere, nihil agere (nihil acti esse)" are the more prominent—have no fixed meaning and it would be useless to try to systematize them.[93]

d. Even granting that the ancient and modern Church usage of "invalid," "irrita," "vacua" and the like meant "null, void, non-existent,"—it must be remembered that this "nullity," at least according to contemporary canonical usage, pertains only to the *"juridical efficacy"* of an act[94]—not to its theological or its sacramental efficacy at its most profound level. Failure to heed this distinction, which will be clarified below, is responsible, in my judgment, for the fact that so many manuals of theology say little more than canonists when speaking of the validity or invalidity of sacraments. The authors of such texts think their work is done once they have discussed the criteria for validity (deficient as this discussion was). But they fail to move to the properly theological task of discussing what validity and invalidity mean theologically.

e. The terms "valid" and "invalid" have at least two theological senses and corresponding applications. One kind of invalidity or in-validating condition totally vitiates what purports to be, but is not in reality, a sacramental act. Such is the case when someone outwardly

---

Kuttner and J. Ryan, eds., *Proceedings of the Second International Congress of Medieval Canon Law: Held at Boston, August, 1963* (Vatican, 1965), pp. 221-225; McSorley, "The Roman Catholic Doctrine of the Competent Minister of the Eucharist in Ecumenical Perspective," *LC,* pp. 121-125; Gurrieri, pp. 28-32.

[92]Gurrieri, p. 31.

[93]*Das römische Privatrecht* (Munich, 1955), p. 214; cited by Gy, p. 194.

[94]R. Naz, "Nullités," *Dictionnaire de Droit Canonique* 6: 1036; my emphasis. According to current Roman usage, ordinations performed in defiance of certain canons are "illegitimate" and lacking in "juridical effect." Even though they may be "valid" the Church does not recognize them and will not as long as the defiant spirit continues: "Decretum circa quosdam illegitimas ordinationes presbyterales et episcopales," *AAS* 68 (1976): 623; THE JURIST 37 (1977): 170-171.

performs a Christian sacramental sign without in any way intending its Christian meaning, or when someone shares bread and wine but with no reference whatever to Jesus Christ. Here what has been called the "substance" or the very nature of the sacrament has not been achieved and it is really no sacrament—neither canonically nor theologically. Such deficiencies cannot be overcome, "healed," "supplied" or "recognized" by any ecclesiastical "power."

Another kind of invalidity is that incurred due to lack of a condition required by what theological textbooks have called "the positive will of Christ."[95] Such would be the requirement of baptism on the part of the ordaining minister and the ordinand. Congar has drawn attention to the way in which precisely such a case was treated by Pope Innocent III: the pope did not require that those ordained by such a bishop be reordained, and this on the principle of "Christus supplet."[96]

In the first kind of invalidity one is justified in saying both canonically and theologically: nothing happens sacramentally. In the second case we have an example of an ordination canonically invalid but not devoid of theological and sacramental substance, owing to the belief that, all other conditions being realized, Christ would not deprive the Christian people of theologically effective ministries. Because of the *theological* substance that was recognized, a *canonical* ruling was then made upholding the validity of the ordinations in this case.

This distinction of kinds of invalidity helps clarify a point at issue between J. Coventry and E. Yarnold in connection with the question of Anglican orders in particular and the meaning of validity in general. Coventry captures the thought of many Catholic theologians today when he says validity is a determination "that one's church recognizes it; to say that it is invalid is simply to say that one's church does not recognize it. . . . Hence a declaration by Rome of the invalidity of orders does not in principle close the door to . . . arguments . . . that a considerable means of effectiveness and perhaps full effectiveness should now be recognized in those orders."[97]

---

[95]Vagaggini, p. 259. See pp. 269-275 for his discussion of three kinds of invalidating conditions deriving from (1) the nature of the sacrament, (2) the positive will of Christ, and (3) the positive law of the Church. Among the third kind he lists the requirement of masculinity and of ordination by a bishop.

[96]*Heilige Kirche: Ekklesiologische Studien und Annäherungen* (Stuttgart, 1966), pp. 299-301; cf. *Decr.* III, tit. 43, c. 3.

[97]J. Coventry, "'Valid'," *Faith and Unity* (1968): 91-93; cited by Hughes, p. 3, n. 5. See also Coventry's contribution to the Tenth Downside Symposium, *Intercommunion*

Yarnold argues that the bull, *Apostolicae Curae*, presupposes "that invalidity of orders is a fact which the Church cannot alter except by conferring new orders." Those who contend "that invalidity is not a fact independent of the Church's judgment, but simply the absence of the Church's approval" are wrong. For "there are some ordinations which the Church *could* not . . . regard as valid: of babies or madmen (because consent is required), of the unbaptized (because membership in the Church is required), of horses . . . (because humanity is required)."[98]

Taken in isolation, Coventry's remarks would seem to overstate the power of ecclesial recognition by failing to note certain pretensions to sacramentality the Church *cannot* recognize. Yarnold, on the other hand, is in danger of overstating the case for sacramental objectivity. Correct with regard to *some* ordinations the Church could not recognize (although his absolutizing of the baptismal requirement is, as we have just seen, questionable), Yarnold fails to see the implications of the fact that this is true of some, but not all ordinations. There are other "invalidating" conditions, especially those associated with the requirement of "form," for which the Church can "supply."

f. In view of the many problems and ambiguities associated with the terms "valid" and "invalid" it is not surprising that some theologians have suggested abandonment of those categories.[99] I, too, agree that canonists may wish to define more precisely what they have meant by "validity" in the recent past, perhaps as a first step in developing a less ambiguous terminology. And in the light of the important distinction made above of kinds of "invalidity," there is merit to the suggestion

---

and Church Membership, J. Kent and R. Murray, eds. (Denville, N.J.: Dimension Books, 1973), pp. 77-82.

[98]E. Yarnold, *Anglican Orders—A Way Forward?* (London: Catholic Truth Society, 1977), p. 10. Yarold further argues that if the view of Coventry and others were correct, and orders would be valid simply because the Church says they are, then *Apostolicae Curae* was a vain undertaking since it was concerned precisely with determining whether Anglican orders were valid. This, I think, is to trivialize Coventry's view by making it appear arbitrary. Surely Coventry's stress on Church recognition as the crucial element in determining validity does *not* eliminate the need for ascertaining grounds on which to base the recognition.

[99]See McDonnell, p. 211, n. 1; and H. M. Legrand, "Bulletin d'Ecclésiologie," p. 657: the "problematique" of validity "doit précisement être depassée." As was pointed out in part II above, however, K. Lehmann cannot be rightly invoked to support such a view.

that a distinction be made between what the Anglican historian B. J. Kidd has called "sacramental validity" and "canonical validity."[100]

Kidd's distinction corresponds to that developed by Karl Rahner on the basis of his reflection on the Church's highly flexible sacramental theory and practice over the centuries, between a basic sacramental validity and a sacramental-canonical validity.[101] Integral to this distinction is the awareness that the Church "does" many things tacitly and implicitly and not just officially and publicly. The principles of "ecclesia supplet" and "economy," above all the power of the sacramental sign, are at work regardless of official recognition or even awareness of them, as soon as the essential conditions of sacramental faith and practice are fulfilled when other normal standards of canonical validity are unable to be met. In such situations "valid" ministry and sacramentality are present even before official recognition takes place, as G. Tavard had already maintained before Rahner.[102] The whole purpose of his *Vorfragen*, says Rahner, "is to make it thinkable that the extent of that which is sacramentally valid by means of an 'economy' is not simply identical to that which is explicitly recognized as valid in sacramental-canonical (*sakramentsrechtlich*) terms."[103]

It is in the context of the newer state of the question that we ought appropriately to hear Rahner's answer to the question he posed to the pre-Vatican II concept of determining the validity of orders which we cited in part I: How can any priest know he is validly ordained?

> Why can't we look at the matter this way: The valid ordination of a priest or bishop is present when he is recognized as such without contradiction by the ecclesial society? This factual public recognition of a bishop or a priest by the Church constitutes their valid state of being ordained (*Ordiniertheit*). What we usually regard as conditions and presuppositions of a valid ordination is in reality the fulfilling of the "normal" rules,

---

[100]Gurrieri, p. 57.

[101]*Vorfragen, passim.* I find hard to comprehend Legrand's almost scornful dismissal of Rahner's historically and theologically well-argued case as an example of "post-Tridentine ecclesiology" (p. 687) and a "rationalisme abstrait" of interest only to those Catholics who find no difficulty working with the categories of schism, heresy and power that have issued from "school theology" (p. 679-680). Legrand thus misses the point of the entire book by failing to see Rahner's intention to challenge and shake up the immobilty of post-Tridentine school theology.

[102]See *LC,* p. 304, n. 5.

[103]*Vorfragen,* p. 12.

according to which the (hierarchically constituted) public of the Church forms its judgment of recognition. These rules, however, because they are promulgated by the Church in its concreteness, are rules which the Church itself makes with an obligation whose degree and extent depends on the Church's will. They are thus not a tribunal against the Church public and its judgment and thus they can be disregarded without harm if the Church itself wishes to depart from its usual course of action, that is, if it wishes to recognize an ordination as valid despite such violations of the norm.[104]

In terms of Rahner's analysis, it is possible to offer a simple but sound response to a difficulty raised by a committee of the Catholic Theological Society of America against the statement of the Catholic participants in the Lutheran-Catholic dialogue on ministry that was discussed above. The committee agreed with the Catholic statement that it is unnecessary to "solve the problem" of Lutheran orders in the past "before recognizing the validity of" that ministry today. Yet they think that the Catholic members "leave the basis for the recognition ambiguous" by not deciding whether recognition by the Roman Catholic Church would constitute validity or simply be confirmatory of existing validity.[105] Since Rahner holds that a "basic sacramental reality" can be present in the absence of sacramental-canonical validity, his reply to the above question would be that recognition of Lutheran, Anglican, or Protestant orders by the Catholic Church constitutes validity in the sacramental-canonical sense, but confirms it in the former sense of basic sacramental validity. The true basis for such recognition can only be an already existing sacramental reality. Without such a sacramental basis, any merely canonical determination of validity would itself be null and void.

The only reservation I have of Rahner's position as enunciated in *Vorfragen*, apart from the monological style that occasionally leads

---

[104]Ibid., pp. 40-41. Lest one think Rahner is also open to the criticism Yarnold made of Coventry, this statement must be read in the context of the entire book. On p. 63, for example, Rahner makes it clear that, in the unusual circumstance he is describing, he presupposes that those who celebrate the Eucharist without the presence of an ordained priest "are united with the Church through good faith and salvific faith." Where there is public contempt for the normal requirements for validity, the presumption of bad faith "makes these rites sacramentally invalid." This is quite similar to Grelot's analysis mentioned above.

[105]*CTSA Proceedings* 27 (1972): 201.

him to looseness of expression, is that he winds up with two kinds of validity. The term, as we have seen, is complex enough. Why then have two kinds of it? Rahner might answer: you always have been using the same term in two different senses without being aware of it. Now at least you know what you're talking about. That makes sense. But it still must be rejoined: the term "validity" is incapable of dealing adequately with *both* levels of Church life, the level that is official and canonical and the level that is not foreseen by canon law and which is non- (not anti-) canonical, but nevertheless ecclesial.

The distinction of two senses of validity is acceptable but inelegant. Since "validity" is a juridically inspired term, should it not be possible for theologians to get along without it and to coin their own vocabulary for expressing what is intended by the phrase "basic sacramental validity"? In view of the widespread acceptance of the term "recognition" in connection with ministry, sacramental "recognizability" might be a leading contender for the favor of theologians, while the canonists might reserve the term "invalid" for acts which are only pretensions to sacramentality, and use "not recognized" for ordinations which have not yet been judged to be "sacramentally recognizable" by theologians and bishops. Leaving the term "valid" to the jurists, at any rate, while urging them to clarify it and perhaps find a substitute for it may redound to the good of both canon law and theology.

So much, by way of conclusion, for the sub-title of the essay: determining the meaning of "validity".

For a succinct conclusion about determining the "validity" of orders in terms of the various data and arguments considered in this essay, it can be said that the Christian Church, which includes Christ's Roman Catholic Church, can recognize (or recognize as "valid") as its own sacraments those orders or ordained ministries which include the intention and some effective sign of continuing the apostolic ministry of the Church insofar as that ministry is able to be continued.

While this sparse statement about determining the "validity" of orders does not mention the role of the bishop, it must be said for the sake of Christian realism that, statistically speaking, bishops in the "historic succession" have been the ordinary, authorized ministers of this sacrament, with some competition from presbyters over the past 450 years in the West. There is today every indication that that competition will relatively soon be over as more and more Christian churches seek to recover episcopacy where it has been lost and to recognize the bishop as the person authorized by the Church to transmit the ministerial commission. To refuse to be ordained by a bishop will, therefore, increasingly be regarded as a *theological* indication of the lack of "valid" orders, not because such an attitude is anti-episcopal, but because it is anti-ecclesial.

"FULLNESS OF ORDERS": THEOLOGICAL REFLECTIONS

BERNARD COOKE
Holy Cross College
Worcester, Massachusetts

For the Roman Catholic Church with its stress on preservation of religious tradition in both doctrine and practice the present evolution of Christian ministry offers a double challenge. There is the challenge to nurture those creative developments which promise to make the Catholic community more effective in serving humanity's needs (and therefore the kingdom of God). There is the challenge to develop such new ministries in clear continuity with the centuries-old understandings of the sacrament of orders and the centuries-old monopoly of Christian ministry by church officials. That there will be more diversified and more charismatic exercise of ministries by all Christians, including Catholics, is very likely and seems intrinsic to the "recovery of the laity." But it is not clear whether we will see the emergence of new structures of ministry that are recognized by church officialdom, included as part of "approved" church activity, and related cooperatively to long-standing Catholic institutions.

Obviously, the resolution of this tension between new needs and energies on the one side and established power on the other must be the task of the entire Catholic community; it cannot be achieved by theological reflection on the matter. Yet, a number of theological issues are intrinsic to the problem, none of them more basic than the correct understanding of "fullness of orders." But why focus on this particular issue?

Until quite recently (and even now in some quarters) the popular understanding was that all acceptable exercise of ministry within the Catholic Church must relate to, even derive from, official levels of the Church. Central to this view was the belief that any Catholic who ministered did so by participating in the fullness of pastoral authority and power possessed by the hierarchy. Since (in this view) Christ himself gave the Church this hierarchical character, all ministerial structures and processes must be grounded in, spring from, and "extend" this basic and perennial ministerial institution.

Dominant as this view has been, some change in understanding is unmistakably occurring, as witnessed for example in the shift from Pius XI's designation of lay activity as participation in the apostolate of the episcopacy to Vatican II's teaching (in *Lumen gentium*, 33) that men and women are commissioned to the apostolate proper to the laity by the Lord himself. This rapid shift in perspective has been accompanied by an increasingly autonomous involvement of lay men and women in a range of ministerial services. There is, then, a clear need for theological research and reflection to determine the accurate understanding of "fullness of orders" and to examine critically how intrinsic to orthodox Catholic faith is the belief in such a prerogative of the hierarchy.

PERSPECTIVE OF VATICAN II

Let us begin, then, with the present official understanding of the Catholic Church. Since in recent decades no expression of Catholic belief has matched Vatican II in doctrinal authority, we can justifiably concentrate on that council's view of the issue.[1] That a certain ambiguity marks Vatican II's treatment of the question is not surprising. The council was not a forum for creative theological reflection nor even for critical theological analysis; rather, its discussions and documents represent a broad consensus of present Catholic understandings, a consensus in which competing views at times stand side by side and unresolved in the conciliar literature.[2] There are more specific reasons why "fullness of orders" received less than final theological clarification at the council. For one thing, the council's interests and deliberations were directed more pointedly to the relation between papacy and episcopacy, trying to reconcile Vatican I's emphasis on papal prerogatives with the emerging awareness of episcopal collegiality.

The rather obvious *locus classicus* for our question is the third chapter of *Lumen gentium*. In that chapter, as well as in other chapters of

---

[1]The present study will need to be updated by examination of "fullness of orders" in the new Code of Canon Law. Essentially, however, the doctrinal bases for theological reflection will remain unaltered because of the relatively greater importance of the Vatican II statements.

[2]K. Rahner, commenting on *Lumen gentium* in H. Vorgrimler, ed., *Commentary on the Documents of Vatican II*, (New York: Herder, 1967), I, pp. 200-205, gives a mild reference to this unresolved tension: "The text leaves many questions open." See also E. Schillebeeckx, *The Real Achievement of Vatican II* (New York: Herder, 1967), pp. 15-18.

Lumen gentium,[3] there is a certain diversity of language regarding "fullness of orders."[4]

1. Episcopal consecration confers "the fullness of the sacrament of orders" (21). This fullness is immediately equated with the "high priesthood" of Christianity and called the "apex of the sacred ministry." In the cultic activity of the Church the highest dignity and highest worship role belong to those who have been fully empowered as cultic agents by their episcopal ordination. So, whatever the sacrament of orders is as a continuing sacramental reality in the Church's life, the episcopacy is that fully.

The following paragraph makes it clear that "the sacred ministry" is one of sanctifying the faithful. Though the text immediately adds that the offices of teaching and governing are also conferred in the ordination, there seems to be a certain primacy given the *priestly* office. At this point in the text there is no explanation of the manner in which the bishops carry out their sacred empowerment to sanctify others or how this relates to teaching and ruling. It is simply stated that they carry on pre-eminently Christ's own role of shepherd, teacher, and high priest— the bishops act *in persona Christi*.[5]

Whatever this fullness of the sacrament of orders is, it is possessed fundamentally by the episcopal order, by the college of bishops. Each bishop shares in it, but does so by virtue of his pertaining to the *collegium*. Even the bishop of Rome exercises his special role only when he acts in his relationship to the rest of the episcopal body.[6]

[3]The decree on the episcopacy, *Christus Dominus*, while amplifying the pastoral implications of *Lumen gentium*, adds nothing to the doctrinal understanding of "fullness of orders."

[4]The terms *plena potestas ordinis* or *plenitudo potestatis ordinis* do not occur as such in the text; the closest (26) is "Episcopus, plenitudine sacramenti Ordinis insignitus . . ." *AAS* 57 (1965): 31.

[5]Discussion of ministry, priesthood, orders, etc. is frequently bedeviled by imprecision in the use of the term "priesthood" (or "priest") (1) It can be used (apart from its theological appropriateness) as a sociological denomination referring to those who occupy a certain position and exercise certain functions in a religious group. (2) It can be used to refer to a specific cultic function (and to those exercising that function). (3) It can be used to designate an aspect and certain functions of a broader pastoral office. (4) It can be used to refer to the entire pastoral office (of which it is a part), in which case it includes other functions such as teaching and ruling. (5) It can be used to refer to the basic (sacramental) mode of existence of the Church (or of an individual or group within the Church). Usage of Vatican II involves all of these, at times without discrimination.

[6]This exercise of the papal office in relationship to the episcopacy remains, of course, one of the tensions within Vatican II teaching. On the "clarification" of this issue provided by the *nota explicativa praevia* cf. K. Rahner, pp. 198-199.

2. It is this episcopal community, including and relating to the pope, that is the subject of supreme and *full* power over the Church. The text singles out the power to loose and bind, but mentions also teaching authority and pastoral rule. This power is specified somewhat by equating it with the supreme *authority* possessed by the *collegium*; but this equation is a bit difficult to integrate with the earlier focus on this power as one of priestly sanctifying.[7] However, one is not justified in looking in the text for theoretical clarification of the *collegium*'s fullness of power; it is quite clear throughout chapter three that the principal concern is to recognize the collegial nature of the episcopacy without diminishing any of the papal claims to supremacy established at Vatican I.[8]

3. A slightly different aspect of "fullness of orders" is mentioned as the chapter moves to a description of the individual bishop. Here there is mention of the bishop being "marked with the fullness of the sacrament,"[9] which singles him out as the high priest who in celebration of the Eucharist functions as a unifying symbol for the local church and a symbol also of the larger Christian Church. It is the bishop who is *the* offerer of eucharistic worship and therefore has the role of regulating all eucharistic practice. Through his role in sacraments, through preaching the gospel, through all his prayer and works the bishop channels the fullness of Christ's holiness to his people.

4. Even if *Lumen gentium*'s discussion of episcopacy focuses on the sacred power of the bishop, that power associated with his high priesthood, the power of jurisdiction connected with episcopal rule is never far from view. This is clear when (27) the *sacred* power in question is described as "proper, ordinary, and immediate, although its exercise is ultimately regulated by the supreme authority of the Church . . ." Such language places us squarely in the context of jurisdiction; the remainder of the passage confirms the point. In the conciliar view, "fullness of orders" seems to involve not only what classically was associated with

----

[7]However, the integration is simplified if one sees the bishops' power to sanctify as flowing directly from the possession of official authority; but this is an element of soteriology that requires examination.

[8]For the need to stress increasingly the collegial side of this tension, cf. K. Rahner, "Towards a fundamental theological interpretation of Vatican II," *Theological Studies* 40 (1979): 726.

[9]At this point in the text there is no direct mention of "the sacramental character of ordination" but the "mark" mentioned in this passage does seem to carry that implication, especially since there had been an earlier (21) clear statement: ". . . et sacrum characterem ita imprimi ut Episcopi . . . in Eius persona agant." *AAS* 57 (1965): 31.

potestas ordinis but also that indicated by *potestas jurisdictionis*.[10] Indeed, the council situates jurisdiction increasingly within the realm of the "sacred powers" previously identified with the "power of orders".[11] Acting as Christ's vicar, bishops have the "sacred duty to make laws for their subjects, to pass judgment on them, and to moderate everything pertaining to the ordering of worship and the apostolate. The pastoral office or the habitual and daily care of their sheep is entrusted to them completely." (27)

5. One element of Vatican II's understanding of the fullness of episcopal power comes into somewhat sharper perspective if we inquire how the unmitigated claim to *full* episcopal possession of ministerial power is compatible with the council's statements that the laity have a share in Christian ministry that is properly their own (31). It would seem that there is no possibility for something, namely the particular role of the laity, to be added to the all-embracing and total role in which the hierarchical college acts for Christ himself. The solution may lie in the distinction (which incidentally has frequently functioned in statements of Pope John Paul II) between two spheres of activity: the bishops' ministry is a *sacred* one that deals directly with God's own saving activity, whereas the laity are meant to deal with the secular world as their proper arena, preparing it for the eventual acceptance of God's saving grace in Christ.[12] There is a constant use of the adjective "sacred" to describe the bishops' role and power and activity.

Summary. It seems that the fathers of Vatican II, without wishing to give any doctrinal clarification of the matter, teach that what is conferred by sacramental ordination is possessed and exercised *fully* by the episcopal college and by any individual bishop in virtue of his communion with this *collegium*. The element that is uppermost in

---

[10]For recent discussion of the relation of these two *potestates* cf. J. Cuneo, "The Power of Jurisdiction: Empowerment for Church Functioning and Mission distinct from the Power of Orders," THE JURIST 39 (1979): 183-219.

[11]This seems to fit into the historical development in which, as the claims to and exercise of temporal jurisdiction diminished through political changes in Europe, ecclesiastical claims (especially by the Papacy) to authority shifted increasingly to teaching and sanctifying.

[12]Such limitation of properly lay activity to the realm of "the secular" runs counter to what *Lumen gentium* itself (33) speaks of as the role of lay people: "The lay apostolate, however, is a participation in the saving mission of the Church itself. Through their baptism and confirmation, all are commissioned to that apostolate by the Lord himself." This position is reiterated in the decree on the laity *Apostolicam actuositatem*, e.g. 3-6. But this decree does stress the laity's special role "ad extra": "The laity must take on the renewal of the temporal order as their own special obligation" (7).

Vatican II's view of "the fullness of the sacrament of orders" is Christian high priesthood, though this is inseparable from the teaching and ruling aspects of the pastoral office which a given bishop exercises for his church (and the *collegium* exercises for the entire Church) as Christ's vicar, *in persona Christi*.

DOGMATIC AUTHORITY

To what extent, then, does Vatican II's *Constitution on the Church* contain normative teaching that sets the limits within which change of ministerial structure can occur in Roman Catholicism? First, the strict dogmatic issue must be settled by going beyond Vatican II itself: the council fathers propose their text as teaching but not as solemn teaching.[13] In matters pertaining to relative powers in the Church they rest upon Vatican I in large part, in matters concerning Christian sacraments they draw from Trent.[14] So, the dogmatic status of texts from these two councils that carry over into Vatican II must be evaluated in their original *Sitz im Leben* as well as in their usage (or modification) by Vatican II. Secondly, in the delicate task of situating all this in the centuries-long history of Christian tradition and process of doctrinal development, the text of *Lumen gentium* (and the process from which it emerged) provides relatively little assistance, since the utilization of biblical and patristic sources is governed by the proof-text mentality and takes little account of critical textual or historical methodologies.[15] Thirdly, the statements of Vatican II (and the understandings that produced them) rest on a number of theological and doctrinal presuppositions whose verifiability conditions the normative force of the council's teaching.[16] The remainder of this essay will be directed to

[13]Foundation for the normative limitation on changes within the Church, if there is such, would have to be the element of "divine institution" of the episcopacy; and it is precisely on this point that the text (20) says: ". . . this sacred synod teaches that by divine institution bishops have succeeded to the place of the apostles as shepherds of the Church . . ." Cf. K. Rahner, *Commentary*, p. 191.

[14]The council text itself indicates this in the notes relating to the key sections of chapter 3.

[15]As an alternative approach to many of the same texts, cf. the historical portions of my *Ministry to Word and Sacraments*, which try to give a contextual understanding of the biblical and patristic statements relative to episcopacy and Christian ministry.

[16]Christian faith today is to be guided by the *faith* of earlier councils more ultimately than by the (historically relativized) expressions of that faith found in council statements. Trent's discussion of original sin and its removal by baptism provides a classic instance of the need to distinguish between the truth attached to underlying faith insights

reflection on some of these theological issues. Mere listing of them makes it evident that the understanding of "fullness of orders" lies close to the center of present-day ecclesiology and soteriology.

THEOLOGICAL QUESTIONS

1. Vatican II's approach to episcopal power brings us immediately into contact with the tension between differing "models" for thinking about the Church. Both New Testament scholarship and emphasis on the Church as a community that lives by faith have brought to the fore an "organic" model—the Church as Body of Christ, animated by the Spirit, growing into eschatological fulfillment by increasing participation in the new life of the risen Lord.[17] Yet, the "hierarchical" model, whether stressing its more political aspect or its "causation from above" aspect, is quite clearly that which controlled the bishops' understanding of themselves at Vatican II. Now, one need not, probably should not, opt for only one model as *the* way of thinking about the Church—the Pauline mixture of body/building/bride imagery indicates this. Yet, it does make a basic difference whether one views the Spirit as working "from outside" upon the community through the mediation of the hierarchy who to some extent stand above the faithful, or whether the Spirit is viewed as working from within the community and as "the mission of the Church," bringing into being those agencies (including the bishops) that are needed for the Church's life and priestly ministry. Again, it makes considerable difference whether one uses a "participation" or a "*communio*" model for understanding the sharing of Christian ministry.[18] And it does make a difference in

---

and the truth of those interpretative elements that influence a given formulation of that faith: contained in any Tridentine statement about baptism removing original sin is the understanding that there was an actual historical happening in which two historic personages, our "first parents," performed a gravely sinful act. The truth or falsity of this understanding clearly affects the normative role of Tridentine statements about baptism (and original sin); we are driven to seek the deeper norm of Tridentine faith in baptism as salvation from sin.

[17]Cf. A. Dulles, *Models of the Church* (Garden City: Doubleday, 1974).

[18]This is not to say that one identifies the missionary teleology of the Church with the Spirit; rather, the Spirit is the indwelling though transcendent principle of that teleology. On the N.T. roots of this view, cf. James D. G. Dunn, *Jesus and the Spirit* (Philadelphia: Westminster, 1975). It would make an interesting theological study to combine Dunn's insights with the various points of view expressed in the Canon Law Society's seminar on the Church as *mission* (published in THE JURIST 39 [1979]: 1-288).

appraising the normative force of official teaching about the nature of the Church to be conscious that these official statements are employing one or other model. Even if such statements do legitimately and rather accurately reflect the reality of the Church, they do not do so adequately.[19]

2. Interlocking somewhat with this shift in models is the dialectic between function and institutional structure, a dialectic that exists both in reality and in our view of that reality.[20] For a variety of reasons, recent theological thought has moved away from a long-standing attention to the structures and dealt more with processes. The change in approach has affected all facets of theological consideration, from trinity to eschatology.

The ecclesiological explanation one gives of the relation between form and function will ground any judgment about the continuity or discontinuity of structures such as the episcopate. Moreover, it will radically affect the way in which one interprets the historical evolution of tradition in the Church. Diversity of viewpoints on this matter underlies much of the Reformation and post-Reformation controversy about the nature of the Church and of its ministering agencies.

Because function and form are inseparable in the actual historical reality of the Church, the view one takes of their relationship conditions one's understanding of the Church's history.[21] And to that extent it conditions the judgment one makes about the necessity or contingency of any particular ecclesistical institution.

3. To make the last remark more precise, one could point to the ambiguity of *koinonia* in Acts 2: does it denominate the observable social reality of the early Christian community or the process of sharing that unites them?[22] Closer to our present discussion would be the

[19]What this means is that the principle *Ecclesia semper reformanda* has to be applied to the cognitive order, and that the complementarity intrinsic to genuine religious pluralism must be respected as an asset to faith.

[20]For an interesting and productive application of this dialectic cf. the December 1976 issue of *Theological Studies*, especially the interacting articles of R. Haight and R. Sears.

[21]For the most part, histories of the Church have concentrated on the structural elements and on official activities; there is surprisingly little historical study of the faith and prayer and inner spiritual life of the Christian people, even little study of the activities of evangelization or sacramental celebration. Even exceptions like H. Bremond's classic on the "French school" deal more with the more notable expressions of Christian faith and do not describe the spiritual state of the community as a whole.

[22]Cf. R. P. C. Hanson, *The Acts* (Oxford: Oxford University Press, 1967), p. 70, note 42; E. Haenchen, *Apostelgeschichte* (Goettingen, 1961), pp. 152-153.

multivalence of the key term *munus*[23] which is the operative word in Vatican II discussion of the episcopal function. In itself *munus* can refer to a responsibility or function whether societally stabilized or not, though it tends to denominate something fairly permanent.[24] It can, of course, refer to a publicly (even legally) established role and authority, in which case it can be translated "office."

This imprecision of *munus* carries over into present discussion of Christian ministry. For one thing, questions are being raised about the appropriateness of jurisdictional power in the Church, especially when this notion is applied to teaching and sanctifying.[25] Responding to such challenges (which obviously touch the Catholic episcopacy's claim to fullness of orders), some theologians, Karl Rahner among them,[26] stress the intrinsic need for structure and order in any on-going human society. Such a response does not really come to grips with the issue. Granted that enduring human communities need some stable, even explicitly established institutions, including some recognized leadership roles, this need not involve jurisdiction. An educational institution, for example, *only accidentally* (for purposes of service and management) includes some jurisdictional functions and roles—though often this principle is forgotten as education becomes controlled and administrators conduct themselves as rulers. Essentially, achievement

[23]The word *officium* occurs three times in the chapter (25, 26, 28), but with the meaning of "duty," not as an alternative to *munus*; what does occur as something of an equivalent for *munus* is *ministerium*.

[24]*Oxford Latin Dictionary*, edit. P. Glare (Oxford: Clarendon, 1976), p. 1146.

[25]Given the importance of the notion for the thesis of this present essay, it might be well to clarify the meaning of "jurisdiction" as used here. Basically, the historical use of the term grew out of the legal function of *passing judgment*, especially in Roman law. Christian ecclesiastical use broadened that meaning to the more general sense of "the power to govern." Mörsdorf in the article on jurisdiction in *Lexikon für Theologie und Kirche*, col. 1220, sees the church usage as including the classic three functions: legislative, executive and judicial (*Gesetzgebung, Rechtsprechung, Verwaltung*); and in his article in *Sacramentum Mundi*, K. Rahner, C. Ernst, K. Smyth, eds. (New York: Herder and Herder, 1969), vol. 3, p. 229, he points out that jurisdiction is intrinsically linked to *office*. So, it is quite clear that the notion of jurisdiction is one that belongs to a legal/political model for the Church, i.e. to a particular context and manner of governing. There are many other ways of guiding and directing a community, even other ways of governing; jurisdiction (as we have just described it) is an appropriate way of governing the Church only if the legal/political model is an appropriate way of understanding the nature of the Church.

[26]See, for example, "Aspects of the Episcopal Office," *Theological Investigation* 14, p. 188: "The existence of this office is justified, rather, on the grounds that in the concrete it constitutes the legitimate and, in the long run historically speaking, indispensable way of ensuring the necessary continuity of the community of Jesus with its origins."

of a school's purpose and the leadership guiding that achievement are grounded in the knowledge possessed by the teachers and in their pedagogical skills; that is its own kind of authority, but quite other than official jurisdiction. One can find examples also in the religious sphere. Enduring religious communities, such as Rabbinic Judaism or Zen Buddhism, have functioned with leadership that is other than jurisdictional.

Given the difficulties involved in unifying the millions of humans who comprise the Catholic Church, it may be strategically prudent, perhaps practically necessary, to introduce some jurisdictional government into the Church's life. But if so, these institutionalized functions are not those through which the Church primarily attains its goals. It does the latter through other authority and other ministry: the authority and ministry of faith correctly understood, accurately communicated in teaching, and authentically witnessed to in sacrament. Some governing may be helpful in enabling the Church's ministry to the saving Word and Spirit of God; this governing is not the heart nor the source of such ministry.[27]

Without retreating from the view that some governing function may well be required in the Church—a charism of governing has been recognized from Christianity's beginnings as a gift of the Spirit to the community[28]—we might begin to stress more the need for unifying *leadership* within the Church. Such leadership is distinct from official administration or legal regulation, though there is still a widespread presumption in the Church that they are meant to coincide. At the same time there is a centuries-old tension in Christianity, which has remained one of the principal sources of potential division, between the leadership of office and the leadership of sanctity.[29] Given the oft-remarked shift in the nature of leadership in today's world, the new modes and worldwide scope of communication which have qualitatively altered the manner in which the symbolic aspects of leadership can influence people, and the fact that in discussing episcopal fullness of orders we are dealing with a sacramental (i.e. symbolic) reality, it

[27]Obviously, this runs counter to the soteriological view that salvation can be effected precisely through *official* power.

[28]Cf. 1 Cor. 12:28.

[29]I have tried to examine this issue at various points in my *Ministry to Word and Sacraments*, not just in the context of recurrent Donatism, but also as part of the differentiation between Latin and Eastern Christianity and part of a continuing tension between episcopacy and religious orders.

seems that we need serious and detailed theological discussion about the ministry of leadership within the Church.[30]

4. Any Catholic analysis of the sacramental aspect of ministry raises rather quickly the question of the priestly identity of the hierarchy. Though *Lumen gentium* speaks of the high priesthood of the bishops as axiomatic, the history of the first two Christian centuries raises serious questions about this claim.[31] But even if one accepts the legitimacy of such an attribution, there is need to ask what it means. On the basis of the classical explanation, the priestly role possessed in fullness by the hierarchy consists in (a) worship and (b) sanctification of the people.

Clearly, one's interpretation of episcopal priesthood rests on a given understanding of the nature of Christian worship, above all on a particular understanding of the eucharistic act. This is not the place to suggest any given approach to eucharistic theology. But it does make a great deal of difference in our understanding of the bishops' high priesthood whether we see Eucharist as an action of the entire community as Body of Christ, or whether we view it as the action of the celebrant attended by the people; whether we see it as an enactment of a sacred somewhat hidden mystery, or as the celebration of the community's daily experience of being humanly Christian.[32] Any claim to a privileged role in Christian worship is, then, basically relativized by the nature of the worship in question, and any theological insight into the bishops' high priesthood is conditioned radically by one's theology of Christian worship. Again, the distinctiveness of the bishops' power as *sacred* power is certainly affected by current theological reflection on

---

[30]Such study would have to examine in depth the symbolic role of the bishops. This has already begun with recent reflection upon episcopal power as essentially *sacramental*. Karl Rahner has increasingly stressed this aspect of the episcopal function, which is significant in the light of his strong emphasis also on the juridical aspect of episcopacy. Cf. *Theological Investigation* 12, pp. 44-45. This stress on the sacramental aspect is, of course, completely in line with Rahner's view of the Church's role as expressed in his *The Church and the Sacraments* (New York: Herder and Herder, 1963). On the evolution of Rahner's ecclesiology, cf. L. O'Donovan, M. Fahey, P. Schineller, J. Galvin, "A Changing Ecclesiology in a Changing Church," *Theological Studies* 38 (1977): 736-762.

[31]Cf. bibliography accompanying pp. 523-553 in Cooke, *Ministry*.

[32]Vatican II's constitution on the liturgy points towards increased emphasis on the human aspects of Eucharistic celebration; without denying an element of "mystery" in Christian sacraments, it stresses the pastoral need for sacraments (especially Eucharist) to be easily intelligible to people and to relate to Christians' daily lives.

the relationship of sacred and secular, both in life and in worship.[33]

The second element in Vatican II's description of episcopal priesthood is the bishops' power to sanctify the faithful, particularly through administration of sacrament. Not only does the understanding of this sanctifying activity rest on a view of the way in which sacraments function; it rests on a particular soteriology. But, quite noticeably, a revolutionary development is taking place today in our soteriology—in our understanding of "grace," "divine providence," the presence of God to history, "resurrection," etc. For one thing, there has been renewed recognition that the individual person must be the principal human agent of his or her own salvation. This changing view of the reality of God's saving action in human life is already having major impact on Catholics' practical attitudes towards the ordained ministry; and probably the impact will grow.

One element of soteriology prominent in Vatican II's description of episcopal ministry is the notion that the bishop acts *in persona Christi* (*Lumen gentium*, 21). This expression has received various interpretations historically (e.g. the bishop is a sacrament of Christ, or is a legate of Christ); but all concur that the bishops, particularly as sacramental celebrants, somehow signify to the people Christ's own presence. Through the bishop Christ makes himself salvifically present to the faithful; somehow the bishop embodies this presence.[34] However, such a view of the bishop acting *in persona Christi* has long stood in tension with the view that the liturgical celebrant acts *in persona ecclesiae*. This more ecclesial view of the celebrant's role has recently received increased attention and acceptance among Catholic theologians. Edward Kilmartin, for instance, in his 1975 article in *Theological Studies*, makes a convincing case for the position that the bishop sacramentalizes first and foremost the faith of the community.[35] Such a view points to those statements of *Lumen gentium* that speak of the Church in its entirety as the sacrament of the risen Christ.[36]

---

[33]Developments in "theologies of liberation" are perhaps the most striking example: it is precisely in the domain of "secular" activity (political, social, economic involvement) that the intervention of God's saving (sacral) action is seen to occur.

[34]Though grounded in the theology of Augustine and Chrysostom, the formal theology of the *sacerdotium* (bishops and presbyters) sacramentalizing Christ's presence is largely a medieval creation; cf. pp. 575-582 in Cooke, *Ministry*.

[35]E. Kilmartin, "Apostolic Office: Sacrament of Christ," *Theological Studies* 36 (1975): 243-264. On the historical use of *in persona Christi* cf. B.-D. Marliangeas, *Clés pour une théologie du ministère* (Paris: Beauchesne, 1978); also Cooke, *Ministry*, pp. 574-590, 609-610.

[36]Cf. *LG* 7-8, 38-39.

This is not to deny a genuine sacramentality to the episcopate; it is just a question of *what* is salvifically signified. While this may seem an abstruse bit of theoretical distinction, it actually has great bearing on the objectives and therefore the practice of liturgical ceremonies. Vatican II apparently wished to link the episcopal office and episcopal power most basically to the sacramental order: the fullness of the sacrament of orders; it is the fullness that comes precisely with episcopal ordination. Since the council, theologians have picked up this clue and given increased attention to the sacramental dimension of the episcopate. Not only is episcopal power rooted in sacrament; episcopal power is itself sacramental power, the episcopacy is meant to function as sacraments function.[37]

If this line of thinking about the episcopate is legitimate—and Vatican II seems quite clearly to support, even encourage, it—it means that the principal source of episcopal effectiveness lies in the bishops' *operative significance*, in what they symbolize to the Church as a whole and beyond that to the world. The power involved in such an exercise of ministry operates within the realm of faith, precisely that faith which makes the risen Christ and his Spirit present to and transformative of human life. Because the preservation of authentic faith, grounded in the original apostolic experience of Jesus as the Christ and evolving through centuries of Christian discipleship, is critical to Christianity's very existence, the bishops function as a central and sacramental witness to their collegially-shared faith which in turn reflects the faith shared by Christians throughout space and time. Such a role involves real power, real authority; but it is the authority and power of faith (sacramentally expressed) in the Word and Spirit of God, the authority and power of religious commitment to the establishment of God's rule of justice and peace. Such a role is truly a unifying force in the life of Christian communities and in all exercise of Christian ministry; but it unifies in the way that key societal symbols (including symbolic people) integrate and dynamize human communities.

Such a role finds paramount expression in sacramental liturgy where the celebrant's profession of his (and the episcopal college's) faith activates, enriches, grounds, and unifies the faith of the assembled people,

---

[37]"In the bishops . . . our Lord Jesus Christ, the supreme High Priest, is present in the midst of those who believe . . . He is not absent from the gathering of His high priests, but above all through their excellent service He is preaching the Word of God to all nations, and constantly administering the sacraments of faith to those who believe." *LG* 21.

helping to shape them into an actively worshipping community that becomes in this act of liturgical worship more intensely believing and more thoroughly dedicated to christian ministry, i.e. more fully the Body of Christ. The word "fullness" can be truly used to describe the sacramental power of the episcopate, because it is the collegial dimension of the bishop's witness (in liturgy as well as in other expressions of episcopal concern for the faith and life of people) that points to the faith of the *entire* Church. The special power exerted by the bishop comes from the public nature of his faith witness as a recognized (ordained) member of the episcopal college.

6. Any discussion about the "fullness of orders" and the claim of the bishops to possess such a fullness leads us inevitably to examine the origin of episcopacy as an institutionalized structure in the Church. In Catholic circles this has for centuries centered around the doctrine (scarcely ever challenged) that the episcopacy is *de jure divino.* It was instituted by Jesus himself in the choice of his twelve closest disciples whose function and authority (i.e. office) the bishops inherit by unbroken historical succession. It all seemed so simple to prove: the New Testament literature testifies to Jesus' choice and empowerment of the Twelve; the Pastorals witness to handing on of office; and historical evidences to the process of succession are traced back to the first Clementine letter, Ignatius, Irenaeus, Hegesippus and Eusebius. But things are not so simple and direct as they had seemed. Modern critical scholarship has raised a number of issues that Catholic teaching must honestly face if it is justifiably to maintain the claims it has made for the episcopacy's origin and authority.

Perhaps the most basic question raised for us by critical study of the historical evidence is: what exactly did Jesus do that might be seen as "the institution of the episcopacy"? It is highly unlikely that he actually empowered the Twelve with a discernible office in a religious community or even granted them authority as the basis for the emergence of such an office. As a matter of fact, though there is no possible verification in such questions, it is rather unlikely that Jesus himself thought of establishing an institutionalized religious body. Even if one maintains, as genuine Catholic belief does, that Jesus Christ did institute the Church, the essence of such institution was his dying and rising. What preceded death and resurrection was somehow an integral element in Jesus' role (not just "preliminaries") and pertained to the action of institution, but the manner in which it pertained remains to be clarified—though we know enough to know that earlier simplistic statements should not be repeated.[38]

Also, historical study raises questions about the actual emergence of episcopal structures from the Twelve. Careful study of the New Testament gives us no basis for saying that any of the Twleve functioned as an *episkopos*; nor is there any foundation for the contention that the various episcopal sees came into existence by branching off from sees begun by Jesus' own Apostles. At the very least, Catholic explanations of the present episcopacy's links to the Twelve will have to be modified in a way that takes account of responsible critical scholarship.

One of the needed adjustments in understanding has to do with the notion of "institution by Christ" and the closely related notion of *de jure divino*.[39] Really, to see "institution" as something not limited to actions of the historical Jesus would accord quite well with the basic Catholic view that the ongoing historical life of the Church is an essentially positive growth of a community directed by God. The activity of Christ that might be seen as "institution of the Church" pertains more to that post-resurrectional period in which, present to the Church through his Spirit, the risen Lord works continuously to bring into being whatever can serve the advance of the kingdom of God. Even if (which, of course, is not the case) the episcopacy had not come into existence until the sixth century, this would not necessarily mean that one could not see its emergence as resulting from divine institution.

Karl Rahner has made this point quite forcibly. Though several diverse patterns of church order may well have existed side by side in primitive Christianity, and it may have taken some time for the Church to realize what form was most in accord with its nature, this does not mean that a structure such as the episcopacy after having once emerged as the universal and recognized form is not thereafter a perennial and necessary element of institutionalized Christianity. The *de jure divino* claim for the episcopacy is not grounded on some explicit establishment by Jesus himself, but on the fact that it is a necessary means of ensuring that the believing community throughout history will remain in contact with its origins. Though the circumstances of the hierarchy's

[38]For a review of some of the recent theological study of the relationship of Jesus' life, death, and resurrection to one another, cf. J. Galvin, "Jesus' Approach to Death: An Examination of some Recent Studies," *Theological Studies* 41 (1980): 713-744.

[39]For a survey and analysis of much of present discussion of *ius divinum* cf. A. Dulles, "*Ius divinum* as Ecumenical Problem," *Theological Studies* 38 (1977): 681-708.

origin were historically contingent, this does not mean that the episcopacy is a contingent element of the Church's existence.[40]

Applying this understanding to an episcopacy that historically claimed and exercised jurisdictional authority according to a *monarchical* model[41], one has to raise a basic question: is it possible for there to emerge, as an element attributable to the Spirit's influence, something that is contradictory to Jesus' (and primitive Christianity's) understanding of "the kingdom of God"? The question would seem to demand a negative answer: Catholic theology is faced with the need to resolve earliest Christianity's repudiation of dominative authority (starting with Jesus' rejection of a political interpretation of Messiahship) and the historical episcopate's claim to monarchical power of rule. Simply put: episcopal fullness of power cannot relate to anything other than that kind of power that is appropriate to the Church as agent of God's kingdom and extension of Jesus' own exercise of power. But what kind of power did Jesus himself claim and exercise, and how did earliest Christianity understand itself and its leadership to be empowered? What emerges in the historical episcopate is at least partially of a different order. The question is: can this *different* element be seen as an organic outgrowth of what begins with Jesus, or can it even be seen as intrinsically reconcilable with Jesus' own establishment of the kingdom? Understanding and justification of episcopal "fullness of orders" and its relationship to the broader reality of Christian ministry presuppose a clearer knowledge of the continuity between Jesus and the bishops than we now possess.

Given this element of uncertainty, what conclusions can one draw in the practical order? Certainly, the ministerial activities of Catholics should be carried on with regard for continuity with the deepest levels of tradition; we should cherish our history and remain constantly open to learning from our present experience. In the overall endeavor of the community, theology has a specific task: not to legitimate or defend either the past or the new, but to examine critically by research and

---

[40]K. Rahner, "Reflection on the Concept of 'jus divinum' in Catholic Thought," *Theological Investigations* 5, pp. 226-240; "The Episcopal Office", *Theological Investigations* 6, pp. 313-360.

[41]In his "Open Questions in Dogma Considered by the Institutional Church as Definitively Answered," *Journal of Ecumenical Studies* 15 (1978): 211-226, Karl Rahner proposes the possibility that the episcopal office need not be exercised by an individual. It seems that this would move us away from *monarchy*, but still leave us within the political model for understanding the governing power proper to the Church.

reflection that stream of belief and devotion and life that flows from Jesus himself up to and beyond the present. More specifically, this means a serious study of the *sacramentality* of the episcopal college, a clear analysis of the *authority* intrinsic to the ministries (or ministries), and a candid examination of the kind of *power* that is appropriately exercised in the Church.

CLERGY, LAITY, AND THE CHURCH'S
MISSION IN THE WORLD

JOSEPH A. KOMONCHAK
The Catholic University of America

In December, 1977, forty-seven members of the Roman Catholic Church in Chicago issued a brief document entitled "The Chicago Declaration of Christian Concern."[1] In brief, the Declaration expressed regret that since the Second Vatican Council, the distinct and proper roles and responsibilities of the laity had ceased to be appreciated and promoted. Instead, the advancement of the laity in the Church had taken the form of their greater "participation in work traditionally assigned to priests and sisters"; "lay ministry" had come to be seen as "involvement in some church related activity." Meanwhile, "the unique ministry of lay men and women," which is "essentially the service performed within one's professional and occupational milieu," not only had been neglected but had in many cases been taken over by the clergy and religious. A new clericalism threatened, this time from the left. Priests and religious no longer saw their role as encouraging the laity to assume their proper responsibility "to transform the world of political, economic and social institutions." They often neglected the laity and undertook that task themselves. The result had been not only the decline of the many organizations which had formerly promoted the mission of the laity in the world, but a depreciation of the role of the ordinary layperson in his worldly occupation and even, perhaps, "the loss of a generation of lay leadership." The Declaration ended with an expression of concern:

> In the last analysis, the Church speaks to and acts upon the world through her laity. Without a dynamic laity conscious of its personal ministry to the world, the Church in effect, does not speak or act. No amount of social action by priests and religious can ever be an adequate substitute for enhancing lay responsibility. The absence of lay initiative can only take us down the

---

[1] The Declaration may be found, along with commentaries, in R. Barta, ed., *Challenge to the Laity*, (Huntington, Ind.: Our Sunday Visitor, 1980), and in *Commonweal* 105 (1978): 109-16.

road to clericalism. We are deeply concerned that so little energy is devoted to encouraging and arousing lay responsibility for the world. The Church must constantly be reformed, but we fear that the almost obsessive preoccupation with the church's structures and processes has diverted attention from the essential question: reform for what purpose? It would be one of the great ironies of history if the era of Vatican II which opened the windows of the Church to the world were to close with a Church turned in upon herself.

The Chicago Declaration aroused a good deal of mixed comment, not least of all because among its signers were leaders of lay movements before the council and many other figures known to be sympathetic to the conciliar reforms. Even among those who did not agree with the Declaration's basic position, there often was agreement that it addressed a genuine problem in the post-conciliar Church. Nor is the Declaration the only expression of the concern.

Since he became pope, John Paul II has made the Church's right to promote social justice and peace a prominent part of his ministry and message. The social, political, and economic conditions of the many countries he has visited have regularly been brought under the judgement of the Christian gospel. But in his many addresses the Pope has also warned several times of the danger of confusing the respective roles of the clergy, religious, and laity with regard to the Church's social mission. The Pope's speeches in Mexico in 1979 are typical. He reminded the bishops at Puebla that, according to the council, "secular duties and activities belong properly, although not exclusively, to laymen." He went on:

It is necessary to avoid supplanting the laity, and to study seriously just when certain ways of substituting for them retain their *raison d'être*. Is it not the laity who are called, by virtue of their vocation in the Church, to make their contribution in the political and economic areas, and to be effectively present in the safeguarding and advancing of human rights?[2]

Similar remarks were addressed to priests:

You are not social directors, political leaders or functionaries of

[2]Pope John Paul II, "Opening Address at the Puebla Conference," III, 7, cited from J. Eagleson and P. Scharper, eds., *Puebla and Beyond: Documentation and Commentary*, (Maryknoll: Orbis, 1979), p. 69.

a temporal power. So I repeat to you: Let us not pretend to
serve the gospel if we try to "dilute" our charism through an
exaggerated interest in the broad field of temporal problems.
. . . Do not forget that temporal leadership can easily become a
source of division, while the priest should be a sign and factor of
unity, of brotherhood. The secular functions are the proper field
of action of the laity, who ought to perfect temporal matters
with a Christian spirit.[3]

Pope John Paul has repeated these positions on several occasions
since 1979[4] and he has taken steps to discourage and prohibit priests
from continuing direct political activity, the best known cases being
those of Fr. Robert Drinan and the priests involved in the government
of Nicaragua. The Pope's position is a complex one, aimed at avoiding
several dangers: the reduction of the gospel to political purposes or
programs, confusing the Christian principles of social action with particular ideologies, the usurpation of the laity's proper role, the com-
promising of the unifying role of the priest, and the loss to both
Church and world of the witness to the transcendent given by religious.
He does not entirely preclude the possibility of clergy and religious
engaging in social and political activities; but it is clear that for him
these activities are typically the role of the laity.

In both the Chicago Declaration and in the speeches of the Pope,
several issues are involved. First, there is the canonical and theological
distinction between clergy and laity. Second, there are the customary
assumptions about their respective roles, which need not be what the
canonical and theological definitions would lead one to expect. Third,
there is the Church-world relationship as defined theologically. And,
finally, there is the Church-world relationship as in fact realized in the
remote and proximate past and in the contemporary situation. This
essay will address these issues in the course of an exposition and
critique of Vatican II's teaching on the laity and on the Church's
mission in the world.

VATICAN II ON THE LAITY

Two different approaches to the clergy-laity distinction and relationship are visible in the conciliar documents. The first of these is canonical, reflecting "the divine and hierarchical structure of the Church"

---

[3]Pope John Paul II, "Address to Priests in Mexico City," *Origins* 8 (1979): 548-549.
[4]See *Origins* 10 (1980-81): 10-12, 15-16, 136.

(LG 43). From this perspective there is a twofold differentiation among the members of the Church, that between the ordained clergy and all others. Thus, the religious life is not "an intermediate state between the clerical and lay condition; rather some Christians from both groups are called by God to enjoy a special gift of grace in the life of the Church" (LG 43). Canonically and hierarchically, then, there are only two conditions of Christian life, the clerical and the lay.

A second approach is visible when the Council goes on to say of the religious state that, "while it does not enter into the hierarchical structure of the Church, it belongs undeniably to her life and holiness" (LG 44).[5] The concrete self-realization of the Church is not adequately described solely in terms of its hierarchical differentiation. The neat twofold distinction is disturbed by the presence of religious who may be either clergy or laity in the canonical sense.

But there is a further complication when the life of all three groups, clergy, religious, and laity, is looked at more concretely. Now again there is a twofold differentiation, but now it is between clergy and religious on the one hand and the laity on the other. This distinction appears in *Lumen Gentium* 31, where the Council explained at length what it understood by the term, "the laity."[6]

The term is first explained by means of a negative delimitation: "The term 'the laity' is here understood to mean all the faithful except the members of a holy order or of a religious state approved by the Church." This is immediately followed by a positive description: the laity are "the faithful who, incorporated into Christ by baptism, established in the People of God, and made in their own way sharers in the priestly, prophetical, and kingly office of Christ, exercise their own role in the mission of the whole Christian people in the Church and in the world." While this description is a fine statement of the dignity and responsibility of all Christians, laity included, it also clearly applies equally well to the clergy and religious. It was necessary, then for the council to state more precisely the distinctive character of the laity:

[5]The distinction between the "hierarchical structure" and the "life and holiness" of the Church recalls Yves Congar's attempt to construct a theology of the laity in terms of a distinction beween "structure" and "life"; see *Lay People in the Church: A Study for a Theology of Laity* (Westminster: Newman, 1954). Congar's theology had a visible influence on Vatican II's teaching on the laity.

[6]See E. Schillebeeckx, "The Typological Definition of the Christian Layman according to Vatican II," in *The Mission of the Church* (New York: Seabury, 1973), pp. 90-116.

A secular character is proper and peculiar to the laity. For members of a sacred order, although they can sometimes engage in secular affairs, even by practicing a secular profession, still by reason of their particular vocation are principally and expressly ordained to a sacred ministry. At the same time, religious by their state give outstanding and striking witness that the world cannot be transfigured and offered to God without the spirit of the beatitudes. As for the laity, it is their proper vocation to seek the Kingdom of God by engaging in temporal affairs and ordering them according to God's will. They live in the world, that is, they are engaged in each and every work and business of the earth and in the ordinary circumstances of social and family life which provide, as it were, the texture of their existence. There, in the world, they are called by God so that, led by the spirit of the gospel as they carry out their role, they may, like a leaven, contribute to the sanctification of the world as if from within and thus, resplendent especially by the witness of their life, by faith, hope and love, they may manifest Christ to others. It belongs to the laity in a peculiar way to illuminate and to order all temporal things, with which they are so closely associated, in such a way that they may be realized and grow according to Christ and may be for the glory of the Creator and Redeemer (LG 31).

This secular character of the lay Christian life is presupposed in the remainder of this chapter where the council explains how the laity have roles in the twofold task of establishing and building up the Church and of ordering the world according to God's will. So, for example, the lay apostolate is "a participation in the very saving mission of the Church," and it is their "special vocation . . . to make the Church present in those places and situations in which only through them can the Church be the salt of the earth" (LG 33). The laity exercise their share in Christ's threefold office in the ordinary circumstances of the world, where in fact it is they who have "the principal role" in bringing the world to its goal in justice, love and peace (LG 36).

This teaching is echoed in the Decree on the Apostolate of the Laity, which begins with a programmatic statement:

In the Church there is a diversity of ministry but a unity of mission. To the apostles and their successors Christ entrusted the office of teaching, sanctifying and governing in his name and by his power. But the laity, made sharers in Christ's priestly, prophetical, and kingly office, carry out their roles in the mission of the whole People of God in the Church and in the world. In reality, they exercise their apostolate by their work for the evangelization and sanctification of people and by their efforts to make the spirit of the gospel permeate and perfect the temporal order, so that their efforts in this area may bear clear witness to Christ and serve the salvation of people. But, since it is proper to the lay state that they lead their lives in the midst of the world and of secular affairs, laypeople are called by God in their Christian fervor to exercise their apostolate as a leaven in the world (AA 2).

Chapter II of this Decree, which is devoted to the objectives of the lay apostolate, begins by distinguishing two goals of Christ's redemption and of the Church's mission: salvation and the renewal of the whole temporal order (AA 5). The next two paragraphs vindicate the right of the laity to participate in this twofold purpose. The task of evangelization and sanctification, while "committed in a special way to the clergy," also is borne by the laity (AA 6). The whole Church is to work to renew the world, with pastors offering the principles and moral and spiritual assistance.

As for the laity, they have the proper responsibility to take on the restoration of the temporal order and, guided by the light of the gospel and the mind of the Church and prompted by Christian love, to act within that order directly and definitely. As citizens among other citizens, they cooperate with their specific competence and by their own responsibility; everywhere and always they are to seek the justice of the Kingdom of God (AA 7).

Later, the Decree states that "the apostolate in the social environment, that is, the effort to inform with the Christian spirit the mentality and behavior, laws and structures of the community in which one lives, is so much the duty and responsibility of the laity that it can never be properly fulfilled by others" (AA 13).

These descriptions of the laity's proper role in secular affairs should be seen against the background of the three basic concerns of these two conciliar documents.[7] The first was to vindicate the laity's right to share in the building up of the Church and in its central saving mission.

[7]See E. Schillebeeckx, "A New Type of Layman," in *The Mission of the Church*, pp. 117-131.

They were to be shown to be more than the passive objects of the clergy's ministrations.

The second concern was to clarify the nature and basis of the lay apostolate. The council asserted the sacramental and charismatic basis of that role. Christians were deputed by God himself, in virtue of their baptismal incorporation into Christ, to carry out their own role in the Church. Several possible types of relationship with the hierarchy were envisaged, of which Catholic Action and its "mandate" is only the strictest.[8] Essentially, a genuine initiative and autonomy was granted the lay apostolate.

Thirdly, the council wished to affirm the truly Christian and ecclesial character of the laity's daily secular activity. Laypeople are to act in the world as Christians; it is as workers, as married, as parents, that they serve Christ, and this activity, prior to any official ecclesiastical authorization, constitutes their ecclesial role. In turn, this involvement in the world grounds their contribution to the self-constitution of the Church. In the world they are to act as Christians. In the Chruch they are to speak and act as *laypeople*; *i.e.*, as persons whose secular involvement itself qualifies them to make a unique and irreplaceable contribution to the Church. As Schillebeeckx puts it:

> The layman's Christian relationship with the world colours his whole (active) being as a Christian—his life of prayer, his forms of faith, love and hope, his contribution as a non-office-bearer to the primary, religious mission of the Church and even his specifically lay collaboration with the hierarchy in their apostolate (either in an organized form or not).[9]

On the whole, then, the council sought to establish the Christian and ecclesial significance of the everyday life of the layperson as in itself a real share in Christ's and the Church's mission and to establish also that the Church itself, in its primary task of self-realization, needs from the laity precisely those insights, perceptions, orientations, which only life in the world makes likely or even possible.[10]

Before a theological critique of the council's statements on the laity can be offered, it is necessary to examine what precisely the council

---

[8]See P. Guilmot, *Fin d'une Église cléricale? Le débat en France de 1945 à nos jours* (Paris: du Cerf, 1969).

[9]Schillebeeckx, "Typological Definition," p. 115.

[10]As Guilmot and Schillebeeckx both show, the council's positions clearly reflect the state of the theology of the laity reached at the end of the 1950's.

intended to do in the fundamental paragraph (LG 31) in which it explained the term "laity." In the *Relatio* which introduced Chapter IV of *Lumen Gentium*, the council fathers were asked to note that "this chapter does not offer an *'ontological' definition* of the layperson, but rather a *'typological' description*," which was only to be taken "in the context of the matter and purpose of this schema."[11] A similar explanation introduced paragraph 31:

> The council does not intend to give a definition that would settle discussions in the schools, as, for example, whether religious and, *a fortiori*, members of a secular institute are to be considered laypersons and in what sense. Furthermore, the council is not proposing an "ontological" definition of the layperson, but rather a "typological" description.[12]

The statements on the secular character of the laity simply offered "a *typology of the layperson* in the world, as compared with clerics and religious."[13]

Because these clarifications of the council's intent are not always kept in mind in discussions since the council about clergy and laity, it is worthwhile pointing up some of their features. First, the council does not proceed from a definition of the "essence" of the lay condition (I take this to be what an "ontological" definition might offer). Instead, the council presents a "typological description." This appears to be a terminological innovation in church documents, and the *Relator* offered no help in explaining it. We are, it is clear, offered a description, and, it seems, a description of a type, that is, of what typifies a layperson's situation and activity. A layperson typically is married, has a job, lives in the world, etc.

Second, the source of this typification is clearly not metaphysical. It also seems not to be theological, at least not in the sense of some biblically, traditionally, or dogmatically required notion of the layperson. Not only does such a notion not exist, but the *Relator* made it clear that the text offered only a description and one which was not intended to settle disputed theological points, as, for example, whether the theological notion of a layperson coincides with the canonical. It remains, then, that the council offered simply a description that reflects

---

[11]*Acta Synodalia Sacrosancti Concilii Oecumenici Vaticani II*, III/III (Typis Polyglottis Vaticanis, 1974), p. 62.

[12]Ibid., III/I, p. 282.

[13]Ibid.

typical differentiations among the members of the Church that have become customary. As such, it would seem, the description need not necessarily apply to every previous age of the Church nor be considered to preclude future developments which might alter the customary typical differentiations of roles.

Third, like ideal-types in the social sciences, the council's descriptions admit exceptions. Laypeople can be quite closely involved, even in full-time occupations, in Church-internal activities; in exceptional circumstances, they may even be entrusted with offices normally reserved to the clergy.[14] Similarly, the clergy may occasionally be involved in secular affairs or have a secular occupation.[15]

Fourth, it can be asked whether, if the description of the lay person is only "typological," the same might not be true also of the descriptions of the clergy and religious, at least with regard to their secular involvement. If so, the council's typifications of the latter as *not* having a "secular character" could be regarded as having the force only of descriptions of customary role-distributions.

Acceptance of this suggestion is perhaps impeded by the council's use of the language of "states of life." The *Relator* explained that the phrase, "the state of those Christians called laypeople" (LG 30), was used rather than "condition and mission," so that "the laity would be acknowledged to have the honor of constituting a *state* in the Church, at least in a broad sense."[16] Neither here nor anywhere else did the council specify what it meant by a "state," a question on which both theologians and canonists have disagreed.[17]

But a perhaps unintended sociological consequence of conceiving clergy, religious, and laity as distinct "states of life" can be noted. The phrase can, of course, be used purely descriptively, to refer simply to different typical situations or conditions. But it can also easily become prescriptive, so that the typical or customary becomes normative. "States" then take on almost ontological status, and this can serve the useful purpose of legitimating the taken-for-granted and ensuring the

---

[14]See LG 33, 35; AA 24.

[15]See LG 31; PO 8; GS 43. See the *Relatio* for LG 36: "Although clergy and religious may sometimes exercise some 'lay' activity, especially to supply for certain deficiencies, in other words, in supplementary fashion, still, generally speaking, they cannot take the laity's place for this sort of activity" (*Acta Synodalia*, III/I, p. 288).

[16]*Acta Synodalia*, III/I, p. 218.

[17]See F. Klostermann, "The Laity," in H. Vorgrimler, ed., *Commentary on the Documents of Vatican II* (New York: Herder and Herder, 1967), I, p. 235.

continuance of the customary. "Ontological" definitions of the priest-hood and religious life are not uncommon at all.[18]

Other essays in this volume study the development and implications of an "ontologizing" of the "states of life"; here mention may be made of how it affects an understanding of the relationship between the various "states" and secular activity. Particular historical forms, say, of the priesthood are canonized and then provided with a theological legiti-mation which sees in them the very "essence" of the priesthood. The essence, determined prior to any set of concrete situations, on theolog-ical or canonical grounds, is then examined to determine the legitimacy of priests' involving themselves in particular types of behavior. Typical forms and characteristic behavior, which arose historically in response to particular conditions, now are removed from history, ontologized, and made normative for any conceivable set of circumstances, even ones quite different from those in which the typical forms and behavior first arose.

But if the *Relator*'s remarks about the merely typological character of the description of the laity can be extended also to the clergy and religious, then it would seem that the council's remarks about the latter need not be assigned prescriptive force. Certainly the council was at least describing typical relations between all three conditions and secu-lar activities. It was probably also intending to be prescriptive at least in the sense that the typifications were not considered to be inappro-priate in the past and, probably, for the future as the council saw it. It is legitimate at least to ask whether the councils' typifications continue to be appropriate; and an answer to that question will very much depend on an evaluation of the council's understanding of the relation-ship between the Church and the world.

VATICAN II ON CHURCH AND WORLD

It is by now a commonplace that the Second Vatican Council expressed a far more positive attitude towards the modern world than had been reflected in many earlier official statements and actions by Catholic authorities. This went beyond a mere acceptance that, after all, the Church was living in the twentieth century and ought finally to

[18]For perceptive comments on the effect of such an approach on contemporary discussions of ministry, see C. Duquoc, "Concepts of Ministry," *The Tablet* 350 (1979): 101-113. For the historical development, see E. Schillebeeckx, *Ministry: Leadership in the Community of Jesus Christ* (New York: Crossroad, 1981), esp. pp. 52-65.

give up all hope of the return of a vanished era. The council acknowledged a legitimate and proper secularization of the world and used the
word "autonomy" to refer to its effect.[19] It regularly sought to avoid
any suggestion that it wished to see the world and its affairs again
under the control of the Church or the clergy.[20] It acknowledged the
benefits the Church could receive from the world, many of which have
resulted from the very developments which have given the modern
world its distinctive character (GS 44). In this positive description of
the modern world it is not unjust to see a conciliar equivalent of the
"theology of secularization" which had its brief moment of glory
around the time the council was meeting.

The council's understanding of the relationship of the Church to the
world may be studied in its statements about what the Church is to do
in and for the world. Thus, according to *Lumen Gentium*, the laity are
to engage in temporal affairs in order to direct them in accordance with
God's will; by fulfilling their specific duties, laypeople will contribute to
the sanctification of the world; their efforts are so to illumine and order
temporal matters that these may be realized and grow according to
Christ and for the glory of God (LG 31). By their everyday activities,
the laity "consecrate the world itself to God" (LG 34). They work
"so that the world may be filled with the spirit of Christ and may the
more effectively attain its destiny in justice, love, and peace," Christ
himself by their efforts "illumining the whole of human society with his
saving light" (LG 36).

The abstract and strictly theological language of those statements
makes it difficult to know precisely what the council intended. In the
Decree on the Apostolate of the Laity there is a formal statement:

> The work of Christ's redemption concerns essentially the salva-
> tion of people; it takes in also, however, the renewal of the
> whole temporal order. The mission of the Church, conse-
> quently, is not only to bring people the message and grace of
> Christ, but also to permeate and improve the whole range of the
> temporal. The laity, carrying out this mission of the Church,
> exercise their apostolate therefore in the world as well as in the
> Church, in the temporal order as well as in the spiritual. These
> orders are distinct; they are nevertheless so closely linked that

---

[19]See LG 36; AA 7; GS 21, 36, 41. The council did not make use of the term
"secularization."

[20]See F. Klostermann, "Decree on the Apostolate of the Laity," in *Commentary on
the Documents of Vatican II*, II, pp. 323-334.

God's plan is, in Christ, to take the whole world up again and
make of it a new creation, initially here on earth, in full realization at the end of time (AA 5).

Paragraph 7 describes at some length the second of the two purposes of
the Church. God's design for the world is the renewal and perfecting of
the temporal order. This requires acknowledging the autonomous
value of that order, but also its infection by sin and consequent need of
the Church in order to fashion people able to restore a proper set of
values and to "direct it towards Christ."

Gaudium et Spes begins with the statement that the Church "feels
itself to be intimately linked with the human race and its history"
(GS 1) and then offers its own description of the world the Church
wishes to serve:

> The world which the council has in mind is the whole human
> family with the totality of realities among which it lives, the
> world as the theatre of human history, marked by human labor,
> failures, and triumphs, the world which Christians believe to
> have been established and sustained by the Creator's love,
> reduced to slavery to sin yet freed by the crucified and risen
> Christ who has broken the power of the Evil One, so that it
> might be transformed according to God's plan and attain to its
> perfection (GS 2).

Such a world the Church now addresses, offering to clarify its problems in the gospel's light and to supply the Spirit's saving help. For
"the human person must be saved and human society restored. The
hinge of our discussion will be the human person, one and whole, body
and soul, heart and conscience, mind and will" (GS 3).

Progress in bringing societies better to promote the good of persons,
the council says, reveals the presence of the Spirit, and the gospel is like
a yeast which arouses an unbreakable demand for human dignity
(GS 26). People may not be content with a purely individualistic morality (GS 30). Human activity in the world has, by God's own will, an
inherent dignity and value (GS 34-36). If history shows that the
greatest accomplishments have been threatened by sin, Christians
preach the possibility of their purification and perfecting in Christ.
Recognizing the divine author of the goods they possess, people will
learn how truly to possess them (GS 37). Christ continues to act in the
world by his Holy Spirit not only by arousing a desire for the world to
come, but also "by that very fact quickening, purifying, and streng-

thening the generous aspirations of mankind to make life more human and to subject the whole earth to this purpose."

> But there are diverse gifts of the Spirit: while he calls some to give manifest witness to people's desire for their heavenly home and to keep it vividly before their minds, he calls others to dedicate themselves to the earthly service of people, by this their ministry preparing the material for the kingdom of God. But all are freed by the Spirit so that, putting aside self-love and integrating all earth's resources into human life, they might reach forth towards that future when humanity itself will become an offering acceptable to God (GS 38).

When that day will come and what the new and transformed earth will be like, we do not know, except that it will surpass all our desires. Expectation of this future should not diminish our concern to develop this earth, "where that Body of the new human family grows which already foreshadows in some way the new age. That is why, although earthly progress is to be carefully distinguished from the growth of the Kingdom of Christ, still it is of vital concern to the Kingdom of God insofar as it can contribute to the better ordering of human society" (GS 39).

Against this background, the council considers the relationship between Church and world. The Church knows itself to be a society of divine origin, nature, and purpose. Still it exists here on earth, sharing the world's lot, and called to be "a leaven and, as it were, the soul of human society, which is to be renewed in Christ and transformed into the family of God." This leads to a programmatic statement of the Church's role:

> In pursuing its own saving purpose, the Church does not only communicate the divine life to the person, it also casts its reflected light in some way over the whole world, especially by healing and elevating the dignity of the human person, by strengthening the cohesion of human society, and by endowing the daily activity of people with a deeper sense and meaning. The Church thus believes that through each of its members and its whole community it can contribute much to make the human family and its history more human (GS 40).

The following paragraphs explicate this statement. Paragraph 41 discusses the Church's defence of human dignity. The Church's role in strengthening society is the subject of paragraph 42: although "the proper mission, which Christ entrusted to his Church, is not of the political, economic, or social order—the purpose he gave it is of the religious order," still the Church can contribute to the making of society, but by faith and love and not "by some external dominion exercised by purely human means." Paragraph 43 attributes Christian significance to daily activity in the world, which it is one of the great errors of the day to think can be separated from faith. "Secular duties and activity belong properly, even if not exclusively, to the laity." While they may look to their pastors for guidance and spiritual support, they must assume their own responsibility in and for the world. "The laity, who have an active role to play in the whole life of the Church, must not only imbue the world with a Christian spirit; they are also called to be witnesses to Christ in all circumstances, in the very heart of the human community." Bishops and presbyters are to preach the gospel so that it illumines all the earthly activities of the faithful and, with the religious and the laity, to "demonstrate that the Church with all its gifts by its presence alone is an inexhaustible source of all those resources of which the modern world is in so great a need" (GS 43).

In turn, the Church receives from the world. Past experience, scientific progress, and cultural diversity cast great light on human nature and open new avenues to truth. The Church has used and will use the language and thought of various peoples to articulate its own message. Its own social structure "can be enriched by the development of human social life, not of course as if anything were lacking in the constitution Christ gave it, but in order to understand it more deeply, to express it better, and to adapt it more successfully to our times." In general,

> whatever contributes to the development of the community of humanity on the level of family, culture, economic and social life, and national and international politics, by God's plan also contributes in no small measure to the community of the Church insofar as it depends on things outside itself. Indeed, the Church admits that it has benefitted and still benefits from the very opposition of its enemies and persecutors (GS 44).

The three documents reviewed here do not clearly offer a single and coherent view of the relationship between Church and world. This is perhaps no surprise, given that they were drawn up by different groups of bishops and theologians and that each of them was often the fruit of considerable compromise.

Moreover, many of the statements are on such an abstract theological level that it is difficult to give them specific enough content to make
them subject to theological evaluation. As in other teachings, we often
find different statements set alongside one another, like beads on a
rosary, with little internal connection. The great question which a
concrete theology would ask, for example, is how the vindication of
the world's autonomy is to be reconciled with the statements about its
need to be "sanctified," "consecrated," or "infused with a Christian
spirit,"—and all this without a new clerical or ecclesial domination.
How does one relate again what the council accepts as now distinct
orders: the religious and the political, economic and social, the spiritual and the temporal, the divine life and its reflected light? At least one
group of critics maintains that the council has not succeeded in overcoming the old distinction between a natural and a supernatural destiny.[21] The world's "autonomy" can sound a great deal like the *finis
naturalis* which the council seems to have repudiated with regard to
the individual. But can the individual have a single, supernatural destiny and the world and society only a natural one?

In two respects the council's statements reflect the theology of the
years in which they were composed. The first of these is the confident
acknowledgement of the world's autonomy. This effect of secularization is presented as a legitimate development, in accord with God's
creation and not threatened by the need for Christ's redemption or by
the Church's mission. It is not hard to recognize here the "theology of
secularization" and the confident optimism of the early 1960's of which
it was only a reflection. The Church's role in society, for example, is
presented as that of strengthening social cohesion; little attention is
given to social conflict, and the atmosphere is quite different from that
of later documents such as *Octagesima adveniens* or the 1971 Synod's
"Justice in the World," not to mention the theologies of revolution and
liberation which soon succeeded the theology of secularization.

The second of these reflections of the state of contemporary theology
is visible in the council's tendency to present the Church's mission as
directly and immediately affecting individuals. The council appears to
have no difficulty in articulating the meaning of the faith in terms of the
situation, needs and desires of individuals, but its discussion of its
significance for the social, economic, and political realm is, theologically, quite tentative and even hesitant. The council fathers were

---

[21]See *Les deux visages de la théologie de la sécularisation: Analyse critique de la
théologie de la sécularisation* (Tournai: Casterman, 1970), pp. 24-25.

not able to agree upon a clear and strong statement on the relationship between the central Christian message and mission and the social realm.[22]

One wonders also if there is not some correlation between this hesitation before the social implications of the gospel and the fact that, in its typologies of Christian activity, the clergy and religious typically see to the Church-internal affairs while the laity have as their primary and typical role the mission of the Church to the world. One must be careful here, for the council certainly affirmed the right and duty of the laity to be involved in the immediate self-constitution of the Church and it did not exclude entirely the worldly activity of clergy and religious. Still, typologies do count for something, as, for example, when the word "also" must be introduced into the descriptions of roles.[23] The primary means by which the Church is present and active in the world is the laity. The growing autonomy of the world has meant the banishment of clergy and religious from the secular world, where, however, the laity still reside.[24] Having one foot in both realms, the religious and the political, economic and social, they are uniquely placed to make Christianity effective in the larger world. It would probably be an exaggeration to say that in its insistence on the autonomy of the secular and in its role-typologies, the council is simply making a virtue out of necessity and coping as best it can; but one is entitled at least to some reservations about a view of the Church-world relationship that bears so great a resemblance to modern Western society's notions about the appropriate social role of religion.[25] One suspects that political and economic liberals would have far less difficulty with the conciliar teaching than, for example, with the Church-world understanding of many liberation-theologians.

This correlation between the Church-world relationship and the clergy-laity relationship is confirmed by an unexpected paragraph of Yves Congar. In a discussion of the ecclesiological problem raised by the new question of the relation between the spiritual and the temporal, Congar notes that the single mission of the Church, precisely

[22]See G. Gutierrez, *A Theology of Liberation; History, Politics and Salvation* (Maryknoll: Orbis, 1973), pp. 168-172.

[23]See Schillebeeckx, "A New Type of Layman," p. 129.

[24]See *Les deux visages de la théologie de la sécularisation*, pp. 26-27.

[25]See *Les deux visages de la théologie de la sécularisation*, pp. 173-200, and, in the same volume, F. van den Oudenrijn, "La théologie de la sécularisation: une idéologie religieuse de la société unidimensionnelle," pp. 155-172.

because it includes both orders, raises the question whether "the full exercise of the Church's mission does not surpass the structures and means of the Church insofar as it is an original society of divine right." In the world that mission is exercised by the clergy through their prophetical preaching, but only the laity can make it truly effective. He goes on:

> The laity are, in their very life, the living link between the Church and the world. Once again they are then acting insofar as they are Christians. The distinction will not so much be between "acting as a Christian" and "acting insofar as they are Christians," that is, as the Church. It will rather be between the Church as a positive institution of divine right (with its hierarchy and sacraments) and the Church as the People of God immersed in human history and marching on the same journey. In the end, there will no longer be a distinction between "laity" and the "apostolate of the laity." The distinction will be between what derives from the jurisdiction of the Church and what derives solely from its prophetical element. . . .[26]

After repeating that "it is the person, the *Christian* person, *i.e.*, a member of the messianic people, who is the link between 'the Church' and the temporal order," Congar suggests the need for another distinction in the meaning of the word "Church":

> Between the Church in the strongest and most dogmatic sense of the word, engaging the whole body by the voice of its public authority, and the faithful considered individually, there exist either in fact or, in varying degrees, in law, concrete communities of whom the word "Church" can be used in a lesser and relative, but still real, sense.[27]

It is surprising to find that Congar, who more than anyone else was responsible for recovering the general reference of the word "Church," should here use it in a sense which appears to exclude the laity, whose task, he says, is to be a link between *Church* and world. Congar certainy has stressed often enough that the laity *are* the Church in the world; but his slip is perhaps an indication that the view that the Church really is integrally constituted before it faces the world in the

---

[26]Y. Congar, "Apports, richesses et limites du Décret," in *L'Apostolat des laics,* Unam Sanctam 75 (Paris: du Cerf, 1970), p. 179.

[27]Congar, "Apports, richesses et limites," p. 180.

persons of the laity is still very powerful and is easily taken for granted. Congar's suggested distinction of another sense of the word "Church," to cover small communities of Christians actively involved in the world, may be an attempt to face the difficulty raised by that view's tendency to restrict, at least typically, the Church's temporal mission to individual lay people. Those small communities seem to mediate between the two senses of "Church" which he had already proposed, the hierarchical and sacramental Church of divine institution and the Church as the People of God on pilgrimage in and with the world. It is clear that the difficulties in conceiving the relationship between Church and world or between the two missions of the Church directly relate to the clergy-laity relationship and vice-versa.[28]

CHURCH AND WORLD RECONSIDERED

The obscurities and difficulties in the council's view of the Church-world and clergy-laity distinctions derive, it will here be argued, from an incomplete reflection on the Church's new situation in a secularized world and from a consequently ineffective pastoral response. "Church" and "world" have come in the modern era to mean different things than before, in part precisely because their mutual relationship has so remarkably changed. Some may find it easier to admit that the meaning of "world" has changed than to say that "Church" has also changed in meaning. But there is a sense in which these are correlative terms, each defined by the other, and, if that is so, then "world" cannot change in meaning without "Church" also changing.

This becomes clearest if one makes the "political turn" in theological method. Political theologians claim that they are engaged in something quite different from a "theology of politics."[29] The latter is another "regional" theology, another "theology of . . . ," adding another topic to the already long list of possible objects of theological inquiry. A "theology of politics" is represented by one of the questions asked by Gustavo Gutierrez: "What is the meaning of the struggle against an unjust society and the creation of a new man in the light of the Word?"[30] The form of the question is familiar: What, in the light of

---

[28]Congar defends his distinction in *Un peuple messianique: L'Église, sacrement du salut; Salut et liberation* (Paris: du Cerf, 1975), pp. 171-177.

[29]See, for example, C. Davis, *Theology and Political Society* (Cambridge University Press, 1980), pp. 2-3.

[30]Gutierrez, *A Theology of Liberation*, p. 149.

revelation, is the meaning of X, Y, or Z? Most of the council's statements about the world reflect this sort of "theology of . . . "; they
respond to the question, What, in the light of the Word, should the
Church say or do about the modern world?

The political theologians claim to be doing something quite different, to be asking quite different questions. They are illustrated by
another question with Gutierrez poses: "What is the *meaning of the
faith* in a life committed to the struggle against injustice and alienation?"[31] This sort of question does not concern faith's implications for
some particular aspect of human life, but the significance of a prior
commitment *for the interpretation of faith itself.* Now the form of the
question is: What, in the light of this commitment, is the meaning
of X, Y, or Z, where these letters represent various constituents of
Christian faith. Faith is not being asked to illumine an endless series of
particular problems; faith itself is being illumined by the prior commitment. Since the commitment stands prior to all theological questions, a political theology is not merely regional, but foundational
and comprehensive.[32]

The necessity of this "political turn" appears in the very anthropocentric "turn to the subject" of which it is a critical corrective and
extension. For an anthropocentric theology, existence as a human
problem and project has central hermeneutical significance. Revelation
is not an arbitrary intervention by God, surprising and challenging an
inexpectant humanity. It is a fulfilment of desires which the Creator
has inscribed in every human heart and mind, a response to needs
experienced by every sinner's heart. For such a theology, faith can only
be rendered intelligible by reference to the problems involved in the
free self-realizations of concrete men and women. While there are
many council statements which do not employ this hermeneutical
stance and simply use biblical, traditional, or dogmatic language, it is
safe to say that this language need not be incompatible with an anthropocentric approach and that the latter is even in evidence in certain
documents, particularly in *Gaudium et Spes.* It is in fact this sort of
approach that determines the council's definition of the Church in
distinction from the world. The council has asked, "What, in the light
of the problem of human existence, is the Church?"

[31]Gutierrz, *A Theology of Liberation,* p. 135.
[32]This, of course, does not mean that the commitment itself goes unquestioned.
Gutierrez asks *both* types of questions. And both types are needed if there is to be a
genuine and critical correlation between contemporary practice and Christian faith.

But the political theologians object to such an anthropocentric theology that it does not really deal with human existence in its full concreteness. It ignores the fact that concretely existence is a political problem,[33] and so works with an abstract individual. The "incarnate subjectivity" which it acknowledges and to which it refers the gospel's message is incarnate in the human body, but its political, social, and cultural embodiments are overlooked. As Dorothee Sölle remarked of Bultmann's theology, this interpretation "neglects the conditions of its own preunderstanding."[34] It takes for granted the validity and even universality of its analysis of the problems of human existence which serves as its *Vorverständnis*. But these existential problems are not (or at least are not merely) universal problems; they are concrete problems, politically, socially, and culturally conditioned if not determined; and, if they are universal, it is only because they are concrete problems everywhere.

If the political character of human existence is neglected, an anthropocentric theology will attempt to interpret the meaning of the faith or of one of its constitutents (the Church, for example) by reference to an imaginary and abstract individual. Such a theology will not, of course, consider that its reference-point is abstract or imaginary, but that is because it takes for granted and universalizes the specific political conditions in which human existence is a concrete problem. That human existence poses the concrete problems that it does pose in part at least because the political, social and cultural order is what it is, is neglected or trivialized. A truly concrete and self-critical anthropocentric theology can only be a political theology, for which existence is known to be a political problem and project.

It is neglect of this political dimension of human existence that permitted the council to define the Church prior to considering the world and to suggest that there is a first moment in which the Church constitutes itself as the Church before it turns to consider its mission in and to the world. Clearly, the Church is not defined or constituted without reference to the problem of human existence, but the world does not enter into the definition or constitution of that problem. The council did ask, "What, in the light of the Word, is the meaning of the Church?" Its answer to that question included in part the asking of the other question: "What, in the light of the problem of human existence,

---

[33]See J.B. Metz, "The Church and the World in the Light of a 'Political Theology,'" in *Theology of the World* (New York: Herder and Herder, 1969), pp. 108-110.

[34]D. Sölle, *Political Theology* (Philadelphia: Fortress, 1974), p. 45.

is the meaning of the Word (including the Word about the Church)?" It did *not* ask, "What, in the light of human existence as a political problem, is the meaning of the Word (including the Word about the Church)?"[35]

If, however, existence is a political problem and project, then the world cannot be considered to be external or subsequent to the real business of human living. The world (or at least the world as intended in discussions of the Church-world relationship) is not simply "the theatre of human history," as the council called it; the world *is* human history, it is what human beings not only have made together but *are* together. Individuals are individuals within that world; it makes them what they are and they make it what it is. Individual self-realization occurs within the general political, social and cultural self-realization of the world; the world realizes itself through the individual self-realizations. To paraphrase Peter Berger and Thomas Luckmann, the world is a human project, and the individual is a worldly product.[36]

As, from an earlier anthropocentric standpoint, the religious question is not separable from the problem of individual self-realization, so, from the standpoint of political theology, the Church's self-realization is not separable from the problem of the world's self-realization. As an individual's faith is a particular instance of the project of human existence, so the self-constitution of the Church is an instance of the self-realization of the world. The Church does not come to be except in the world, in reference to the world, and even in part because of the world. The Church is a moment in the world's self-realization.

These conclusions suppose, of course, that what Christian revelation interprets is not only the drama that defines an individual's existence but the tragi-comedy of political existence as well. This is something of what Gutierrez, for example, means when he tries to make concrete Karl Rahner's abstract statement that the Church is the sacrament of what God's grace is doing also outside the Church.[37] For Gutierrez this

---

[35]See, for example, the extremely limited significance assigned to the world in the self-constitution of the Church in *Gaudium et Spes* 44.

[36]See P. Berger and T. Luckmann, *The Social Construction of Reality: A Treatise in the Sociology of Knowledge* (Garden City: Anchor, 1967), p. 61. Their statement is that "Society is a human product" and that "Man is a social product."

[37]"The Catholic must think of and experience the Church as the 'vanguard,' the sacramental sign, the manifestation in history of a grace of salvation which takes effect far beyond the confines of the 'visible' Church as sociologically definable"—K. Rahner,

formal statement means that the Church "must be the visible sign of the presence of the Lord within the aspiration for liberation and the struggle for a more human and just society."[38] This too helps to explain what he means when he speaks of the Church's self-consciousness being mediated by the consciousness of the world in which it lives.[39]

Something like this view of the Church-world relationship seems implied in the perspectives of *Octagesima adveniens* when Pope Paul VI says that "at the heart of the world there dwells the mystery of man discovering himself to be God's child in the course of a historical and psychological process in which constraint and freedom as well as the weight of sin and the breath of the Spirit alternate and struggle to prevail."[40] At the heart of the *world* the mystery of sin and grace, constraint and freedom, constitutes the great issue of human history. History, the world, is constituted by what constitutes the Church; if the world is unintelligible at its heart without the Church, the Church is by that fact unintelligible without the world. Church and world define one another.

It remains, however, that there is nothing to relate if Church and world are not distinct. The distinction lies in the fact that the Church is that community of men and women who constitute themselves around the person of Jesus Christ, because of him, in his name, and for his sake. The problem of human existence, individual and social, is for them interpreted and resolved in Christ. This is not a private moment nor an act of withdrawal from "the world." It occurs in the world, and it is a moment in the world's self-realization. For the world is not what lies outside the Church; the world includes the Church, and without the Church, the world would not be what it is. Christian believing, hoping, loving are political acts, moments in the realization of the world. If this is the case, then there is not some first moment in which the Church becomes the Church and a second moment in which the Church considers its relation to the world. The Church's self-constitution is itself an act within and with reference to the world.

A recognition of this may be impeded by the fact that historic,

---

"The New Image of the Church," *Theological Investigations* X (New York: Herder and Herder, 1973), p. 16.

[38]Gutierrez, *A Theology of Liberation*, p. 262.

[39]Gutierrez, *A Theology of Liberation*, p. 260.

[40]Pope Paul VI, *Octagesima adveniens*, 37.

especially Catholic, Christianity includes certain objective representations and bearers of its constitutive meaning and value: the Scriptures, the living memory of its tradition, patterns of worship, creeds, etc. Without these, Catholic Christianity would not recognize its own distinctive self-realization: these are constitutive of the Church's coming-to-be in the world.

But the objectivity of these bearers of the Church's self-constitutive meanings and values is misunderstood if it is thought that they bear those meanings and values prior to or independently of the questions about human existence that mediate the Church's self-interpretation and self-realization. Meanings and values are borne only when they are received by persons and communities. Such reception is always a concrete act, in concrete circumstances, with concrete personal and social significance. Only the assumption that the reception of the constitutive Christian meanings and values is exhausted by the problem of individual existence allows one to think that the objective bearers carry meanings and values constitutive of the Church prior to its engagement in the world. The reception of those meanings and values, even when they are restricted in reference to questions of individual existence, *is* the Church's engagement in the world. But when the questions are given their full reference to questions of existence, both individual and political, that engagement can become self-conscious and self-critical.

Clergy and Laity Reconsidered

Vatican II's typologies of clergy, religious, and laity describe their respective relationships to the world. The clergy and religious typically do not involve themselves in the world, but minister to the Church's self-constitution and testify to its transcendent destiny. The laity typically realize their Christianity in the world by their worldly activities, although they also have roles in the Church's self-constitution.

It was suggested above that this role-differentiation implies a priority to a distinct moment of ecclesial self-constitution. Schillebeeckx, for example, in an early essay, refers to evangelization as the "primary, religious" mission of the Church.[41] This causes no problem if the word "primary" refers to the distinctive centering of its constitutive meanings and values around Jesus Christ. But there would be some problem if this were to be taken to mean something prior to a second and secondary mission of the Church to the world. To identify the primary

[41]Schillebeeckx, "Typological Definition," pp. 114-115.

mission of the Church as "religious" is also unfortunate if it suggests that the secondary mission is not religious. This is possible only on the assumption that the meaning of the religious is exhausted by the private and individual realms.

If, however, the relationship between Church and world is reconsidered along the lines suggested above, then the council's typologies also need to be reconsidered. The central and constitutive meanings and values, to which the clergy minister, are themselves politically significant. The religious "state" is in itself a political statement; and the life for which the vows free a person may be a life in the world.[42] It is not only, and not even typically, the laity who mediate the political significance of the Church's faith; this is an inescapable part of its meaning for and in the lives of all christians. As Schillebeeckx puts it:

> The relationship between the Church and the world was clearly not fully thought out in all its consequences at the council and the "definition" of the layman and, although less obviously, that of the office-bearer is consequently not entirely satisfactory. Every form of being a Christian, in whatever kind of service or function in the Church (either lay or clerical), is a manner of being a Christian in the world. Even religious life cannot be interpreted in any other way than as a specific manner of being in the world. The Church is the "universal sacrament of salvation", . . . the sign of salvation in and for the world. All Christians are implicated in this sign, each according to his own service or function in the Church.[43]

The immediate political significance of Christian existence is most clearly visible in grass roots communities, particularly but not only in the Third World, in which the gospel is preached and received through the mediation of an interpretation of the social and political context and the group gathers in conscious opposition to the structures and styles of life of the larger society.[44] That there is a danger, as the Latin

[42]This is well recognized in a recent document of the Congregation for Religious and for Secular Institutes, which quite transcends the limited perspective of *Lumen Gentium* and other conciliar documents; see "Religious Life and Human Promotion," *Origins* 10 (1980-81): 530-541.

[43]Schillebeeckx, "A New Type of Layman," pp. 129-130.

[44]See *Les groupes informels dans l'Eglise* (Strasbourg: CERDIC, 1971) and the sociological study of K. Dobbelaire and J. Billiet, "Community formation and the Church: A Sociological Study of an Ideology and the Empirical Reality," in M. Caudron, ed., *Faith and Society*, (Gembloux: Duculot, 1978), pp. 211-259.

American bishops at Puebla and Popes Paul VI and John Paul II have pointed out, that these communities may reduce the principles on which they gather to particular political interpretations and programs is undeniable; but it would be a mistake to think that the great Church does not run a similar danger in the secularized societies of the West. For their privatized understanding of the constitutive meanings and values of Christianity is itself of immense political significance. These Churches show a tendency to locate the *specificum Christianum* primarily in a cultural opposition to a vaguely described "materialism" and a specifically described sexual morality. The political and economic structures and practices of the society tend to be taken for granted.[45]A sign of this is that direct political action is typically assigned to the laity who remain in a world from which the Church, in the persons of the clergy and religious, has effectively and even on principle emigrated.

But that attempted or recommended emigration is itself, at least on the analysis given above, a political option based on a particular, although often unconscious and uncritical, interpretation of the relation between the Church and the world, an interpretation which, somewhat ironically, has been taken over from the liberal political theory of the Enlightenment. The clergy and religious are not typically to be involved in the world because the world is now regarded as "autonomous," and its autonomy is the condition as well for the freedom conceded at the council to the laity in their typical sphere of activity in the world.

But if the autonomy of the world—at least in the form in which it was asserted both in the council documents and in the "theology of secularization"—must be called into question, then so must the allocation of typical responsibilities to clergy, religious, and laity. The growing sense that there is not only a distinction but also, in certain senses of the words, an opposition between Church and world makes it difficult to represent that opposition practically by the council's opposition of the typical activities of clergy, religious, and laity. What is really needed is a return to the original opposition which did not counterpose clergy and laity, but the whole Church, clergy, religious, *and laity*, to

---

[45]It is this form of Christianity, which he calls "bourgeois religion," that is the object under criticism in J.B. Metz' two recent books, *Faith in History and Society: Toward a Practical Fundamental Theology* (New York: Seabury, 1980), and *The Emergent Church: The Future of Christianity in a Postbourgeois World* (New York: Crossroad, 1981); for a summary statement, see the latter, pp. 1-16.

the world.[46] Becoming a Christian would itself then be seen as a political act within and over and against the world, and the differentiations within the Church would be so many different ways in which the directly political significance of belonging to the Church is articulated.

There is, then, a valid point to the concerns expressed in the Chicago Declaration. But it consists less in the growing activity of priests and religious in the world than in the danger that the greater involvement of the laity in Church-internal activities may itself reflect or result in an ecclesiastical narcissism and privatization of the laity themselves. But this restricting of the gospel's implications ought also to be stressed with regard to the clergy and religious as well. The authors of the Declaration appear to confine the political significance of the gospel in rather narrow channels in general and particularly with regard to the ministries of the clergy and relgious. They fear, perhaps not without reason, a new clericalism; but that danger will not be overcome by having clergy and religious stick to their own "religious" and supposedly "pre-political" tasks. The clericalism really to be feared is that of those clergy, religious, and even laity whose efforts to make explicit and critically effective the political character of the gospel are undertaken without competence or critical inquiry. What constitutes such competence and inquiry is, of course, a nice question, on which, it seems, the authors of the Declaration would differ from at least some of the clergy and religious who have become involved in secular and political issues. Many of the latter are likely to feel that the Declaration is far too accepting of the differentiation of the Church and world typical of modern liberal and secularized societies in the West.

There will, of course, remain different gifts in the Church, some of which will be more useful and suitable than others for articulating in theory and practice the political character of the gospel. But these differences will not be based on some mythical pre-political religious meaning, nor are they likely to be distributed neatly within the lines of the canonical and theological distinctions among clergy, religious and laity. None of these groups is, except by custom and, of course, training, less likely to be the recipient of the needed gifts and competence. In any one of them may appear the critical intelligence, the willingness, and the courage that constitute a call to the special ministry of articulating the political implications of the gospel and of provoking and challenging the whole Church to assume, consciously and critically, its inescapable political responsibility.

[46]See Schillebeeckx, "A New Type of Layman," pp. 117-121.

TOWARD A RENEWED CANONICAL
UNDERSTANDING OF OFFICIAL MINISTRY

JAMES H. PROVOST
The Catholic University of America

Yves Congar has observed that any renewal effort in the Church must become rooted in legal structures if it is going to have lasting effect.[1] The renewal of ministry is no exception. There is a need, therefore, to explore some of the fundamental issues in the canonical understanding of official ministry and to evaluate elements where a renewed sense of ministry might take root.

Legal structures are part of the broader field of canon law. Church law must not be collapsed into the Code. Rather, it consists in a broader set of principles, precedents, procedures and decisions which evidence considerable variety even under a system of codification. This diversity is due in part to the various legal cultures from which the Church has drawn in developing its law. It is also due to the fact that the way we are as Church is political; church structures are not so much a matter of abstract principles as the "art of the possible." Politics is a cultural reality, and church structures for official ministry are in fact culturally conditioned.[2]

Structures for the organization of official ministry vary among the diverse ritual churches or rites of the Catholic Church. For example, married clergy are part of the structuring of ministry in the Eastern Rites outside North America; celibate clergy are the norm for all the Western or Latin Rite. Official ministry includes catechists, leaders of local communities, and other non-ordained persons in Africa and Latin America. It tends to be more exclusively clerical in Europe and North America, but even there the numbers of non-ordained in "official" roles peculiar to various countries are increasing.

---

[1]Y. Congar, *Vraie et fausse réform dans l'Église* (Paris: du Cerf, 2nd ed. 1968), pp. 177-178. See also J. Provost, "Canon Law—True or False Reform in the Church?" THE JURIST 38 (1978): 257-267.

[2]See J. Coriden, "Law in Service to the People of God," THE JURIST 28 (1968): 129-148; J. Provost, "The People of God: Law or Politics?" *CLSA Proceedings* 42 (1980): 44-59.

A global evaluation of this complex diversity is beyond the possibilities of this paper. Given the cultural conditioning of church structures and the cultural variations in what constitutes official ministry even within the Latin Rite, I will confine myself to the canonical understanding of official ministry within the United States.

By "official ministry" I mean ministry which is organized into offices, structured according to the norms of law, and carried out in the name of the Church. The "canonical understanding" of such ministry means both the practical organization of it according to the norms of canon law, and the underlying view or concept of such ministry which forms the basis for the practice. Such an underlying view can frequently be perceived by a careful analysis of the various interconnected elements in the provisions of the law, even though a somewhat different view may be proclaimed in theory. The ideology, in other words, is not always the actual working conceptual framework reflected in legal practice.

The focus of these reflections is to seek an understanding of what canonical situation persons in official ministry are, as a matter of fact, experiencing; and consequently, what type of canonical understanding of official ministry seems to await others who seek to expand the ranks of official ministry in this country. Because priests have formed the most organized and central body of official ministers in the United States, I will concentrate on them in this study, using secular priests as the major referent.[3]

HISTORICAL FRAMEWORK

1. *The American Scene*

There have been some remarkable peculiarities in the structuring of offical ministry in the United States. Originally a Church staffed and governed by priests, the nineteenth century saw the growth and organization of a hierarchically governed Church accompanied by some bitter disputes and, briefly, several schisms.[4] By the end of the last century

---

[3]Differences between secular and order priests can be characterized in terms of the kind of work they do—whether "secular" work, or ministry in a more traditional form. Secular clergy, who do primarily official ministry rather than what is usually considered secular work, form the major referent for this study. See T. M. Gannon, "The Impact of Structural Differences on the Catholic Clergy," *Journal for the Scientific Study of Religion* 18 (1979): 350-362.

[4]See R. Trisco, "Bishops and Their Priests in the United States," in J. T. Ellis, ed., *The Catholic Priest in the United States: Historical Investigations* (Collegeville, MN: St. John's University Press, 1971), pp. 111-292; G. Fogarty, "American Conciliar Legislation, Hierarchical Structure, and Priest-Bishop Tension," THE JURIST 32 (1972): 400-409.

much of this activity had died down and the American church in this century has been characterized by outspoken loyalty to the Apostolic See and, generally, by the outward docility of official ministers toward their superiors. Underneath, however, vestiges of hostility and mistrust continue to plague the relationship of various official ministers, a legacy from a time when structures for ministry were so fluid that the priests themselves clamored for "canon law" in this country.[5]

Since the middle ages official ministry in the Catholic Church has been structured through a system of offices, funded by the institution of benefices, and exercised by a class of ministers (clergy) set apart from the rest of the people of the Church.[6] In the United States the missionary condition of the Church precluded the establishment of parishes in the last century, and even the benefice system was generally unknown in view of the regular free-will offerings of the faithful. As communities became better organized with a church building and priest of their own, "quasi-parishes" as well as missions were set up with missionaries, rectors and quasi-pastors staffing the basic structures of official ministry.[7]

Trusteeism was, in part, a movement to have greater lay control of the structures of official ministry in the United States. Beginning with the premise that constructing the church building gave parishioners a right to name and determine the tenure of their priest, trustees claimed a very American version of the *ius patronatus*. The bishops and, eventually, the Apostolic See rejected this claim.[8] The struggle against trusteeism was so bitter that residual suspicions can be noted today.

---

[5]"There are systematic and substantial differences between bishops and priests on almost every matter" investigated in the National Opinion Research Center's sociological study of American priests; NORC, *The Catholic Priest in the United States: Sociological Investigations* (Washington, DC: USCC Publications, 1972), p. 312. The nineteenth century call by priests for canon law was forcefully stated in the anonymous work, *The Rights of the Clergy Vindicated, or A Plea for Canon Law in the United States* (New York: James Sheehy, 1883).

[6]D. Heintschel, *The Medieval Concept of an Ecclesiastical Office in the Major Sources and Printed Commentaries from 1140–1300*, Canon Law Studies 363 (Washington, DC: Catholic University, 1956); V. de Reina, *El sistema beneficial* (Pamplona: EUNSA, 1965); "Ministères de direction dans l'Église: colloque de Strasbourg 1972," *Revue de Droit Canonique* 23 (1973); R. Schwarz, *Die eigenberechtige Gewalt der Kirche,* Analecta Gregoriana 196 (Rome: Pont. Univ. Gregoriana, 1974).

[7]See F. Macdonald, "The Development of Parishes in the United States," in C. J. Neusse, ed., *The Sociology of the Parish: An Introductory Symposium* (Milwaukee: Bruce, 1951), pp. 45-71.

[8]A detailed history is provided by P. J. Dignan, *A History of the Legal Incorporation*

Reacting against trusteeism and faced with some irresponsible priests, bishops in this country developed an autocratic approach to church governance which had definite impact on the structures of official ministry. Trisco states the relationship between bishops and priests in the United States has been marked by four issues, all in some way related to the canonical understanding of official ministry: greater say in the selection of bishops; some way to influence the authority of the bishop, for example through a board of consultors; security of tenure through the creation of irremovable pastors; and protection through strict judicial procedures in cases where priests were accused of serious misdeeds.[9] To some extent these remain major issues today.

In 1908 the United States ceased to be a missionary territory and came under the general law of the Church. More significantly, the structuring of official ministry was given renewed clarity in the codification of Church law promulgated in 1917. Three key concepts mark the Code's approach to official ministry: ecclesiastical office; clerics as the sole possessors of ecclesiastical power; and the requirement of a title to become an official minister.

2. The Code of Canon Law

Office in the Code admits of a broad meaning: any function which is done legitimately for a spiritual purpose (CIC 145, §1).[10] But the Code uses as a matter of course a more strict definition. In this latter sense an office is a stably constituted function (*munus*) of either divine or ecclesiastical law which is conferred according to the norms of canon law, and which entails some participation in ecclesiastical power whether of orders or of jurisdiction. Since only clergy can obtain the power of either orders or jurisdiction (CIC 118), official ministry was effectively restricted to clergy alone. Clergy, moreover, form a separate classification from laity, and this by divine institution (CIC 107).

To be ordained to major orders, and thus to have the qualifications for major ministerial offices, a cleric must have a "title" (CIC 979).[11]

---

of Catholic Church Property in the United States (1784-1932) (Washington, DC: Catholic University, 1933).

[9]Trisco, p. 112.

[10]*Codex Iuris Canonici* (Vatican: Typis Polyglottis, 1917); canons from this Code will be cited: CIC.

[11]The obligation of title expressed here applies to the secular clergy. Religious are assured the same support through their communities if they have made perpetual profession; otherwise, they are bound to the law which applies to seculars—CIC 982.

This is an assured source of income which will provide for adequate support of the cleric throughout his life. The Code prefers benefices, personal patrimony, and then pensions as the source for this income. As a last resort it is willing to permit men to be ordained "for the service of the diocese" or, in missionary areas, "of the mission" (CIC 981). The system preferred to see clergy supported independently from the central administration although still accountable to it. Parishes were established not only to provide for the care of souls, but also to provide income for the support of the priest who held the parish as a benefice.[12]

The American structures for organizing ministry did not have all the features of the new Code but official interpretations made it clear the new law was to have full force in the United States.[13] The restriction of ecclesiastical power to clerics had already been achieved as a result of the trusteeism disputes of the previous century. The title for ordination in the United States was standardized as the "service of the diocese," giving bishops effective control and responsibility for their clergy. The concept of office was admitted in principle, but previous civil arrangements for the ownership and administration of parishes and dioceses continued under the new Code. In practice the independence legislated for pastors in the 1917 codification was conditioned by the role of the bishop in parish corporations or through the diocesan corporation sole, American bishops retaining thereby more influence on the organization of official ministry than many of their counterparts in other areas of the world.

3. Vatican II

The Second Vatican Council introduced significant changes in all three concepts of the Code's approach to official ministry. A broader meaning was given to ecclesiastical office; the fundamental equality of all the People of God was affirmed; and the funding of ministry was given a new organization.

More specifically, the broad meaning of office was adopted as normative: "From now on [an ecclesiastical office] should be understood as any function which has been permanently assigned and is to be

[12]P. M. Hannon, "The Development of the Form of the Modern Parish," in Neusse, ed., *The Sociology of the Parish*, pp. 17-44.

[13]The most significant decision from the perspective of official ministry was that U.S. parishes are true canonical parishes; see letter from the Apostolic Delegate to the bishops of the United States, November 10, 1922: *Canon Law Digest* [*CLD*] 1: 149-151.

exercised for a spiritual purpose" (PO 20).[14] Not only clerics but also lay persons can participate in this official ministry: "Finally, the hierarchy entrusts to the laity some functions which are more closely connected with pastoral duties, such as the teaching of Christian doctrine, certain liturgical actions, and the care of souls. By virtue of this mission, the laity are fully subject to higher ecclesiastical direction in the performance of such work" (AA 24).

While only the ordained receive *sacra potestas*, this is not to obstruct the basic equality which obtains among all Christians, ordained and non-ordained: "if by the will of Christ some are made teachers, dispensers of mysteries, and shepherds on behalf of others, yet all share a true equality with regard to the dignity and to the activity common to all the faithful for the building up of the Body of Christ" (LG 32).[15]

Even the funding of ministry received a new direction. "The chief emphasis should be given to the office which sacred ministers fulfill. Hence the so-called benefice system should be abandoned or at least it should be reformed in such a way that the beneficiary aspect, that is, the right to revenues accruing to an endowed office, will be treated as secondary, and the main consideration in law will be accorded to the ecclesiastical office itself" (PO 20). The recompense for clergy should be standardized so it "should be fundamentally the same for all those operating in the same circumstances" (PO 20).

Post-conciliar implementation of these changes has been mixed. While limited term has been introduced to assure greater stability in office as well as reasonable turn-over in various positions, and personnel boards assist in making placement decisions,[16] bishops continue to exercise broad powers through the system of church ownership and administration in force in the United States. The inclusion of other persons in ministry has not diminished this episcopal role. There have been successful efforts to standardize and equalize the remuneration for clergy, but similar efforts on behalf of non-ordained ministers and even ordained deacons are lacking in most dioceses.

[14]Translations are from Abbott.

[15]See P. Krämer, *Dienst und Vollmacht in der Kirche. Eine rechtstheologische Untersuchung zur Sacra Potestas Lehre des II Vatikanischen Konzils*, Trier theologische Studien 28 (Trier: Paulinus, 1973).

[16]J. A. Janicki, "Limited Term of Office and Retirement," *CLSA Proceedings* 41 (1979): 39-59; J. S. Teixeira, *Personnel Policies: A Canonical Commentary on Selected Current Clergy Personnel Policies in the United States of America*, Canon Law Studies 503 (Washington, DC: Catholic University, 1981).

4. *Toward a New Code*

A new Code of Canon Law is in preparation.[17] It will address these same issues and propose norms to implement some of the conciliar changes. Incorporating the broad meaning of office, it will provide structures to include non-priests in pastoral positions even while restricting the office of "pastor" to ordained priests. Official ministry by non-ordained persons in other aspects of Church life will also be recognized. A greater sharing in the powers to teach and sanctify will be accorded all the people of God, although non-ordained participation in the power to rule will be kept under tight restrictions. Attention will be given the adequate remuneration of all who work for the Church, including permanent deacons, although the practical systems for doing this will be left to local determination.[18]

What will the impact of this new Code be on the American approach to official ministry? Given the manner in which the 1917 Code was modified when it was applied in this country, it is not unreasonable to assume the peculiar conditions affecting official ministry will continue to be a factor in how the universal law is applied locally. Even more important will be the underlying understanding of official ministry which is put into operation, for the council called not only for a change in practical structures but even for a broadening of the meaning and practice of official ministry.

It is to this underlying understanding of official ministry as it applies in the United States that I now turn. Even as the new Code is being drafted, canon lawyers have begun debating the very basis for the structuring of official ministry—is it an *ordo*, or is it a *status*? Even

---

[17]Pope John XXIII called for the revision of the Code of Canon Law at the same time as he announced the Second Vatican Council. Drafts developed by working groups assigned to various portions of the law have been circulated for comment by the bishops, and a revised *Schema Codicis Iuris Canonici* (Vatican: Libreria Vaticana, 1980) has been circulated to Code Commission members in anticipation of an October, 1981 meeting to finalize the work. For an evaluation of the effort to date see T. J. Green, "The Revision of the Code: The First Decade," THE JURIST 36 (1976): 353-441; idem, "The Revision of Canon Law: Theological Implications," *Theological Studies* 40 (1979): 593-679; F. G. Morrisey, "The Revision of the Code of Canon Law," *Studia Canonica* 12 (1978): 177-198.

[18]See *Schema Codicis Iuris Canonici* [draft canons from this schema will be cited: Sch], Sch 142 (on office); 456, §2 (non-priests in charge of communities under the direction of a pastor); 273 (lay persons in ecclesiastical offices); 714 and 791, §1 (on teaching and sanctifying); 126 and 244 (on power of ruling); 1237 and 255 (on adequate remuneration).

more fundamentally, what is the operative understanding—ministry as a profession, or ministry as a bureaucracy?

"Ordo" or "Status"

One effort to clarify the canonical understanding of official ministry has been to determine whether this ministry is the prerogative of a separate class or caste in the Church (a "status"); or, does the function a minister provides bring about the special standing which characterizes an official minister in the Church (an "ordo"). Here are some examples of positions which have been taken in this discussion.

A leading exponent of the *ordo* side is the Spanish canonist Juan Fornes.[19] He argues the canonical understanding of ministry has shifted over the course of the Church's history. Originally, the basic equality of all in the Church was emphasized over against the fundamental stratification into unequal levels which characterized the Roman Empire (civil *status*). Within this fundamental equality in the Church there were various services or functions; those who provided them in an on-going manner were formed into *ordines*. The distinction was not on the basis of caste or class, however, but on the basis of service or function.

Fornes and others argue that a caste system developed within the Church when it took on the structures and trappings of the Roman Empire. Even the concept of *ordo* as it was practiced in the Roman State had become a caste type of stratification; when it was taken over into formal ecclesiastical usage, the element of stratification carried over with it.[20] Basic inequality became the cornerstone of the ecclesial structure even to the extent that the caste difference between clergy and laity was claimed to be based on divine institution.[21] The Second Vatican Council's teaching on the fundamental equality of all believers is viewed as a return to the early Church's understanding of ministry; it is seen to imply a function rather than a status or caste basis for ministry.

A more critical appraisal of the conciliar teaching is presented by the

---

[19]J. Fornes, *La nocion de "status" en Derecho Canonico* (Pamplona: EUNSA, 1975).

[20]A. Faivre, *Naissance d'une hiérarchie. Les premières étapes du cursus clerical* (Paris: Beauchesne, 1977); see also discussion on related aspects of this historical development in the studies by Collins and Osiek in this volume.

[21]A. Ottaviani, *Institutiones Iuris Publici Ecclesiastici* (Vatican: Typis Polyglottis, 4th ed. 1958), vol. 1, pp. 348-349.

French Dominican Christian Duquoc.[22] He faults the approach to ministry which bases itself on a "sacerdotal state" as hindering effective and creative responses to serious crises facing the Church. But he also contends that Vatican II did not address the underlying issue effectively. It was content, he claims, to put side-by-side approaches which emphasize the service or functional character of ministry, with statements about *sacra potestas* and the divinely willed distinction between clergy and laity.

The Italian canonist Dario Composta voices the other side of the discussion.[23] He examines the Scriptures and early church writers to refute historical arguments similar to those advanced by Fornes, and concludes the reality of the distinction by *status* is present from the very beginning even if the language to express it was not developed until later. Theologically, he argues, a faulty methodology and limited perspective typical of the "Atlantic" countries has led to the rejection of the special status due ordained ministers. He offers an interpretation of ordained ministry as rooted in the common status of all Christians, but differentiated from it by a consecration whereby the ordained are made representatives of Christ. The social expression of this consecration is found in the separateness (or "setting apart") of the ordained within the ecclesial community.[24]

At this stage in the debate it seems fruitless to try to resolve the issue historically, and the theological arguments will probably not convince either side. The significance of the issue is the understanding it represents of official ministry—service as the primary focus, or special status.

One cannot deny that ordained ministers—and even non-ordained ones—have a special social status. The canonical question is whether this role is essential to ministry and must be expressed and protected by a separate legal structure apart from the rest of the community. The special social status could be a function of the sociological typology of the church organization,[25] and the "divinely willed" distinction

---

[22]C. Duquoc, "Théologie de l'Église et crise du ministère," *Études* 350 (1979): 101-113. He cites three "crises": ordination of women, lack of priests in various third world countries, and the law on celibacy.

[23]D. Composta, "Lo stato clericale e i suoi problemi giuridici-teologici," *Apollinaris* 52 (1979): 442-477.

[24]See, however, Kilmartin's critique of a christomonostic approach to ministry elsewhere in this volume, and Collins' analysis of the status elevation language used for ordination.

[25]Formation of a professional elite for ministry is an element in the institutionalization of religion, and is subject to the dilemmas this process entails. See T. F. O'Dea,

(according to Trent) between clergy and laity might be respected without the full legal apparatus called for in the Code of Canon Law. While the attempts of Vatican II to place the issue in a better perspective have not been without criticism, they do offer the possibility of going beyond the ideology which lies at the core of the *status* versus *ordo* debate.[26]

PROFESSIONAL OR BUREAUCRAT

Legal structures cannot be understood adequately outside their political and cultural contexts. The understanding of official ministry in the United States is not untouched by the *status* versus *ordo* controversy, but it does seem to be affected more directly by a different kind of division not uncommon to the American culture. This is the tension between a professional and a bureaucrat.

Two people with the same training and commitment can become one a professional, the other a bureaucrat. An example might be accountants, one of whom helps you as your personal consultant in preparing your income tax form; the other, the person who audits your return as an official of the Internal Revenue Service. The tension between servng as a bureaucrat and operating as a professional is common to a number of specialties in the United States.[27] Several studies have used this fact as a way to understand the dilemma priests find themselves in today. As official ministers, are they professionals, serving the needs of the people? Or, are they agents of the organization, serving the needs of the church institution?

Hall and Schneider found the key factor for psychological success of priests to lie in the challenge of the work they do. Mary Ellen Reilly documented a general consensus among priests of all age categories that they see their work to be in terms of priest as teacher and priest as leader of ritual. Ventimiglia observed that seminarians become social-

---

"Five Dilemmas in the Institutionalization of Religion," *Journal for the Scientific Study of Religion* 1 (1961): 30-39.

[26]For example, Vatican II emphasizes service as the rationale for ministry, and the distinction of clergy-laity is rooted in the distinction between the common priesthood and the ordained priesthood. See P. Lombardia, "Estatuto juridico de los ministros sagrados en la actual legislacion canonica," in J. Lindemans and H. Demeester, eds., *Liber Amicorum Monseigneur Onclin* (Gembloux: J. Duculot, 1976), pp. 259-280.

[27]See R. Hall, "Professionalization and Bureaucratization," *American Sociological Review* 33 (1968): 92-104; J. Blau, "Expertise and Power in Professional Organizations," *Sociology of Work and Occupations* 6 (1979): 103-123.

ized into an identity as an official minister primarily through the reaction of people to whom they attempt to minister.[28] In other words, factors which are key to a priest's self-identity as priest, his psychological success and his desired work, are all related to a professional mode of behavior. The professional approach focuses on the relation of individuals to their work and the needs of one's client.[29]

The bureaucratic approach, on the other hand, stresses the way people relate by means of a system. Bureaucrats must perforce be primarily interested in maintaining the system. Typical experiences which reinforce a bureaucratic self-awareness for priests are the centralization of significant decisions affecting their work, including placement and tenure; content they are expected to include in their preaching; emphasis on rules and canon law; the expectation of both people and superiors that they will represent the system (diocese, or even the Church universal) to the people they serve; major administrative responsibilities which are restricted to them, or for which they are at least ultimately responsible.

The priest is not alone in finding himself at once a professional and a bureaucrat. Doctors in community health facilities, architects in various sized firms, lawyers who serve in corporations or large law firms find themselves faced with similar seemingly conflicting role expectations.[30] The difference seems to be that priests are in a closed system, a profession which cannot be exercised outside the Church without violating the very faith commitment which constitutes the essence of their call to be a priest in the first place.[31] Hence, priests find themselves peculiarly faced with the contrasting and even opposed principles of bureaucratic and professional modes of organization, without a ready escape from the resulting tension by transfer, change of firm, or the option of private practice.

[28]D. Hall and B. Schneider, *Organizational Climates and Careers: The Work Lives of Priests* (New York: Seminar Press, 1973); M. E. Reilly, "Perceptions of the Priest Role," *Sociological Analysis* 36 (1975): 347-356; J. C. Ventimiglia, "Significant Others in the Professional Socialization of Catholic Seminarians," *Journal for the Scientific Study of Religion* 17 (1978): 43-52.

[29]J. A. Struzzo, "Professionalism and the Resolution of Authority Conflicts Among the Catholic Clergy," *Sociological Analysis* 31 (1970): 92-93. The description of professionalization will be developed below.

[30]See Blau, "Expertise and Power."

[31]W. R. Headley, *The Departure of a Priest: Management of a Deviant Identity* (Ann Arbor: University Microfilms, 1974) deals with the priesthood as an "encapsulated profession" (pp. 4-16).

Let me analyze for a moment what this means.[32] As bureaucrats priests are subject to a centralized leadership, while as professionals they respect leadership on the basis of expertise. As representatives of the institution they must emphasize and enforce standard procedures, whereas as professionals they seek to adapt procedures to the needs of individual parishoners. From a bureaucratic point of view, they look to simplifying tasks so these can be done piecemeal and routinely; as professionals, they seek a comprehensive grasp of the total work. Little initiative is fostered in a bureaucracy, whereas broad initiative characterizes professionals. Corporate responsibility is emphasized in their bureaucratic mode, with obedience the primary virtue; personal responsibility is the most prized dimension of their professional work. As a bureaucrat the priest is expected to be able to deal equally with all sorts of other priests, somewhat impersonally, so he can be transferred to wherever the institution needs to place him; as a professional he seeks close colleague relationships with priests of like mind or challenging talent. Priests enjoy a certain prestige and status from office, an "ascribed" status; as professionals, many priests desire to be respected for their competence and not merely because they are pastors or officials of some agency.

In all this the priest is caught between the bureaucratic mode of organization which is designed to serve the system, and the professional mode in which he seeks to serve his parishoners. Let me stress again that this tension is due not to anything intrinsic to holy orders, but arises from the canonical understanding and the social organization of official ministry in the Church in the United States. The same dilemmas await anyone who would become involved in official ministry.

PREFERENCE TO BE PROFESSIONALS

Priests prefer to consider themselves professionals. At least, this seems to be the implication from various studies. Mary Ellen Reilly's findings note a preference for professional activities such as providing instruction and celebrating liturgy, but very low priority to such a critical institutional concern as recruiting new vocations.[33] Greeley reports priests view themselves as comparable to other professionals

---

[32]This analysis is based on the "comparison of the contrasting principles of organization in the bureaucratic and professional systems" developed by J. H. Fichter, *Religion as an Occupation: A Study in the Sociology of Professions* (Notre Dame, Ind.: University of Notre Dame Press, 1961), p. 224.

[33]Reilly, p. 351.

such as doctors and lawyers on the general characteristics of their professionalism.[34] Psychologically, priests in the United States are generally either underdeveloped or still in a stage of developing, according to the research of Kennedy and Heckler. That is, they are not at a mature level of self-motivation, although neither is the average American male. Kennedy and Heckler recommend greater freedom and responsibility for priests—typical of professional modes of operating—to foster a climate in which psychological maturity will develop.[35]

What is it that makes an occupation a "profession"? Professions have been analyzed according to various structural or objective elements, and according to various key attitudes on the part of those who make up the profession.[36] Structural attributes of a profession include: (1) creation of a full-time occupation; (2) establishment of a training school; (3) formation of a professional association; (4) formation of a code which the professionals enforce upon themselves. Attitudinal attributes include: (1) use of professional organization as a major reference group; (2) belief in service to the public; (3) belief in self-regulation; (4) sense of calling to the field; (5) professional autonomy.

Hall points out that the degree to which these attributes are verified can vary even within the "established" professions.[37] It is not necessary that all elements be clearly demonstrable for the priest to consider himself a professional. Yet most of these attributes can be demonstrated both in the factual experiences of official ministers, and in the organization of their ministry according to the Church's teaching and law.

For example, official ministry is a full-time occupation. This fact is reinforced by the conciliar teaching on priests (PO 3) and, negatively, by the prohibition from engaging in other activities besides ministry (CIC 138, 139, 142; Sch 259, 260, 261). Training schools or seminary formation, required at least since the time of Trent and mandated in the law (CIC 972; Sch 206) are promoted by a special decree of Vatican II (*Optatum totius*). Priests are encouraged to form and join associations (PO 9), the right to which will soon be stated in law (Sch 252); in

[34]A. M. Greeley, *Priests in the United States: Reflections on a Survey* (Garden City, NY: Doubleday, 1972), p. 118.

[35]E. C. Kennedy and V. J. Heckler, *The Catholic Priest in the United States: Psychological Investigations* (Washington, DC: USCC Publications, 1972), pp. 178-179.

[36]R. Hall, "Professionalization and Bureaucratization"; H. L. Wilensky, "The Professionalization of Everyone?" *American Journal of Sociology* 70 (1964): 137-158.

[37]R. Hall, pp. 93-94.

practice, various types of associations for educational, social, spiritual and professional purposes have developed among priests.

A profession normally sets its own code to which the professionals bind themselves. There is nothing directly comparable in the Church. Official ministers are bound by the teachings of the Church as well as the code of law imposed on them by the hierarchy. They do not have an active role in determining these, and Fichter points out this is a special factor about religious professionals—even their life style is set for them.[38]

Attitudes toward professionalism vary among the clergy. Struzzo proposes that it is the development of a professional attitude which differentiates the way priests resolve authority conflicts.[39] Fichter claims the professionalization of the clergy is promoted by increasing specialization in many aspects of ministry, including pastoral ministry; but his argument reads more as a plea than as an observation—he is urging that this mentality be adopted.[40] Nevertheless there are various indications of a professional mentality among the clergy, and some encouragement of this even in Church teaching and law.

Here are some examples of official encouragement of a professional attitude. Using the professional organization as a major reference group is encouraged by PO 8 (all priests are to help one another in many ways, including through professional priestly concerns), and Sch 248 encourages a spirit of fraternity among priests. Service to the public underlies what most priests have identified as their primary goal; this is encouraged by PO 3. A belief in self-regulation is encouraged by PO 8 where priests are called to look after one another, admonishing and correcting each other as needed. A sense of calling is reported by most priests, is encouraged by PO 3, and is one of the traditional elements tested before admission to ordination. Professional autonomy has traditionally been assured through the system of offices and

---

[38]Fichter, *Religion as an Occupation*, pp. 213-219.

[39]Struzzo, pp. 92-106.

[40]J. H. Fichter, *Organization Man in the Church* (Cambridge, Mass.: Schenkman, 1973), p. 49. Gannon indictes a complex effect when such professionalization is attempted, depending n whether the priest is secular or religious; see T. M. Gannon, "The Effect of Segmentation in the Religious Clergy," *Sociological Analysis* 40 (1979): 183-196. Gannon's categories of "accomodation" and "exchange model" address some of the issues of professionalism and bureaucracy, but from more of a social-interactionist perspective; see his "The Impact of Structural Differences" cited in note 3, above.

the ordinary jurisdiction attached to them (CIC 197; Sch 142, §2).[41]
Pastoral initiative is encouraged under the lead of the "loving Spirit
who breathes where he will" (PO 13).

TENSION ABOUT BEING A PROFESSIONAL

Priests expect to be professionals. There is solid backing for such an
expectation in the official documents and in the law of the Church. Yet
it is a frequent observation that precisely these expectations lie at much
of the tension priests experience today. Greeley claims "the curate is a
professional caught in a feudal structure."[42] Fichter associates the professionalism of the priest with his "subsidiary role"; his key role, like
that of other religious professionals (sisters, brothers) is a member of
an organization.[43] This becomes problematic when the "church professional who finds satisfaction in his work may be dissatisfied with the
authoritarian structure in which he works."[44]

Struzzo proposes that conflicts with authority faced by priests—who
are professionals within an authoritarian bureaucratic structure—arise
from the fact that two different principles of organization are at
work.[45] Expecting a professional approach which emphasizes the role of
individual activities and colleague relationships, they find instead a
bureaucratic subordination of the individual to the organization.

There are several aspects of the structuring of official ministry where
this conflict can be observed. For example, promotion in a professional
setting ideally depends on expertise, although seniority is taken into
consideration.[46] The law reinforces this expectation within the Church
by calling for appointment of those "more suited" to vacant parishes
(CIC 459, §1), or at least "suited" in keeping with the situation of the

---

[41]This canonical assurance, however, is somewhat negated by the American practice
of using delegates (chancellors) instead of vicars general, and stressing the direct intervention of the bishop rather than the pastoral responsibility of the office-holder.
See below.

[42]A. M. Greeley, "The Parish Assistant," in G. Sloyan, ed., *Secular Priest in the New
Church* (New York: Herder & Herder, 1967), pp. 157.

[43]Fichter, *Religion as an Occupation*, p. 165.

[44]Fichter, *Organization Man in the Church*, p. 28.

[45]Struzzo, p. 29.

[46]Blau finds this has special significance for lower-level professionals such as staff
architects; "Expertise and Power," p. 115.

parish (Sch 463). However, the fact is that among priests seniority has been the dominant element which explains advancements.[47]

Conflict has been evident when priests are asked to enforce certain rules in the context of their pastoral ministry (i.e., their professional work) which to them appear to be bureaucratic rather than pastorally based. Interestingly, this applies even to the sacraments; delays in processing marriage cases or inconsistencies in granting permission for eucharistic hospitality or general absolution are leading to the same kind of marginalization for these norms as seems to have occurred relative to the official teaching on birth control.[48]

The bureaucratic-professional conflict has been most evident, however, relative to expectations about the priest's personal life-style. The celibacy issue is such an obvious point of conflict that it has been a major occasion for several recent sociological studies about priests. But questions of clerical dress and personal living quarters have also been points of conflict between what priests consider their professional autonomy and what they perceive to be bureaucratic efforts to control their lives.

BUREAUCRATIC DIMENSION

What is this "bureaucracy"? Max Weber presents a study of the "ideal-type" of bureaucracy; that is, he studies the ideal features of such an organization, and presents frankly positive connotations of efficiency and fairness.[49] Mouzelis has summarized Weber's position into six elements:[50] (1) high degree of specialization and division of labor; (2) hierarchical authority structure with limited areas of com-

---

[47]R. Peterson and R. A. Schoenherr, "Organizational Status Attainment of Religious Professionals," *Social Forces* 56 (1978): 794-822.

[48]The NORC study documented a reaction in 1970 which indicated that "insofar as [*Humanae vitae*] was designed to obtain the consent of the American clergy in moral teaching," it was not successful; support for the position in the encyclical *declined* in all age categories after its promulgation. See NORC, *The Catholic Priest in the United States: Sociological Investigations*, pp. 105-115. Developments on the other issues are not thoroughly documented, but discussions with clergy at various meetings around the country indicate they are taking place.

[49]M. Weber, *Economy and Society* (New York: Bedminster Press, 1968), vol. 3, pp. 956-1006. He presents the Catholic Church as an historical example of "relatively clearly developed and quantitatively large" bureaucracies (p. 964).

[50]N. P. Mouzelis, *Organization and Bureaucracy: An Analysis of Modern Theories* (Chicago: Aldine, 1967), p. 39.

mand and responsibility; (3) impersonal relationships between organizational members; (4) recruitment of officials on the basis of ability and technical knowledge; (5) differentiation of private and official income and resources; (6) exercise of control through rules which are based on technical knowledge rather than tradition alone.

These elements clearly apply to the canonical understanding of official ministry. Bureaucratic division of labor has been a canonical tradition since the middle ages through the system of offices (CIC 145; Sch 142). Quite a few specializations have developed among official ministers, as reflected in PO 8. The hierarchical structure is one of Roman Catholicism's most evident features, officially highlighted in Chapter III of *Lumen gentium* and expressed juridically in CIC 108-109, Sch 202. Clergy are to avoid too intimate an involvement with those they serve, even while coming to know their conditions, needs and wants (PO 17); legal principles are given for what to do when objectivity is missing in church administration (CIC 103-104; Sch 121-125), and penalties are set down in CIC 2404-2414 for abuse of power or office. Qualifications for the job are stressed in principles for determining whom to appoint to an office (CD 31), and attention to them is required by law (CIC 459; Sch 460, §3). Official income and church resources are protected through the system of benefices and rules for church administration (PO 17; CIC 1518-1528; Sch 1224-1240). The exercise of control through rules is reinforced in terms of the obedience and reverence official ministers owe their superiors (PO 15; CIC 127-128; Sch 245-247).

Weber's concepts are of an "ideal-type." The practice of bureaucracy in the Roman Catholic Church has characteristics of its own which distance it from such an ideal form. Actually, the Church's bureaucratic system is still in tune with its Roman roots, where bureaucracy was not a pure type but existed in combination with patrimonialism, harmonizing achievement with class ascription.[51] The Church's bureaucracy is set in a familiar (or paternal) setting where the Holy "Father" for the Church universal, the bishop as "father" and pastor of the diocese, control the operations of the bureaucracy. As a result it reaches not only into the efficient operation of the institution, but touches the life-style and personal manner of living of those who at the lower levels staff the bureaucracy (the official ministers).

[51]R. J. Antonio, "The Contradiction of Domination and Production in Bureaucracy: The Contribution of Organizational Efficiency to the Decline of the Roman Empire," *American Sociological Review* 44 (1979): 905.

SOME DRAWBACKS

There are potential dangers in either the professional or the bureaucratic approach when applied purely and simply in the Church. The Church is a communion and a mission; its official ministry cannot be a loose association of independent professionals, for their ministry is directed precisely toward building up the communion and enabling the mission of the body. Neither is the Church a "necessary" institution such as a civil government; today, the Church is a voluntary organization in which people know they have a way out. Purely bureaucratic methods which may work when all are subject to the organization are not adequate to engender the sense of belonging which is critical to continued communion and mission.[52]

However, the evidence seems to support the claim that the dominant mode in church practice is clearly bureaucratic. For this reason, more detailed attention needs to be given the implications of such dominance if we are to grasp realistically the present canonical understanding of official ministry.

When searching for the underlying bond which assures organizational cohesion among ordained ministers, the Church has preferred obedience. While both obedience and pastoral autonomy can be found in Vatican II, the most explicit and direct attention is given to obedience.[53] Obedience is presented not only as a means to assure efficiency in pastoral care, but also as a spiritualized ideology.[54] The very nature of official ministry below the level of bishop is articulated in terms of dependence. Priests, for example, are said to be "prudent cooperators with the episcopal order as well as its aids and instruments" and work "under the bishop's authority" (LG 28). They carry out functions "as co-workers with their bishops" (PO 4) and it is

---

[52]J. Provost, "Structuring the Church as a *Communio*," THE JURIST 36 (1976): 191-245; idem, "Structuring the Church as *Missio*," THE JURIST 39 (1979): 220-288.

[53]PO 15 provides a detailed development on the obedience priests owe the hierarchy, including the following: "Pastoral love demands . . . priests dedicate their own wills through obedience to the service of God and their brothers. This love requires that they accept and carry out in a spirit of faith whatever is commanded or recommended by the Sovereign Pontiff, their own bishop, or other superiors."

[54]PO 15: "This obedience leads to the more mature freedom of God's sons." By it, "priests make themselves like Christ" who by such obedience "overcame and redeemed the disobedience of Adam."

"through the ministry of the bishop" that "God consecrates priests" while "in administering all the sacraments . . . priests by various titles are bound together hierarchically with the bishop" (PO 5). "To the degree of their authority and in the name of the bishop" priests perform their pastoral work (PO 6). Clearly, the council was not talking about independent professionals in private practice, but in terms of subordination and obedience of the official ministers at the professional level to a "ruling elite."

Canonical tradition reinforces this understanding. CIC 127 states that all clerics, but especially priests, are bound by a special obligation to show reverence and obedience to their own ordinary. A cleric must undertake any function (*munus*) assigned him by his ordinary whenever and as often as, in the ordinary's judgment, the necessity of the Church requires this; the cleric can, however, plead a legitimate excuse (CIC 128). The proposed new Code will strengthen the hierarchy's position in both these canons by adding special mention of the obligation of obedience to the pope as well as one's own ordinary (Sch 247), and requiring the ordained minister to accept whatever function the ordinary requires even though the necessity of the Church may not be at stake in the ordinary's estimation (Sch 245).

Efforts to moderate this bureaucratic tendency were made during the Second Vatican Council in special reference to the relationships between bishops and the Apostolic See. Collegiality was adopted as the guiding principle, stressing the professional responsibility of all bishops for the whole Church, and the autonomy of bishops in their respective dioceses. The application of these same principles to professionalizing the official ministry within local dioceses, however, was not developed by the council. Indeed, the paternal mode of relationship was encouraged in the conciliar documents along with more professional-related principles such as shared responsibility. Even with a clear mandate from the council it has been difficult to convert from bureaucratic to collegial relationships at the level of the universal Church. It should not be surprising that at the diocesan level results are equally mixed.

Research indicates that structures for expressing shared responsibility at the diocesan level have been established in a number of dioceses. Most frequently these are priests' senates, but diocesan pastoral councils are also developing. The practical results, however, are disappointing. Three out of four senates and seven out of eight pastoral councils in the United States are, by and large, powerless to affect diocesan decisions in any notable way even though experience shows these groups have a remarkable capacity to do the job well when they do go to work on something.[55]

Legal support for shared responsibility is being weakened in proposals for the new Code, particularly when the 1980 draft is compared with the 1977 version of the book "On the People of God."[56] The earlier version attempted to recognize the significance of episcopal conferences for the life of the Church. Over fifty references to the role of such conferences were deleted in developing the 1980 revision. While a priests' council will be mandated for all dioceses, it is to be totally subject to the bishop who convokes, presides, and sets the agenda for its meetings (Sch 420, §1). When the council's counsel or consent is required by law, only the bishop can make the results public (Sch 420, §§2 & 3). Pastoral councils for the diocese and parishes will be optional, at the determination of the bishop, and will work under the presidency of either the bishop (Sch 431, §1 for the diocesan council) or pastor (Sch 475, §1 for parish councils). It is proposed even to weaken one of the examples of shared responsibility in the 1917 Code; instead of having to consult a pastor before assigning an assistant to the parish (CIC 476, §3), the proposed Code would leave it up to the bishop to determine if such consultation is opportune (Sch 486).

Another indication that the dominant organizational mode in the Church today is bureaucratic is the tendency toward increased middle-level diocesan administration. The reorganization of diocesan administration in recent years has been attempted by several United States dioceses in the name of improving the quality of service. Bureaucracies arise precisely on the promise of increased efficiency.[57] The application of management principles through secretariats, departments, or specialized vicariates is being done by consciously drawing on modern organizational techniques to achieve this same promise. Scheets' analysis of three dioceses discovered an increase of diocesan agencies and

[55]R. A. Schoenherr and E. Simpson, *The Policical Economy of Diocesan Advisory Councils*, CROS Respondent Report 3 (Madison: University of Wisconsin, 1978), pp. 67, 80. See J. Provost, "The Working Together of Consultative Bodies—Great Expectations?" THE JURIST 40 (1980): 256-281.

[56]Pontificia Commissio Codici Iuris Canonici Recognoscendo, *Schema Canonum Libri II De Populo Dei* (Vatican: Typis Polyglottis, 1977). See analysis by J. Komonchak, "A New Law for the People of God: Some Theological Reflections," *CLSA Proceedings* 42 (1980): 38-41.

[57]P. M. Blau and M. W. Meyer, *Bureaucracy in Modern Society* (New York: Random House, 2nd ed. 1971), p. 21.

services from 12 in 1900 to 193 in 1978. He reports a remarkable thirteen percent increase per year in programs since 1970.[58]

Although a comprehensive study of organization in American dioceses remains to be done, it is clear there is a general trend to institutionalize specialized concerns into offices or bureaus, committees or commissions. There has also been an increase in the number of personnel assigned full-time to such work.[59] While such persons may be professionals in their fields, they occupy clearly bureaucratic positions. Moreover, Fichter found job bureaucrats (who happen to have some professional entrance qualifications to the position but are entirely dedicated to the work and career within the bureaucratic system) to be much more prevalent than functional or specialist bureaucrats in the Church (these latter have greater affinity to a professional orientation).[60]

Some Dangers

There are some known dangers in a strongly bureaucratic mode of organization. Weber's ideal-type formulation has been criticized as invalid on several counts, not the least of which is that is presumes bureaucracy will increase efficiency as it claims when in fact the opposite is not an uncommon result.[61] Even Weber recognized another danger; namely, that there is a tendency in bureaucracies to seek domination, since "discipline and hierarchical power relations are the central and integrating attributes" of the bureaucratic mode of organization.[62]

Antonio's study is especially pertinent to an evaluation of the reliance on bureaucracy by the Catholic Church as the primary organizational principle for official ministry. His study is designed to determine the extent to which organizational efficiency contributed to the decline of the Roman Empire. The Church has based its bureaucratic structure on Roman Law foundations, and has even drawn on the organizational patterns of imperial bureaucracy to construct its own

---

[58]F. K. Scheets, "A Sketch of American Diocesan Organization 1900-1978," in *CARA Church Mangagement Program*, Proceedings of the Diocesan Organization Workshop (Washington, DC: CARA, 1980), pp. 28-38.

[59]J. Provost, "Diocesan Administration: Reflections on Recent Developments," THE JURIST 41 (1981): 81-104.

[60]Fichter, *Religion as an Occupation*, p. 231.

[61]Mouzelis, pp. 38-49; P. M. Blau and M. W. Meyer, pp. 23-26.

[62]Antonio, p. 896. He studies "the contribution of organizational efficiency to the decline of the Roman Empire."

hierarchical organization.[63] Increased reliance on bureaucratic efficiency in the Church could well carry the same weaknesses that Antonio discerns in the Roman imperial bureaucracy. This weakness was specifically the centralization of power to assure domination, and while it worked efficiently for that purpose the concern for domination replaced concern for production as the rationale for the bureaucracy itself.

The Roman Empire's wealth was mainly agricultural. "Production" in this sense was influenced by factors independent of human interaction, such as climate, fertility of the soil, and so on. The Church's "production" is specifically in the interpersonal sphere of "care of souls." With the present reliance on bureaucratic organization for official ministry, is there evidence that domination is replacing concern for care of souls, as it did in the Empire? Certainly it has not replaced it in principle or in official policy. But neither did domination replace the ideology of efficient production that surrounded the bureaucracy of Imperial Rome.

Two areas of church life relating to official ministry evidence at least the temptation to let concern for domination replace pastoral production: the question of the availability of eucharistic celebrations for increasing numbers of local communities; and the question of the standing of dispensed priests. An analysis of each of these may help deepen our canonical understanding of official ministry today.

1. Eucharistic Celebrations

The celebration of the Eucharist is the "basis and center" of any Christian community (PO 6). Only a priest (or bishop) can preside at the celebration. The number of priests available for this in the United States is declining at an alarming rate. From 1966 to the end of 1973 there was a 1.46% net average annual decline of active diocesan priests in this country.[64] Careful analysis of entry rates, resignations, retirements and deaths indicates that by the year 2,000 there will be 54 percent fewer active diocesan priests in the United States than there were in the mid-1960s, but they will be called on to serve a Catholic population which will have grown at least thirty-four percent larger

---

[63]Faivre, *Naissance d'une hierarchie.*
[64]R. A. Schoenherr and A. Sorensen, *From the Second Vatican to the Second Millenium: Decline and Change in the U.S. Catholic Church,* CROS Respondent Report 5 (Madison: University of Wisconson, 1981), p. 7.

than in 1969. Moreover, the smaller number of priests will be predominantly older clergy.[65]

This represents a real threat to the availability of eucharistic celebrations in the coming years. In many parts of the world, this crisis situation already exists.[66] Efforts to adjust to these conditions have focused primarily on pastoral care, including the formation of pastoral assistants and the development of lay leadership in base communities.[67] But these do not provide celebrants to preside at the Eucharist, and church officials continue to refuse to ordain competent married men to the priesthood or to permit the ordination of competent women.

Refusal to ordain women, even celibate women, is presented as a theological issue.[68] The position on requiring celibacy of men, however, is clearly a disciplinary norm. It was imposed only after several centuries of married clergy; it has admitted of exceptions. In its present formulation it is peculiar to the Latin Rite, or has been imposed on Eastern Rites contary to their traditions when they are providing official ministry in Western areas.[69] As such, the law on clerical celibacy forms a clear test for the understanding of official ministry today. The law could be changed to ease the crisis of increasing numbers of communities denied the essential experience of Catholic identity, the celebration of the Eucharist. Yet it is maintained. Why?

Paul VI provided several reasons in his 1967 encyclical on priestly celibacy.[70] His arguments can be summarized in four points: the tradi-

[65]Ibid., pp. 38-39.

[66]J. Kerkofs, "Priests and 'Parishes'—A Statistical Survey," in E. Schillebeeckx and J-B Metz, eds., *The Right of the Community to a Priest*, Concilium 133 (New York: Seabury, 1980), pp. 3-11; G. Marc, "Statistical Data, Projections and Interpretations Relating to the Numerical Composition of the Catholic Church," in G. Alberigo and G. Gutierrez, eds., *Where Does the Church Stand?*, Concilium 146 (New York: Seabury, 1981), pp. 87-91.

[67]"What are the Pastoral Assistants of the German Church?" *Origins* 10/32 (January 22, 1981): 503-509; Pro Mundi Vita, *Priestless Parishes in Western Europe: Present situation and attempted solutions*, Europe/North America Dossier 6 (Brussels: Pro Mundi Vita, 1979), pp. 26-27; see also Concilium 133, cited in previous note.

[68]S. Congregation for the Doctrine of the Faith, *Declaration on the Question of the Admission of Women to the Ministerial Priesthood*, October 15, 1976 (Washington, DC: USCC Publications, 1977).

[69]Decree of the S. Congregation for the Oriental Church, "*Qua Sollerti*," December 23, 1929: *AAS* 22 (1930): 99-105, especially §6. See P. Bilaniuk, "Celibacy and Eastern Tradition," in G. Frein, ed., *Celibacy: The Necessary Option* (New York: Herder & Herder, 1968), pp. 32-72, esp. pp. 60-61.

[70]Paul VI, Encyclical Letter "*Sacerdotalis Coelibatus*," June 24, 1967: *AAS* 59 (1967): 657-697.

tion of the Church, particularly in the West; the Christological significance, since the priest stands *in persona Christi*; the ecclesiological
significance, particularly the freedom for ministry and close bonding to
the Church which celibacy provides; and the eschatological witness to
values which go beyond our present experience. John Paul II con-
denses these even further: celibacy is a gift of the Spirit, and it provides
freedom for pastoral service.[71]

By admitting the charism of celibacy is not intrinsically tied to priesthood, and therefore for official ministry it is neither the essential
dimension of Christological significance nor a necessary eschatological
witness, these recent popes have highlighted the ecclesiological or disciplinary importance of celibacy for the present structuring of the
Church. The celibate is bonded in an unusual way to the Church,
which reaches to the most intimate aspects of his personal life. It makes
him free to go wherever he may be sent, without encumbrance of
family to impede total availability to serve as directed.

The history of celibacy is a complex one, frequently overlaid with
cultic and cultural taboos and often imposed as the safest means to
assure continence, the fundamental rationale for imposing celibacy on
the secular clergy in the first place.[72] Economic considerations have also
played their part, for instance in the effort to assure the wealth of the
Church does not fall into the hands of priestly families from one generation to the next.

Today the organizational significance of the law on celibacy is more
evident than cultic or sexual taboos. Likewise, economic considerations have shifted from questions of ownership and inheritance to
issues of support and the heavy investment the American church has
made in buildings and material supports for a celibate clergy. Requiring celibacy as a condition for official ministry—at least, the official
ministry of presiding at the Eucharist, which is central to Catholic
life—despite the evident need for more ministers and the availability of
non-celibates, may be one of the clearest evidences of domination

[71]John Paul II, "A Letter to Priests," April 9, 1979: *Origins* 8/44 (April 19,
1979): 700-701. Pope John Paul calls celibacy "a characteristic, a peculiarity and a
heritage of the Latin Catholic Church, a tradition to which she is resolved to persevere,
in spite of all the difficulties to which such fidelity could be exposed" (p. 701).

[72]Research into the history of celibacy has been extensive. See R. Gryson, *Les Origins
de Celibat Ecclesiastique du première au septième siècle* (Gembloux: J. Duculot, 1970);
idem, "Dix ans de recherches sur les origins du celibat ecclesiastique," *Revue théologique
de Louvain* 11 (1980): 157-185; also, J. E. Lynch, "Marriage and Celibacy of the Clergy:
The Discipline of the Western Church," THE JURIST 32 (1972): 14-38, 189-212.

having taken over as the primary consideration in the canonical understanding of official ministry.

Equally a barrier to official ministry in some parts of the world and for some cultural groups within the United States, may be the seminary system as it has been traditionally structured. Removing a young man from his cultural environment and requiring socialization into a Western European mode of life and thought effectively alienates him from his cultural roots. Rather than adjusting the system to assure professional training for clergy within their own cultural framework, this elite training will soon become specifically a "formation" into the clerical ranks (Sch. 206; 216, §2). Despite the known social drawbacks of insisting on the current system, it is maintained in the face of increasingly critical shortages of priests. Could this be another instance of priority being given to domination concerns?

2. *Dispensed Priests*

Another area of church life where domination may be evident in the canonical understanding of official ministry is the standing of dispensed priests. In October, 1980 new Norms for processing such dispensations were released together with an administrative letter from the Congregation for the Doctrine of the Faith. The letter detailed the position being adopted by the Vatican in such cases.[73] Several factors are of interest in these documents.

First, the reason for granting the dispensation has been reduced to celibacy. Despite considerable evidence to the contrary at least in the United States, the interpretation of why a priest seeks to leave active, official ministry has now been narrowly focused. There is no recognition given to the fact that the current organization of official ministry may itself be leading priests to seek dispensation from clerical status.[74]

---

[73]S. Congregration for the Doctrine of the Faith, "New Vatican Norms for Laicization," *Origins* 10/21 (November 6, 1980): 335-336.

[74]Instead of a dispensation "from all the obligations arising from Sacred Orders, including celibacy, and a return to lay status in the Church," the dispensation is now "*a sacerdotalis coelibatu.*" Various reasons why men seek dispensation are discussed in H. J. Kuehne, "Resignation from the Priesthood and Normal Organizational Development," *Review for Religious* 28 (1969): 783-796; E. Schallert and J. Kelley, "Some Factors Associated with Voluntary Withdrawal from the Catholic Priesthood," *Lumen Vitae* 25 (1970): 425-460; R. A. Schoenherr and A. M. Greeley, "Role Commitment Processes and the American Catholic Priesthood," *American Sociological Review* 39 (1974): 407-426; F. H. Goldner, R. R. Ritti and T. P. Ference, "The Production of Cynical Knowledge in Organizations," *American Sociological Review* 42 (1977): 539-

Second, while the dispensed priest is encouraged to participate in the life of the people of God and to give good example, he is at the same time excluded from activities normally available to qualified lay persons; i.e., he is not to serve as an extraordinary minister of the Eucharist, to teach theological disciplines or subjects related to them in institutions of higher learning, or to have any function in a seminary or similar institute. He may not exercise a directive function pastorally, even one which is now open to lay persons.[75] There is nothing inherently scandalous, giving bad example, or contrary to active participation in the life of the people of God in performing such activities per se; could the restriction not be described as another indication of the domination effect replacing all other concerns, including the inclusion of qualified men for much needed pastoral services?[76]

The danger to the Church in such a domination-centered approach lies in the negative effect it may have on the special ideology of service and concern for the person which the ecclesial community proclaims and which undergirds its institutional structure. Canon lawyers cannot be indifferent to this danger. As practical instances of domination become apparent, especially in the denial of service or opportunities to serve as described above, there is a real possibility that "cynical knowledge" will be produced.

In the context of commitment to an organization, cynical knowledge is "knowledge that presumably altruistic actions or procedures of the organization actually serve the purpose of maintaining the legitimacy of existing authority or preserving the institutional structure."[77] It differs from realism in that it undercuts the basis for commitment,

---

551; J. Seidler, "Priest Resignations in a Lazy Monopoly," *American Sociological Review* 44 (1979): 763-783.

[75]These restrictions are revised from those stated in the "Circular Letter" and "Procedural Norms for Reduction to the Lay State" of January 13, 1971; see *CLD* 7:110-121. Text of the standard rescript now in use, containing the more stringent restrictions, can be found in THE JURIST 41 (1981): 227-228.

[76]Restrictions against involving dispensed priests in some form of ministry are disciplinary law; local bishops theoretically have the power to dispense from such laws (CD 8,b; *motu proprio "De episcoporum muneribus,"* June 15, 1966) but are under considerable pressure from the Vatican not to do so. See analysis of the restrictions and discretionary power of local bishops in J. Provost, K. Lasch and H. Skillin, "Dispensed Priests in Ecclesial Ministry: A Canonical Reflection," *Chicago Studies* 14 (1975): 121-133.

[77]Goldner, et al., "The Production of Cynical Knowledge," p. 540.

whereas realism merely adjusts that commitment more maturely. If people are encouraged to adopt the Catholic understanding of the centrality of eucharistic celebrations, and then are denied the possibility of such celebrations because of bureaucratic concerns for domination that seem to require current restrictions on who may be ordained to official eucharistic presidency, is there not the danger of cynical knowledge resulting as the true reason for the lack of priests becomes apparent? If trained, qualified and willing persons are available for other types of official ministry but are forbidden to serve because they have been dispensed from the obligation of celibacy, can the community avoid the impression that domination of resignees is what counts, rather than service of its needs? If "production" is neglected because of over concentration on domination concerns, there is danger for the continued vitality of the entire organization.

Cynical knowledge affects not only the general population of the Church. It has an impact on official ministers as well. If a bureaucratic mode of organization continues to prevail, and if the temptation to focus on domination as a solution to perceived problems within official ministry is not resisted, the resulting cynical knowledge could further exacerbate the crisis of ministry rather than resolve it. This may indeed be happening already.[78]

SOME IMPLICATIONS

What can be learned from all this? I have tried to illustrate that approaching the canonical understanding of official ministry from a social science perspective may help to clarify some of the options for the organization of ministry as it develops beyond the clerical caste as set in the Code. The following may be some implications from this analysis.

1. Official ministry is not just a profession. That is, official ministers are not private practitioners but are an integral dimension of the life and mission of the Christian community. Neither are they just bureaucrats, and structuring their ministry is not adequately promoted by strictly bureaucratic approaches.

2. Emphasis on a bureaucratic mode of organization in an effort to dominate official ministry and direct it toward the specific ends of those

[78]Goldner, et al., p. 547.

in charge of the organization is self-destructive. It carries with it all the disadvantages of domination, including the real potential for increasing rather than containing what higher officials view as current problems.

3. Canon law, however, is not necessarily bureaucratic nor does it have to be dominative. In its present form, I admit, it lends itself to the bureaucratic mode of organization. But professionals seek civil laws to protect their autonomy and the competence requirements that will maintain the quality of their profession. Canon law has done and can continue to do the same. It has a rich "professional" tradition in the structure of church office, in the understanding of "ordinary" power, and in more contemporary provisions for the right to association and encouragement of peer or colleague relationships. Moreover, it provides for more local or particular legislation which can tailor the canonical structure to conditions within the United States; e.g., through particular councils and decisions of the episcopal conference.

4. Principles and structures which would enable the church community to integrate the professionalism of official ministers and the bureaucratic concerns of the hierarchy are already in place. The Second Vatican Council laid the foundation for collegiality, shared responsibility, subsidiarity and legitimate diversity. These are the principles which are to shape the relationships between various levels of the hierarchical communion in the Church and within the professional dealings of official ministers.[79] Structures such as episcopal conferences, priests' councils, diocesan pastoral councils, and professional organizations of ministers already have some history. They have demonstrated their potential, even though at present they appear to be underutilized and even undervalued.

5. What then, is the problem? It seems to be two-fold: how the law is interpreted and administered; and the general climate within the American church, the "politics" internal to the organization. These deserve closer scrutiny.

a. As with Vatican II, the new Code will contain a variety of perspectives not all of which can be harmonized, and certainly not all of which can be implemented in a way that integrates the bureaucratic and professinal dimensions of official ministry. But canon law in its classical tradition does not expect a mechanical application of norms.

[79]Provost, "Communio," pp. 194-196; idem, "Missio," pp. 228-229.

It is a living, flexible instrument amenable to careful interpretation and development. The principles set forth by the Second Vatican Council set the perspective within which the law is to be received and understood. The structures of shared responsibility and collegiality are the instruments through which it is to be implemented. These certainly temper the present tendency to bureaucratic domination; they must be utilized, however, to be effective.[80]

b. This raises the question of the politics of the church organization, a question which is much more difficult to address. Some of church policies arise from clear cultureal differences which affect such critical elements of church order as hierarchical distance and professional autonomy.[81] Within the American church this may be reflected in the reluctance of bishops to utilize the canonical tradition of "ordinary" power attached to the office of vicar general, or to recognize the appropriate autonomy of parish priests. Instead a system of delegates has been developed, chancellors doing in this country what vicars general do elsewhere; and parish priests seem frequently to be viewed as delegates of the bishop rather than as pastors with the *cura animarum*.[82]

Politics is also a function of persons, their actions and reactions. To the extent a body of persons remains passive and subservient, to that extent a bureaucratic mode can take root and dominate. If a more professional dimension is to be integrated in the understanding of official ministry, the professionals themselves must take responsibility for this.

Priests have already attempted this to some extent through associations and priests' councils. More significant for ministry have been

---

[80]How one interprets the law is as much a function of attitude and general approach to life and the Church as it is a question of technical skill. See J. A. Alesandro, "The Revision of Church Law: Conflict and Reconciliation," THE JURIST 40 (1980): 1-26; L. Orsy, "The Interpreter and his Art," THE JURIST 40 (1980): 27-56; and Coriden, "Law in Service to the People of God."

[81]Such cultural influences are not limited to the Church. For a study of their impact within a multinational corporation see G. Hofstede, "Hierarchical Power Distance in Forty Countries," in C. J. Lammers and D. J. Hickson, eds., *Organizations Alike and Unlike: International and inter-institutional studies in the sociology of organizations* (London: Routledge and Kegan Paul, 1979). pp. 97-119.

[82]Letter of the Apostolic Delegate to the Bishops of the United States, December 3, 1964: *CLD* 6:385, in which the bishops may delegate to their chancellors in this country the faculties in the *motu proprio* "Pastorale munus," November 30, 1963. By general law, these can be delegated only to vicars general. See also J. Provost, "Diocesan Administration," p. 83.

personnel boards the the development of personnel policies in a number of dioceses.[83] As indicated earlier, the effectiveness of such efforts leaves much to be desired.

Effective influence requires that official ministers at the lower levels generate a dependence on them by the hierarchy. This is possible within existing ministerial opportunities. Lower participants achieve power in an organization by obtaining, maintaining, and controlling access to persons, information and instrumentalities.[84] In other words, by building close ties with those they serve and controlling access to them and information about them, official ministers—ordained or not—build a situation where the hierarchy must depend on them. Some pastors have known this instinctively, and influence the bishop by appeals to "my people are not ready for this," or "my people need that." After all, the people are the Church in more than ideology.

The council recongized that "pastors should enjoy in their respective parishes that stability of office which the good of souls demands" (CD 31). However, norms on appointment, transfer and removal from office have been simplified,[85] with the result that clergy appear to have been moved from parish to parish more frequently in recent years than in past practice. Some dioceses have instituted formal time limits to particular offices in an effort to assure some stability, but also with an eye to avoiding the creation of independent power bases by local clergy.[86] While there are advantages to the present approach, it can have the serious disadvantage of keeping the clergy from developing the kind of bond with the people they serve which is needed for the "good of souls." This bond also could generate the base from which to develop influence in the organization.

The early attention by priests' senates and others to the personnel practices in various dioceses was not misplaced. It deserves to be continued. Stability in office, ordinary power, and effective procedures to safeguard these, are rooted in canon law and will find renewed expression in the revised Code. They touch intimately on the professionaliza-

[83]R. F. Szafran, *Preliminary Conclusions About the Creation of Personnel Boards in Roman Catholic Dioceses*, CROS Respondent Report 2 (Madison: University of Wisconsin, 1976). See National Association of Church Personnel Administrators (NACPA), *Report of Professional Development Committee* (Cincinnati, Ohio: NACPA, 1979), for a collection of diocesan policies.

[84]J. Blau, "Expertise and Power," p. 119.

[85]Pope Paul VI, *motu proprio "Ecclesiae Sanctae,"* August 6, 1966, I, 20.

[86]Janicki, "Limited Term of Office and Retirement."

tion of official ministry. Those interested in promoting the professional dimension of ministry would do well to foster these canonical provisions, for they are central to balancing the predominance of the bureaucratic mode in church governance.

Blau finds another significant opportunity to build dependence by the hierarchy: the expertise of lower staff in areas involving uncertainty.[87] As official ministers develop their professional abilities and apply these to the developing areas of ministry, they build a dependence of the organization on them as the Church continues to develop in these areas. For example, professional religious educators have found increasing influence in the system as parishes find they no longer have parochial schools, or as they become aware of the numbers of Catholic youth not in Catholic education.

Fichter points to continuing education as a key to professionalizing ministry.[88] He is correct not only in terms of building the knowledge and self-esteem required to function as a professional. He has also identified a key to gaining influence to move the organization from a highly bureaucratic mode to one that integrates professional considerations more explicitly. Just as attention to personnel issues is critical for the first aspect of this "politics," so attention to assuring programs for continuing education, funding for sabbaticals, and a general climate encouraging regular use of these should be the concern of all who seek expertise in areas involving uncertainty for the Church. This is a proven way to promote the professional dimension of ministry.

Concluding Reflections

I have attempted to illustrate what may be a helpful approach to the canonical understanding of official ministry by drawing on the work of canon lawyers and the findings of sociologists. This work has been available for several years in many cases. It does not seem to have been taken seriously by church officials or by official ministers in the Church. This is regrettable.

It may be understandable, however, in terms of the emotional implications of the research. Hall and Schneider concluded that development of the professional career of priests cannot be divorced from

---

[87]J. Blau, p. 119.
[88]Fichter, *Organizatin Man in the Church*, p. 49.

development of the organization.[89] Seidler proposed that even in the face of evident facts the organization did not respond, evidencing instead the characteristics of a "lazy monopoly" similar to utilities, railroads, and the Post Office.[90] Kennedy and Heckler pose the situation this way: "Those who are responsible for the organization of the Church must review their expectations on their priest-personnel and ask whether they want greater maturity in them or whether the demands of the institution make it necessary to insist on re-emphasizing conformity to the traditional role of the priesthood."[91]

While these questions are focused primarily on priests, they have obvious implication for others interested in joining the ranks of official ministers in the United States. The tensions which have marked bishop-priest relationships since the last century are not limited to holy orders; they are, instead, a tension today between expectations by official ministers to be professionals (and to be treated as such), and the practical governing mode of the hierarchy which is strongly bureaucratic (and becoming even more so). Lay women, the largest group now joining the ranks of official ministers at many levels of the American church,[92] have not been socialized into the clerical caste. Many of them are competent professionals. Will they be treated as such?

The creation of a more adequate canonical understanding of official ministry is possible. It will take careful work within the politics of the Church in this country. It will also require greater respect for the canonical tradition of the Church, for through a system of offices, ordinary power, and adequate procedures the concerns of both professionals and bureaucrats can be met.

[89]Hall and Schneider, p. 230.
[90]Seidler, pp. 774-777.
[91]Kennedy and Heckler, p. 175.
[92]See the detailed findings of the study by the Center for Applied Research in the Apostolate, *Women and Ministry* (Washington, DC: CARA, 1980).

OPTIONS FOR THE ORGANIZATION OF MINISTRY

JAMES A. CORIDEN
Washington Theological Union

Ministry is in disarray. In the Roman Catholic Church today the traditional structures of ministry are disordered and woefully inadequate. The situation is confused to the point of embarrassment, but it has also become pastorally critical because of the frustration and alienation which it causes. Many who feel called to ministry are excluded from it; many others are puzzled about their ministerial roles; and the ordinational and jurisdictional structures stand as barriers to effective ministerial collaboration. The search for serviceable alternatives to or sensible modifications of our present system is an urgent task.

The history of the Christian Church as well as contemporary developments within it suggest a variety of ministerial systems. These reflections will draw upon this diversity and attempt to set forth some authentic alternative patterns for the organization of ministries. Four different ministerial situations will be outlined; they will be briefly sketched, with no attempt at full descriptions or detailed theological analyses, in the hope that the patterns might evoke some possible applications to our present problems. No one organizational arrangement is ideal; none has produced a faultless ministry. They may or may not be improvements upon our present system, but they are legitimate alternatives, and some may be more advantageous, functional and fair than the one we presently employ.

The selection of these particular ecclesial and ministerial situations is based partially on a perception that the following problems are central to our system of ministry today:

—the encouragement, empowerment, and recognition of "lay" ministries, and the integration of these ministries with the traditional ordained ministries;
—the full participation of women in ministry;
—the recognition of legitimate ministries in other churches— the ecumenical problem;
—the shortage of priests which causes more and more local

226

communities to be deprived of the celebration of the eucharist;[1]
—the kind or quality of ministry which is a constitutive element
of an authentic Christian community.

This set of problems should be posed to each of the ministerial patterns
which follow. Each section will conclude with a brief reflection on these
questions.

AN HISTORICAL PRELUDE

Before examining the contemporary developments, it may be helpful
to look back to the shape of ministry in an earlier period of the
Church's life. That time after the New Testament and before the Council of Nicea, the post-apostolic or early patristic period—generally, the
church of the second and third centuries—merits special attention. Not
that it provides an ideal form of Church or ministry; it is not the object
of nostalgic yearning. Rather, in the ministerial patterns of that era
certain values and strengths are discernible which were later lost. They
may be the values and strengths which would provide solutions to our
present problems. They should be borne in mind as we scrutinize current ministerial systems.[2]

---

[1]See J. Kerkhofs "New Forms of Lay Ministry in Western Europe," *Pro Mundi Vita
Dossiers* 9 (June, 1980): 1-20; *The Right of the Community to a Priest, Concilium*, 133,
E. Schillebeeckx and J. B. Metz, eds. (New York: Seabury, 1980).

[2]The following sketch of the post-N.T. church is drawn from these sources: K. Baus,
Handbook of Church History, vol. I, *From the Apostolic Community to Constantine*
(New York: Herder & Herder, 1965), pp. 146-152, 346-367; B. Botte, "Collegiate Charac-
ter of the Presbyterate and Episcopate," *The Sacrament of Holy Orders* (Collegeville,
Minn.: Liturgical, 1962), pp. 75-97; H. von Campenhausen, *Ecclesiastical Authority and
Spiritual Power in the Church of the First Three Centuries* (Stanford: Stanford Univ.,
1969), pp. 149-301; Y. Congar, "The Historical Development of Authority in the
Church: Points for Christian Reflection," *Problems of Authority*, ed. J. Todd, (Balti-
more: Helicon, 1962), pp. 119-127; B. Cooke, *Ministry to Word and Sacrament* (Phila-
delphia: Fortress, 1976), pp. 58-74, 235-253, 350-361, 414-427, 537-553; G. Dix, "The
Ministry in the Early Church," *The Apostolic Ministry*, ed. K. Kirk (London: Hodder &
Stoughton, 1957), pp. 183-227, 266-274; F. Dvornik, "Origins of Episcopal Synods," *The
Once and Future Church: A Communion of Freedom*, J. Coriden, ed. (New York: Alba,
1971), pp. 25-56; H. Hess, "Authority: Its Source, Nature and Purpose in the Church,"
We, The People of God, J. Coriden, ed. (Huntington, Ind.: Our Sunday Visitor, 1968),
pp. 131-144; idem, "The Early Expression of Ecclesiastical Authority and Its Development," *Law for Liberty*, J. Biechler, ed. (Baltimore: Helicon, 1967), pp. 27-38; idem,
"Ecclesial Rights in the Early Christian Community: A Theological Study," *The Case
for Freedom: Human Rights in the Church*, J. Coriden, ed. (Washington: Corpus,
1969), pp. 47-75; J. Leclercq, "The Priesthood in the Patristic and Medieval Church,"

Perhaps the single most important charcteristic of the ministry of the Church of this period was its close ties to the local community. The local churches were small, and personal relationships were key. The leaders were not only known to but also chosen by the faithful. The Church, the assembly of the believers, "the brotherhood", was clearly the primary reality. Ministers exercised functions within the *ecclesia*. "Absolute ordination" or the "translation of bishops" were unknown and would have been abhorrent practices. The linkages between the leaders and members of the community were so close that the eucharistic celebrant or head of the assembly could truly speak for the Church because he was genuinely one with them; he was "of them" and "from there."

The entire community was actively involved in the life and work of the Church; there was no sense of an "active clergy" and a "passive laity" in worship, teaching, and works of charity and mercy. Ministerial roles were many and diverse, and they were widely shared, thoroughly dispersed. People were chosen, because of their gifts, to perform a wide variety of functions, even in small communities. For example, those offices which later became completely symbolic and non-functional, e.g., acolyte, lector, porter, and exorcist, at that time were both real and useful. But the active involvement of the faithful was not limited to those who performed "official" functions. All the members of the Church exercised direction of and responsiblity for the community, both directly and representatively. They directly elected their leaders, celebrated liturgical events, and were consulted on matters of faith and action. They were represented in all decision-making by the college of presbyters which they helped to choose.

Ministry was charismatic in the sense that leaders were chosen because of their recognized gifts, both natural and spiritual, and in the sense that the community was conscious of being directed by the Spirit of God. But ministerial authority was strong, and the early bishops fearlessly asserted it.

The structures of ministry were far from uniform, but the most prevalent pattern was that of a single bishop (overseer) assisted by a

---

The Christian Priesthood, N. Lash and Rhymer, eds. (Denville, NJ: Dimension, 1970), pp. 54-56; H.-M. Legrand, "The Presidency of the Eucharist According to the Ancient Tradition," *Worship* 53 (1979): 413-438; C. Vogel, "Unité de l'Eglise et pluralité des formes historiques d'organization ecclésiastique, du IIIe au Ve siècle," *L'Épiscopat et l'Église Universelle*, Y. Congar & B. Dupuy, eds. (Paris: Cerf, 1961), pp. 591-636.

college of elders (presbyters) and a group of helpers (deacons), and all of these aided by many lesser ministers. The bishop presided at the eucharist and preached; he was the spokesman for the community and its unifying leader. But the *presbyterium* shared leadership with him in matters of faith and governance, as was symbolized by their position around him in the eucharistic assembly. The deacons were the hands and feet of the community in carrying out the works of administration, charity, and justice.

These ministers were chosen by their fellow church members, those who knew their backgrounds and families, their talents and the quality of their Christian lives. They received no specialized training beyond the normal catechesis, continual learning within the community, and an informal apprenticing in their roles. The overseers, elders and deacons were "ordained", that is, recognized, commissioned and inducted into their proper "order" by the laying on of hands. They lived the same kind of lives as the rest of the community members; they were married, and most worked elsewhere for their sustenance.

These early local churches, even though they were small, familial and autonomous, were far from isolated or totally independent. They were linked to the other churches, near and far, by the many ties of communion: common faith and sacraments, correspondence, visits, mutual hospitality and welcome, and structurally, by the synodal system. Aside from a few isolated interventions by outstanding personalities or leaders from prominent cities, the regional synods and local councils, attended by representatives of local churches, were the ordinary means for settling disputes, adjudicating grievances, reaching policy positions, and articulating common faith.

Women were actively involved in the manifold ministries of the early church, often serving with acknowledged distinction, e.g., as deaconesses. However, due to various influences, Graeco-Roman societal structures among them, women did not commonly exercise the leading ministerial roles.

While it is neither appropriate nor especially helpful to address present-day questions to historic situations, it is interesting to reflect on the churches of the second and third centuries and the problems (mentioned above) which beset ministry today. It seems safe to conclude, at least in general, that our problems with the organization of ministry did not exist in those churches.

Having recalled and briefly reviewed this one historical period, and aware of the drastic effects which the political and demographic changes of the fourth century had upon the Church and its ministries, we now look about for significant modern developments.

1. THE "THIRD CHURCH"

Basic Christian communities, base-level ecclesial communities, or Christian parochial cells

This phenomenon may be one of the most significant developments for the structures of ministry in several centuries. It was born and bred in the churches of the "Third World"—the southern hemisphere: Latin America, Africa, and Asia—in the late fifties and early sixties, has enjoyed a remarkable growth in those areas, and now is spreading to Europe and North America.

In 1968 at Medellin the Latin American bishops described the base community:

> It is the first and fundamental ecclesiastical nucleus, which down on that grass-roots level brings richness and expansion to the faith—and to religious worship, which is its expression. This community which is the initial cell of the Church and the radiating center for its evangelizing efforts, is today the most potent factor for human advancement and development.[3]

The 1979 Puebla "Final Document" analyzed the reality this way:

> As a community, the Base-level Ecclesial Community brings together families, adults and young people, in an intimate interpersonal relationship grounded in the faith. As an ecclesial reality, it is a community of faith, hope, and charity. It celebrates the Word of God and takes its nourishment from the Eucharist, the culmination of all the sacraments. It fleshes out the Word of God in life through solidarity and commitment to the new commandment of the Lord; and through the sevice of the approved coordinators, it makes present and operative the mission of the Church and its visible community with the legitimate pastors. It is a base-level community because it is composed of relatively few members as a permanent body, like a cell of the larger community.[4]

---

[3]*The Church in the Present-Day Transformation of Latin America in the Light of the Council*, L. Colonesse, ed., vol. II, *Conclusions* (Washington: USCC, 1968), 15:10.

[4]*Evangelization at Present and in the Future of Latin America: Conclusions* (Washington: NCCB, 1979), p. 641.

There are now many thousands of these base communities in Latin America. Typically they consist of fifteen to fifty neighbors. José Marins, a leading writer on this development, says they look like this. Most are either rural or on the fringes of the larger cities. Those that arise inside the cities tend to be of a homogenous-grouping (vocational, professional, etc.) sort. Lay people usually run them, with a priest's help and counsel. They arise principally among the poor; among the bourgeois they are less frequent; in well-to-do neighborhoods they are as good as non-existent. When they start, they usually want only the celebration of the word, prayers together, and mutual help: some go a whole year before having the full celebration of the Eucharist. Some are socially committed, but not always in an explicitly political way. The conviction is growing, though, that a BCC ought to conscientize people, getting them to be socio-politically involved—not as members of this or that BCC, but as believers in the Christian faith. They are beginning to celebrate the sacraments—baptism, marriage, penance—in the community now.[5]

The base communities are often but not always associated with con-scientization of the people and a theology of liberation.

This ecclesial development is widespread in Africa also. The bishops of Zambia made the building of basic communities a pastoral priority in 1976. In 1979 they described the basic Christian communities as:

> . . . a small group of people believing and baptized in Jesus Christ, who, drawn together in prayer, listening to and spreading the Word of God, celebrate the Eucharist.[6]

With regard to the ministry within these communities, José Marins

[5]J. Marins, "Basic Christian Communities (BCC's) in Latin America," *Basic Christian Communities*, Latin America Documentation 14 (Washington: USCC, 1976), pp. 5-6.

[6]"Bishops' Seminar on Basic Communities," *Ministries and Communities*, Pro Mundi Vita 21 (July, 1979), p. 4.

The Zambian bishops said that it is a unity small enough for its members to experience a sense of belonging and to express it in mutual service and solidarity with the Church universal.

The constitutive elements of the Basic Christian Community are, therefore: faith in Jesus Christ; community prayer; the Word of God listened to and spread; the celebration of the Eucharist; mutual service and a sense of belonging; social and geographic proximity; solidarity with the Church Universal; the promotion of social concern and integral development; and, concern for reconciliation, including ecumenism.

For more recent guidelines for Zambia, see *Origins* 10/11 (Aug. 28, 1980): 161-166.

has gathered these "criteria and conditions for the institution of new ministries" (largely from the Puebla document):

a. that they be autochthonous (i.e. indigenous) and missionary. They ought to be thought of in terms of the particularities of each culture and using their expresssions.

b. that the freedom of the gifts of God be respected. Normally, a ministry is based on a charism that God gives to persons in view of the common good. The personal charisms are for the good of the community and the world.

c. . . . that the people live as inheritors of the goods of the world, being freed from all slavery, becoming brothers and sisters of one another, sons and daughters of God.

d. that they be a service that energizes and multiplies the evangelizing action of the Church.

e. that they respect the unity and profit from the orientation of its pastors.

f. that ministries be created only when the community can no longer respond to a need as a community (the ministries are not given "a priori").

g. that the ministries not be an excuse for the community not assuming responsiblity for a particular service but much to the contrary, the ministries exist so that the community never forgets that particular commitment.

h. that the community participate in the selection and formation of its ministries, searching out persons who are really inserted in the people.

i. that each ministry be exercised collegially. No one can exercise a ministry separated from the ministry of the others. This ministerial body is formed around the one who is ultimately responsible, representing the same Lord as head who inspires and presides over the community. No ministry is autonomous and reaches its maximum, complete expression only in the ministerial body. This means that there cannot be in the Church any task for service that isn't exercised with the "consciousness of being a part"—that is to say, each one seeking an organized integration with the other services. Also the fulfillment of the mission of the Church has to be permeated with the notion of co-responsibility.[7]

[7]J. Marins and Team, *Basic Ecclesial Community: Church from the Roots* (Quito: Colegio Tecnico Don Bosco), pp. 83-84.

Marins enumerates four general types of ministries found in these basic communities:

a. the ministry of coordination—the leadership or presidency, through which the community is linked to the larger Church, normally entrusted to a priest, but here conferred by the priest to a lay person by the laying on of hands or some other symbolic gesture which expresses to the community the public and official nature of the ministry;

b. the ministry of evangelization—the catechists, prophets, leaders of bible groups, etc., who educate in faith by establishing the relationship between the problems of real life and the gospel; these persons are chosen by their own community wherein their conversion, convictions and Chrisian witness are known;

c. the ministry of prayer and liturgy—the ministries of word and sacrament, normally united in the ordained minister, are here separated, and often a liturgy team provides leadership in communal prayer and prayer groups, penance sevices and other devotions, witnesses for marriages, godparents at baptisms, funerals and special liturgies, etc.;

d. the ministry of charity and human promotion—those who aid orphans, widows, and homeless, who care for the sick and promote health, who provide counseling, literacy programs, conscientizing, social assistance and cooperative programs, etc.[8]

These ministers are recruited from within the local village or neighborhood by the other members of the community in dialogue with the "circuit riding" priest or visiting pastoral team. They are often prepared or formed in their ministries by short-term courses or study-prayer sessions at a regional training school or parish center.

The ministerial alignment in the basic ecclesial communities is anything but fixed and uniform; it is clearly quite varied and fluid. However, there are two distinguishing characteristics of nearly all such ministry: it is indigenous and lay. There is much extrinsic stimulation and coordination, and often that is provided by missionaries, both clerical and religious; but the ministerial roles within the local communities themselves are filled by the lay members of those communities. There is an explicit and determined effort to avoid the "clericalization" of the ministries.

Although the formation of these base communities and their ministry structures were occasioned by a reduced supply of priests, lived experience has convinced those involved that the ecclesial and minis-

[8]Ibid, 84-87.

terial pattern is far more than an expedient, an adaptation in an emergency; it is recognized as authentic church, functional ministry.[9]

Some writers believe that the "Third World" experience of base communities is not transferrable to North America, except within disadvantaged or oppressed groups, because of the individualism, materialism and relative affluence here.[10] However, many such small communities of Hispanics exist in the United States, and their formation and development is being warmly fostered.[11] An analogous phenomenon of neighborhood churches or "mini-parishes" within larger parishes is also spreading in the U.S.[12]

---

[9]In addition to the sources already cited, this description of basic ecclesial communities was drawn from: M.-T. Perrin Jassy, *Basic Community in the African Churches* (Maryknoll, NY: Orbis, 1973), pp. 239-251; T. Bissonnette, "Communidades Ecclesiales de Base: Some Contemporary Attempts to Build Ecclesial Koinonia," THE JURIST 36 (1976): 24-58; G. Costello, *Mission to Latin America* (Maryknoll, NY: Orbis, 1979), pp. 154-156, 263-264; articles by G. Gutierrez, L. Boff, and the Final Document in *The Challenge of Basic Christian Communities*, Papers from the International Ecumenical Congress of Theology, 1980, São Paulo, Brazil, S. Torres & J. Eagleson, eds. (Maryknoll, NY: Orbis, 1981), pp. 115-144, 234-239; "The Quest for Truly Human Communities," *Pro Mundi Vita* 62 (1976): 2-5; J. Metz, *The Emergent Church* (New York: Crossroad, 1981), pp. 62-65, 89-94.

[10]G. Mac Eoin & N. Riley, "Parish Communidades de Base," *Parish Ministry* 1:5 (Jan.-Feb., 1980), pp. 1-3.

[11]A recent bi-lingual handbook for promotion of these communities, *Communidades Ecclesiales de Base: Experiencia en los Estados Unidas (Basic Ecclesial Communities: An Experience in the United States)* by the National Secretariat [for Hispanic Affairs, NCCB/USCC] and Hispanic Teams (Liguori, Mo.: Liguori, 1980), p. 159, mentions that there were "more than 100,000 Hispanics in more than 12,000 small communities" in 1977 at the time of the *Segundo Encuentro Nacional Hispano de Pastoral*. The *Proceedings* of that Washington meeting, *Pueblo de Dios en Marcha* (Washington: NCCB/USCC, 1978), pp. 68-80, records the strong encouragement for basic Christian communities and ministry within them among its conclusions. Also confer *Developing Basic Christian Communities—A Handbook* (Chicago: National Federation of Priests' Councils, 1979).

The following theological description was offered at a "special interest session" of the Catholic Theological Society of America convention in Cincinnati on June 11, 1981:

"The Basic Christian Community is a portion of the people of God which constitutes the first and fundamental nucleus of the Church, in which the Church of Christ is truly present and operative at its most basic level, through personal fraternal relationships, in a joint pastoral service which fulfills the filial relationship with the Father, in the brotherhood of Christ and other human beings, through the action of the Holy Spirit, and in the salvation and total liberation of the whole persona and of all persons."

[12]It receives scant attention, however, in the vision statement of the U.S. Bishops' Committee on the Parish, "The Parish: A People, A Mission, A Structure," *Origins* 10/41 (Mar. 26, 1981): 646.

Reflecting on the problems with ministry raised at the outset of this article, it appears that some are solved in the basic community structure and some are not. Obviously, lay persons are fully activated in the *communidades*, women often exercise equal roles in ministry, and the communities themselves seem to be fully constituted local churches— genuine *ecclesiolae*. The organization and operation of these communities offer no special insight into the ecumenical recognition of ministries. But the major shortcoming of these local manifestations of Church is their inability to celebrate the eucharist with regularity, not for lack of desire, but for lack of ordained ministers. The insistence of the Roman Church that only celibate, highly-educated males may lead eucharistic worship prevents thousands of small Christian groups from frequently celebrating the Lord's supper. The central administration of the Church cannot escape the heavy responsibility for the emergence of this lamentable distortion: a virtually non-eucharistic Catholicism.[13]

2. THE SPIRIT CHURCH

Charismatic groups

The neo-pentecostal movement of "charismatic renewal" within the Roman Catholic Church (as well as within the Episcopal, Lutheran and Presbyterian churches) in North America is a truly remarkable phenomenon of these post-conciliar years.[14] After exploratory and diffi-

[13]Confer the persuasive articles in *The Right of the Community to a Priest*, *Concilium*, 133, and E. Schillebeeckx, *Ministry: Leadership in the Community of Jesus Christ* (New York: Crossroad, 1981), pp. 136-142.

[14]This description of charismatic groups and their ministry is drawn from these sources: *Gifts of the Spirit and the Body of Christ: Perspectives on the Charismatic Movement*, J. Agrimson, ed., (Minneapolis: Augsburg, 1974); R. Culpepper, *Evaluating the Charismatic Movement: A Theological and Biblical Appraisal* (Valley Forge, Pa.: Judson, 1977); *Charisms in the Church*, *Concilium*, 109, C. Duquoc & C. Floristan, eds. (New York: Seabury, 1978); J. Fichter, *The Catholic Cult of the Paraclete* (New York: Sheed & Ward, 1975); idem, "A View of Charismatic Parishioners, *Parish Ministry* 1:2 (July-Aug., 1979), pp. 1-10; S. Fahey, *Charismatic Social Action* (New York: Paulist, 1977); D. Gelpi, *Charism and Sacrament: A Theology of Christian Conversion*(New York: Paulist, 1976); J. Jones, *Filled With New Wine: The Charismatic Renewal of the Church* (New York: Harper & Row, 1974); K. McDonnell, *Charismatic Renewal and the Churches* (New York: Seabury, 1976); idem, *The Charismatic Renewal and Ecumenism* (New York: Paulist, 1978); H. Mühlen, *A Charismatic Theology: Initiation in the Spirit* New York:Paulist, 1978); E. O'Connor, *The Pentecostal Movement in the Catholic Church* (Notre Dame, Ind.: University of Notre Dame, 1975); R. Quebedeaux, *The New Charismatics: The Origins, Development, and Significance of Neo-Pentecostalism* (New

cult beginnings on campuses and adjacent communities in the mid-west, it has spread like a prairie fire to all parts of the United States and Canada. At first it was nervously and hesitantly countenanced by the clergy and hierarchy—viewed askance, with doubt and suspicion. But the charismatics have now won acceptance, support, and encouragement from the churches.

Charismatic communities are often parish-related prayer groups within a parish or reaching across several parishes. They maintain communion, reciprocal assistance, and friendly rapport with the official churches. Given the startling and unsettling differences in style between these "Spirit-led" communities and the highly organized and formal churches within which they live, their relatively tranquil acceptance and mutual reciprocity is a wonder. Most Catholic charismatics attend Mass weekly in their home parishes, and they schedule their own meetings and Masses so as to avoid conflicts with their local parish.

The charismatic renewal has been a powerful force for ecumenical understanding and sharing. In fact, the charismatics so often transcend denominational lines in their easy acceptance of one another that they have been accused of ecclesial indifference. However, for the most part, there is careful respect for sacramental practices and disciplinary limitations of their respective churches, even in ecumenically-mixed local communities and prayer groups.

Like the church of the Corinthinan letters, upon which they model themselves, the charismatic groups are not entirely trouble-free. They have been accused of a whole litany of failings: divisiveness, elitism, fundamentalism, lack of commitment to social justice, authoritarianism, subordination of women, and even abandonment of the Church. While these accusations have had some basis in fact, contemporary literature indicates that the problems are receiving serious attention.

The recent charismatic movement is characterized by a keen attention to the scriptures, a high value of and frequent practice of prayer, a lively faith in the Holy Spirit, a personal and communal experience of the Spirit's action, and an awareness of charismatic manifestations—the gifts of the Spirit. It is this final element, the charisms, which constitutes ministry within these communities, and shapes its relations to "official" ministries of the Church. St. Paul's teaching on the gifts of the Spirit is applied like a rule-book.

York: Doubleday, 1976); "The Catholic Pentecostal Movement: Creative or Divisive Enthusiasm," *Pro Mundi Vita* 60 (May, 1976).

The charismatic renewal includes the whole spectrum of Catholic life, lay and clerical. In its broadest expression, however, it is a populist movement. Everyone has some charism to exercise: a prayer to offer, a song to sing, a service to the sick to perform, a teaching ministry to carry out, a community to build. Everybody is a participant. "To each is given the manifestation of the Spirit for the common good" (I Cor 12:7). "Each one of you has received a special gift" (I Pet 4:10).[15]

A person may seek the charisms (I Cor 12:31) but they are essentially spiritual gifts. The gifts are without number, as they are the multitudinous ways that the Holy Spirit comes to visibility in the Church in service functions. To a greater or lesser degree a charism is a ministry to others. The more immediately a ministry or charism is related to the service of others, the higher it is on the hierarchy of gifts. The less immediately the charism is related to the service of others, the lower it is on the hierarchy of gifts. . . . A charism is a manifestation of the Spirit in a ministry to the other members of the body. It is therefore directed outward to others, rather than inward to self.[16]

Because in Paul's view every Christian has a charism the Church is entirely charismatic and entirely ministerly. A Church that is structurally charismatic is structurally directed to ministry because a charism is by definition a ministry to others. At no time does Paul conceive of two kinds of Christians: those who having a charism minister to others, and those having no charism receiving ministry from others.[17]

The influential "Malines Document I," in describing the theological basis of the charismatic renewal, speaks of "the charismatic structure of the Church":

> Though the Spirit manifests himself in different ministries which serve different functions, functions which may differ in kind and degree, the whole Church and all its members are partakers of the Spirit. There are no special classes of Spirit-bearers, no separate groups of Spirit-filled believers. Fullness of

[15]McDonell, *The Charismatic Renewal and Ecumenism*, p. 2.
[16]McDonell, *Charismatic Renewal and the Churches*, p. 6.
[17]McDonell, *The Charismatic Renewal and Ecumenism*, p. 53.

life in the Spirit, participation in the abundant life in the Spirit, is a common possession of the whole Church, although not appropriated in equal measure by all.

This Spirit, given to the whole Church, comes to visibility in ministries to the Church and the world. In this sense the Spirit and his charisms are inseparable but not identical. Though a manifestation (I Cor 12:7) of the Spirit, the charism is not the Spirit himself. A charism is a coming to visibility of the Spirit in a ministerial functon. A charism therefore looks outward in ministry to the Church and world rather than inward to the perfection of the individual. Because the Spirit and his charisms belong constitutively to the nature of the Church as free gifts, it is not possible for the Church to be without either. Without the Spirit and his charisms there is no Church. Therefore, there is no group or any movement within the Church which can claim the Spirit and the charisms in any exclusive way.[18]

Charisms are described as "service gifts" or "ministry gifts" directed toward the service of others rather than for individual sanctification. In scholastic terms the charisms are regarded as *gratia gratis data*, graces given to bring others to union with God; they are looked upon as ordinary endowments of the community. All ministries are looked upon as charisms, some quite customary (teaching, counseling, coordinating, adminstering, distributing aid, etc.); some "more luminous," long forgotten or missing in the Church, are now being rediscovered and put in place (tongues, healing, prophecy, interpretation, etc.).

The harmonious interplay of these ministerial charisms is a real concern and a conscious effort. On the theoretical level the relationship between charismatic ministries and official, ordained ministry seems unsure. Various interpretations have been offered. Some claim that the unique role of the official minister is to coordinate the other ministries, "a charism for other charisms."[19] Others find the uniqueness of the "apostolic charism" in its universality and permanence, that is, the apostle is a member of the college responsible for the universal Church and is permanent (absolute) and transferable—other ministries are

---

[18]"Theological and Pastoral Orientations on the Catholic Charismatic Renewal: Malines Document 1," *Presence, Power, Praise: Documents on the Charismatic Renewal, III*, K. McDonnell, ed. (Collegeville, Minn.: Liturgical, 1980), p. 24.

[19]Mühlen, *A Charismatic Theology*, p. 297.

local, conditioned, and possibly temporary.[20] Neither of these theories seems adequate. However, reflection upon the healthy, vigorous ministries within the charismatic communities and their relations with the structures of ordained ministry may lead to more fruitful theological insights in the future. On the level of practice there seems to be a quite successful integration of charismatic (largely lay) ministries and ordained ministries. Charismatic communities have profound respect for the sacraments and sacramental ministries, and priests seem to relate well to the communities, but are not usually their leaders.[21] The communities are usually led and coordinated by lay persons or mixed teams.

> It is clear that the charismatic ministries do not replace the ordained ministry; . . . Christian communities cannot be formed by the work of either clergy or laity alone. . . . The charismatic renewal of the Church holds promise for a much more balanced state of affairs. The maturing of the charismatic ministries holds promise of a fuller involvement of every member of the Church in building up the body of Christ without jeopardizing anyone's role. It holds this promise because its primary focus is not on the differences between clergy and laity, but on the gifts of service that every follower of Christ receives.[22]

Catholic charismatics describe themselves as a renewal movement within the Church, a phenomenon which will be absorbed into the very life-blood of the Catholic community rather than remain separate as an organization or distinct as a part of the Church. If this revitalizing infusion really does occur, its effect on ministry could be transforming. The conviction that all ministries are gifts of the Sprit given in profusion and diversity for the common good is a radically different point of departure.

Some of the problems with ministry in our Church today, which were raised earlier, may be soluble from the charismatic starting point: ministries are the gifts of the Spirit made visible. Lay members of the charismatic groups feel involved and empowered. In principle women are accepted as equals in leadership roles. Charismatics cross denominational lines with an ease which is sometimes disconcerting; recogni-

---

[20]Gelpi, *Charism and Sacrament*, p. 203-204.

[21]Fichter, *The Catholic Cult of the Paraclete*, pp. 29, 78, 152 n. 30.

[22]G. Martin, "Charismatic Renewal and the Church of Tomorrow," *As the Spirit Leads Us*, K. & D. Ranaghan, eds. (New York: Paulist, 1971), p. 242.

tion of the ministers of other churches is not much of a problem when they are viewed as gifted by the one Spirit. The charismatic approach has not broken through the problem of eucharistic celebration and the necessity of an ordained priest. The groups seem to find the liturgical help they need, and make no pretense at autonomy or self-sufficiency.

3. THE AMERICAN CHURCH

Collaborative ministry

So as not to overlook the obvious, to the preceding ministerial arrangements must be added a domestic and rather prosaic option: the diverse-member group or "team ministry."[23] It is one of the more successful recent developments in North American parish, hospital, and campus ministry.[24] This modern form of group or team ministry stands in rather sharp contrast to the formerly typical pattern of ministry in America.

To use the parish setting as an example, for the first two-thirds of

[23]The "team" concept is not an American invention. For example, it was a pervasive and central feature of the missionary apostolate approach of Abbé Michonneau in the 1940s and 1950s in France. Cf. G. Michonneau, *Revolution in a City Parish* (Oxford: Blackfriars, 1949), pp. xvii, 98-99, 149; idem, *The Missionary Spirit in Parish Life* (Westminster, MD: Newman, 1952), pp. 171-194. However, the notion has received new impetus in North America since the Second Vatican Council and a new configuration, one which often cuts across the clergy-laity dichotomy.

[24]Confer "Canonical Reflections on Priestly Life and Ministry," *American Ecclesiastical Review* 166 (1972): 381-382 (also in *Catholic Mind* 70 [Sept., 1972], pp. 55-56); J. Coriden & M. Mangan, "Team Ministry," *C.L.S.A. Proceedings* 34 (1972): 70-75; R. Cunningham, "Team Ministry: Canonical and Theological Reflections" (JCL Dissertation, Catholic University of America, 1977); D. Donnelly, *Team: Theory and Practice of Team Ministry* (New York: Paulist, 1977); S. Giblin & L. Stanford, "Corporate Ministry: Vision and Ecclesial Implications," *Lumen Vitae* 31 (1976): 209-220; *Growing Together: Conference on Shared Ministry* (Washington: NCCB, 1980); V. Hatt, "The Team Approach to Service and Leadership," *Living Light* 12 (1975): 42-55; K. Kilinski & J. Wofford, *Organization and Leadership in the Local Church* (Grand Rapids: Zondervan, 1973), pp. 150-164; A. MacDonald, *A Sociological Study of Team Ministry in the Roman Catholic Archdiocese of Hartford, Connecticut* (Ph. D. Dissertation, Catholic University of America, 1978); "Diocesan policies and procedures on team ministry," *National Association of Church Personnel Administrators* (Cincinatti: mimeograph, 1979), K: 1-5; "Mixed Pastoral Teams," *Pro Mundi Vita Bulletin* 78 (July, 1979); "Team Ministry: The Hartford Model," *Origins* 5/13 (Sept. 18, 1975): 193-202; J. Sullivan, "The Common Responsiblity of Believers," *Chicago Studies* 16 (1977): 195-202; *Tous Responsables dans L'Église? Le ministère presbytéral dans l'Église tout entière "ministérielle"*, Réflexions de l'Assemblée plénière de l'Épiscopat français (Paris: Centurion, 1973).

this century there were usually two groups identified as ministering full-time in an average parish: the priests and the sisters. The ministry in which each group was engaged was relatively homogeneous. The priests, perhaps two, three or four of them, all did the same things: celebrated Mass and administered the other sacraments, preached, counseled and gave instructions, visited hospitals and homes, led prayers, and looked after the administration of the parish. The priests differed in age and approach, and one (the eldest) was the responsible leader, but their ministerial activities differed little one from the other. Similarly the sisters were usually engaged in education ministries, either in the parish school or in a religious education program (or both). Their responsibilities differed somewhat, but most were related to some form of teaching.

Set aside, for the purposes of this analysis, the immense amount of voluntary lay activity in the parish, both organizational—Altar and Rosary, Holy Name, St. Vincent dePaul, etc.—and individual— ushers, teachers' aides, money counters, choir members, etc. These were anything but unimportant, but they were most often transient and part-time and not really considered part of the "ministry" of the parish.

Within the last fifteen years collaborative groups or teams have been organized to perform parish ministry. They are characterized by a diversity of background, expertise and life style, a division of labor, and cooperation in a common effort. They recognize the variety of talents, preparations and specializations among themselves and they attempt to coordinate their tasks and planning through "staff meetings." Often the team members pray together and make reflective retreats. They represent different ways of living: clerical and lay and religious, celibate and married, solitary and in community. All this diversity is shared in and brought to bear on the ministerial effort within the parish. In terms of human relations and ministerial effectiveness this arrangement appears immensely richer than the foregoing.

It goes without saying that there is a wide range of forms and styles of team ministry; it is also well known that teams frequently fail— many have foundered on conflicts, clericalism, costliness, or lack of acceptance. There is no reason to romanticize about "team"; it is not a panacea. But when the groups are carefully assembled and sensitively facilitated they provide the best pastoral care available in the American church today. Like many other American contributions to Catholicism, team ministry is very pragmatic—it originated largely because priests in eastern dioceses had to wait too long to become pastors—and quite successful.

Team ministry, because it is founded on the principle of the recognition and inter-relation of diverse abilities, draws some lay persons into very meaningful ministerial roles. Women are frequently full and equal partners on the teams which perform ministry. The remaining problems with ministry, mentioned at the beginning of the article, are at least partially illumined by the collaborative or team concept. Some ecumenical parish or campus experiments have effectively utilized a team arrangement for their ministry. And the collaborative pattern alleviates the priest-necessary-for-eucharist problem to the extent that it allows the priest members of the team to focus on eucharistic leadership, while others perform diverse ministerial functions, often more effectively.

4. THE UNITING CHURCH

Ecumenical projections

The Consutation on Church Union (COCU) has provided a most helpful and provocative focus for ecumenical efforts in North America for the past two decades. The Consultation is a forthright, clear-thinking, ambitious striving toward the union of Christian churches. The members of the Consultation are ten of the largest and most influential of American Protestant churches.[25]

In 1966 the Consultation agreed on a set of *Principles of Church Union*;[26] in 1970 it circulated a *Plan of Union* for study by the churches.[27] After receiving reactions from the member bodies and others the Consultation issued a revised plan entitled *In Quest of A Church Uniting* in 1976. However, the chapter on ministry was not completed and approved until January of this year.[28]

COCU's reflections on Christian ministry do not pretend to be a depiction of ministry as it actually exists in any one church now.

[25]African Methodist Episcopal Church; African Methodist Episcopal Zion Church; Christian Church (Disciples of Christ); Christian Methodist Episcopal Church; Episcopal Church; National Council of Community Churches; Presbyterian Church in the U.S.; United Church of Christ; United Methodist Church; United Presbyterian Church in the U.S.A. The Lutheran Council in the U.S.A. and the Roman Catholic Church have observer status on the Theology Commission.

[26]*Consultation on Church Union, 1967: Principles of Church Union, Guidelines for Structure, and A Study Guide* (Cincinnati: Forward Movement, 1967).

[27]*A Plan of Union for the Church of Christ Uniting* (Princeton: COCU, 1970).

[28]*In Quest of a Church of Christ Uniting: An Emerging Theological Consensus*, Chapter VII: Ministry (Revised, 1980) (Princeton: COCU, 1980).

Rather it attempts to describe the characteristics of the ministry in a church uniting. It is a valuable theoretical picture, because of the theological quality and pastoral sensitivity which it contains. But the scenario has practical value as well, because it is based on existing praxis and is aimed at ecumenical acceptance. ". . .These statements describe an emerging theological consensus in whose light the participating churches will continue their serious quest for a Church of Christ Uniting."[29] ". . . We believe that this agreement reflects, in the American milieu, broader world-wide ecumenical agreement."[30]

The chapter on ministry grounds the Church's ministry on that of the Lord:

> The life, death, and resurrection of Jesus Christ was a ministry of God to all humankind. Through the Holy Spirit, God's People are called to share that ministry and are empowered to fulfill what it requires. By the power of the same Spirit, the ministry of God's People appropriates and continues what God sent Jesus to be and do.

> In all its forms and functions, ministry is a rich interweaving of word and worship, work and witness. In different ways, members of the Body share responsibility for the church's government, administration, discipline, instruction, worship, and pastoral care. These activities are to be held together in a visible ordering through which the Church is equipped for its ministry. "Having gifts that differ according to the grace given to us" (Romans 12:26), the several members bring to the one body a wide diversity of gifts, functions, and services. "To each is given the manifestation of the Spirit for the common good" (I Cor. 12:12,13). Each is a distinctive form of a single ministry of Christ as it is realized in mutually complementary and diverse ways in the whole life of the Church and in the world.[31]

COCU's articulation of the ordering of ministry, including the relationship between lay and ordained ministries, is especially insightful.

> The ordained and lay ministries of the Church are differing forms of the one ministry of Christ that is shared by the whole People of God. Because they are forms of one ministry, they share in the same reality and complement one another. Thus,

[29]Ibid., Chapter I., p. 6.
[30]G. Moede in the Foreword to *In Quest*, p. 1.
[31]*In Quest*, pp. 34 & 36.

they must be ordered in relation to one another in the life of the Church.

The ordained ministries serve to strengthen the ministry of all baptized members.

All ministries, lay as well as those of bishop, presbyter and deacon, are to be understood as at once personal, collegial, and constitutional.[32]

The chapter contains reflections on the ministry of lay persons.

In their baptism, lay persons enter into the ministry of Jesus Christ, into a personal relationship to God in Christ, and at the same time into a relationship to other Christians.

Lay persons may be formally appointed to various functions, thereby being acknowledged by the Church, and, in turn, acknowledging their responsibility for particular tasks. They

---

[32]Ibid., p. 39.

"All Ministry in the uniting church will be *personal*. In every minister, lay and ordained, Christ and the Gospel are made present as personal reality and are the source of that life of holiness and devotion which is a mark of ministry. Ministry is exercised by men and women who have been individually called and baptized, and in certain cases, also ordained. Through their baptism, or ordination, they become personally identified with their ministry. They represent in their own ways, the ministry of Christ to the Church and to the world and, in turn, represent the ministry of the Church to humanity. In their varying personal capacities, they serve individuals and groups within and outside the Church.

"All ministry in the uniting church will be *collegial*. Baptism and ordination alike associate the individual with others who share the same call. The ministry is a single task common to many. Collegial relationships obtain among persons in different ministries as well as among those of the same ministry. Such relationships include lay persons as well as bishops, presbyters and deacons. The interpersonal character of collegiality is a basis for partnership in governance and gives life and substance to the institutional structures of the Church.

"All ministry in the uniting church will be *consitutional*. A person enters ministry through formal procedures of membership as well as through election, appointment or ordination. Bishops, presbyters, and deacons, having been selected by a representative process, will be ordained by prayer with the laying on of hands by those authorized to do so, and installed in their ministry. No individual's ministry can be regarded as representative of the Church unless it is constitutional, and remains in communion with, and accountable to, other ministers in ordered assemblies in which all ministries are represented." Ibid., pp. 39-40.

take appropriate roles in the governance of the Church. They carry out their ministries in a variety of ways.

 a) Witnessing to the Gospel
 b) Seeking Justice and Reconciliation in the World
 c) Bringing the World before God
 d) Providing Pastoral Care for Persons
 e) Serving the Cause of Unity.[33]

COCU's chapter on ministry concludes with individual observations on the ministries of bishops, presbyters and deacons; they are acceptable, apt and accurate. The entire treatise merits our serious consideration—for its ecumenical potential and its possibilities as an organizational option for ministry.[34]

Referring again to the problems with our system of ministry mentioned at the beginning, it appears that the theory and plan of ministry put forward by COCU's Theology Commission offers help in encouraging lay ministry and relating it to ordained ministries. It allows for the full sharing of women in ministry, and it is plainly directed at the ecumenical problem: the mutual recognition of ministries and the effective union of the churches. The COCU design does not shed any new light on the eucharistic problem caused by a lack of priests or the level of ministry necessary for an integral Christian community.

CONCLUSION

Do these alternative arrangements of Christian ministry suggest a way out of the confusion and disarray which presently beset Roman Catholic ministry? Do they point toward solutions of the central problems which cause the current disorder? Perhaps. At least these variant organizational patterns provide some insights, some directions in which to look for answers.

[33]Ibid., pp. 40-41.

[34]Also deserving special attention for ecumenical reasons is the splendid statement on ministry approved by the Faith and Order Commission of the World Council of Churches at Accra, Ghana, in 1974. The statement, which is "an attempt to survey the present ecumenical debate on the ordained ministry and to indicate the emerging common perspectives which may lead to the agreement required for the full mutual recognition of the ministries," is found in *One Baptism, One Eucharist, And A Mutually Recognized Ministry*, Faith and Order Paper No. 73 (Geneva: World Council of Churches, 1975), pp. 29-57. A further refinement of the statement, the "Text of January, 1981," is available in mimeograph form from the World Council in Geneva.

All four of the situations described above—basic ecclesial communities, charismatic groups, team ministry, ecumenical plans—take the ministries of the laity seriously, foster them, and coordinate their activities with the ordained. They view ministry as a continuum or broad spectrum of service roles rather than as a narrow, monochromatic, exclusive function. They respect the special place and prerogatives of the ordained, but they realize that many other members of the believing community also have ministerial rights and responsibilities, and that the harmonious collaboration between them is critical.

All four arrangements are, at least in principle, open to the full participation of women in ministry. Whether their starting point is the solidarity of the local people, the recognition of the gifts of the Spirit, the appreciation of personal expertise, or respect for the central realities of ministry embodied in diverse traditions, all welcome women as partners in ministry. None see womanhood as a barrier to full participation.

On the question of the mutual recognition of ministries among the churches, obviously the ecumenical plans were formulated in an attempt to solve this problem. But other situations also suggest helpful approaches. The charismatics focus on the Spirit as the one source for all ministerial gifts. Teams sometimes cross denominational lines to incorporate talented members successfully. The ecumenical problem, which is now largely solved at the levels of theological theory and of personal acceptance, seems to encounter greatest difficulty at the administrative levels of judicatories.

When it comes to the issue of the dearth of vocations to the celibate priesthood and the consequent deprivation of thousands of local communities of regular eucharistic celebrations, no solutions are found in the four paradigms, but one obvious direction is indicated. The leaders of authentic local churches, chosen because of their gifts, should be suitably prepared and then empowered to preside at the eucharist. Whether the "empowerment" is accomplished by ordination or some other form of commissioning or deputation is a secondary question. The primary issue is the tragic inability of basic ecclesial communities to rejoice around the table of the Lord solely because of the ancient and questionable requirements of an ecclesiastical office.

The final problem is closely connected to the previous one, but in a frustratingly circular fashion. If, for its integrity or completeness, a local community of Catholics must have the ability to celebrate the sacraments as well as to hear the word and witness to it, then it is truncated, under present discipline, without an ordained priest. Yet it is unable to find sufficient candidates for the priesthood, given present requirements. It seems clear that other provisions must be made so that the local church can raise up its own sacramental ministers, as it has demonstrated its ability to meet its other ministerial needs.

We must raise our eyes and look beyond our immediate experience for theoretical approaches and practical arrangements which might help us bring order out of the present confusion of ministries. The foregoing alternate ministerial patterns deserve further serious study because of their vitality, authenticity and intrinsic merits.